One Night in America

One Night in America

Robert Kennedy, César Chávez, and the Dream of Dignity

Steven W. Bender

Paradigm Publishers

Boulder • London

green press INITIATIVE

Paradigm Publishers is committed to preserving ancient forests and natural resources. We elected to print *One Night In America* on 50% post consumer recycled paper, processed chlorine free. As a result, for this printing, we have saved:

8 Trees (40' tall and 6-8" diameter)
3,499 Gallons of Wastewater
1,407 Kilowatt Hours of Electricity
386 Pounds of Solid Waste
758 Pounds of Greenhouse Gases

Paradigm Publishers made this paper choice because our printer, Thomson-Shore, Inc., is a member of Green Press Initiative, a nonprofit program dedicated to supporting authors, publishers, and suppliers in their efforts to reduce their use of fiber obtained from endangered forests.

For more information, visit www.greenpressinitiative.org

Letters of Cesar Chavez to Robert F. Kennedy and Martin Luther King, Jr., ™/© 2007 the Cesar E. Chavez Foundation, www.chavezfoundation.org.

Copyright © 2008 Paradigm Publishers

Published in the United States by Paradigm Publishers, 3360 Mitchell Lane Suite E, Boulder, CO 80301 USA.

Paradigm Publishers is the trade name of Birkenkamp & Company, LLC, Dean Birkenkamp, President and Publisher.

Library of Congress Cataloging in Publication Data

Bender, Steven.
  One night in America : Robert Kennedy, Cesar Chavez, and the dream of dignity / Steven W. Bender.
       p. cm.
  Includes bibliographical references and index.
  ISBN 978-1-59451-428-9 (hardcover : alk. paper) — ISBN 978-1-59451-429-6 (pbk. : alk. paper)
     1. United States—Social conditions—1960–1980.   2. Kennedy, Robert F., 1925–1968—Friends and associates.   3. Chavez, Cesar, 1927–1993—Friends and associates.
4. Mexican American agricultural laborers—California—History—20th century.
5. Mexican Americans—California—Social conditions.   I. Title.
  HN65.B4236 2008
  305.5'62—dc22

                                                                2007045363

Printed and bound in the United States of America on acid free paper that meets the standards of the American National Standard for Permanence of Paper for Printed Library Materials.

Designed and Typeset by Straight Creek Bookmakers.

11 10 09 08 07   1 2 3 4 5

I am convinced that the truest act of courage, the strongest act of manliness is to sacrifice ourselves for others in a totally nonviolent struggle for justice.

—César Chávez

My heroes I know by name are few, and most of them, particularly César Chávez, Robert Kennedy, and Dolores Huerta, are connected to the events in this book. They shared a vision for a better world for the underserved, and they resolved to pursue it as their life's work. So I dedicate this book to them and to those ahead who will shoulder the struggle.

Contents

Introduction

Robert Kennedy and César Chávez came from opposite sides of the country and from opposite sides of the "tracks" of class and race that continue to divide so many Americans. But they shared a vision that the lives and promise of all Americans were unfulfilled so long as the American dream failed to extend to the desperately poor farm workers, many of Mexican heritage, who worked the fields in California, the Southwest, and elsewhere. This common bond of desire to help the underprivileged, whether in rural fields or urban ghettos and barrios, drew Chávez and Kennedy together in the 1960s in a brief but inspirational friendship. An assassin's bullet in June 1968 did more than sever a friendship between two devoted family men—it set back the cause for equality for farm workers, for the poor, for Mexican Americans, for us all.

Nearly forty years after that tragic night in Los Angeles, the dream that Chávez and Kennedy shared remains unrealized. Arguably, farm workers today are even worse off than they were in the 1960s—most farm workers make less than $10,000 a year and only a lucky few have health insurance. In 2005, only 2 percent of California's field laborers were represented by a union. After their brief moment in the national spotlight in the 1960s during the grape boycott, agricultural workers faded from public consciousness. Few people eating grapes or a salad today wonder or care about the well-being of the laborer who picked their food, and worker rights have been lost in the shuffle of an increasingly mechanized and globalized economy.

The poverty that Chávez and Kennedy worked to overcome extended beyond the fields to the cities and barrios. Building momentum since the 1960s, U.S. poverty has proven its resilience. Hurricane Katrina in 2005 delivered a tragic reminder that the poor remain among us in urban and rural landscapes, and their numbers are growing.

The story of the relationship and alliance between Chávez and Kennedy is more than an account of a friendship; it is an opportunity to examine the foreground of the issues of race, class, and equality that continue to hold back our pursuit of Camelot. My account is centered in California, and in the struggles for equality of Mexican Americans. Poignantly, California held the best and worst of times for Kennedy, a senator from New York—it was where he broke bread with a weakened and slumping Chávez to symbolize the end of César's hunger strike that aimed to quell emerging violence in the grape strike; it was where Kennedy emerged triumphant in a major victory in the California presidential primary, which he attributed to Chávez's efforts to rouse voters; and it was where he died from an assassin's bullet as he reached to shake the hand of a Mexican American dishwasher moments after he celebrated that victory with the farm workers and other organizers who carried Kennedy's torch. California's role in any story grounded in migrant labor struggles is assured by its strong agricultural industry and its proximity to Mexico. Today, California remains the largest domicile state of migrant and seasonal farm workers.[1] California's central role in the migrant agricultural labor industry brought Kennedy to the state and into a friendship with Chávez through Kennedy's role on the Senate Subcommittee on Migratory Labor. Like California, Mexican Americans and Mexicans play a crucial role in this story; their significance is due not simply to Chávez's Mexican American heritage, but also to the perception and the reality of the substantial Mexican connection to migratory labor—today over 90 percent of migrant farm workers in the United States were born in Mexico.[2]

Mindful of the need to explore in detail the often complex issues of race, class, and equality encircling the relationship between a poor Mexican American labor organizer in California and a wealthy East Coast politician, I start with a biographical account of their friendship in the mid-1960s. Eventually, my account turns to the societal issues of the day, which remain today, ranging from rampant poverty (chapter 10) and the absence of protection for low-wage workers (chapter 7) to foreign war crippling the government's initiative to address poverty (chapter 9). I try to contrast and bridge the activism in rural fields (chapter 7) with mobilization in the urban barrios and ghettos, focusing particularly on the urban activism that marked the Chicano Movement in the late 1960s and early 1970s (chapter 8), and the union-organizing effort in the agricultural fields that Chávez led and Kennedy supported.

Most importantly, the account of their inspirational friendship confronts the emergence since the mid-1960s of the dominant issue today surrounding Mexican Americans and other Latinos—immigration (chapters 11, 15). In the 1960s, Americans regarded the farm worker cause as one of economic reform or, in the eyes of cynics, as economic redistribution. The ready supply of cheap immigrant labor, documented and undocumented, kept Chávez from procuring needed economic reform from employers. But today, the national perception of farm workers and of Mexican Americans generally as undocumented lawbreakers hampers the possibility of meaningful reform because the public sees any betterment of farm labor as encouraging immigrant entry and lawlessness.

Augmenting its inspiration for those working to combat poverty, and toward equality for Mexican Americans, the friendship of Chávez and Kennedy also holds political meaning toward galvanizing the Mexican American vote. Chávez accomplished this in the 1968 California primary, which saw a 100 percent turnout in some Mexican American precincts, an unprecedented turnout then and still unmatched. Looking at the political experience of Mexican American voters in that election and other 1960s elections (chapters 12, 15) gives a window into how Mexican American voters, and others, might recapture the promise of an antipoverty, multi-ethnic coalition, which Chávez and Kennedy envisioned to fulfill their shared dreams of Camelot.

Steven W. Bender

Acknowledgments

My colleague Keith Aoki lent his considerable store of expertise on many subjects, particularly racial politics; as well he constantly encouraged my efforts.

Another source of inspiration was Kevin Johnson, who provided scholarly guidance and marked a pathway of character and conviction for future progressive scholars to follow. I would have been honored to serve under your deanship, Kevin.

I appreciate advance readers of this manuscript, such as Kevin and UNLV's Sylvia Lazos, who provided detailed and insightful comments.

My research assistants at the University of Oregon School of Law, Nancy and Marcos Acevedo, Marisa Balderas, Denise Espinoza, Eulalio Garcia, Sivhwa Go, and Alma Zuniga, aided me greatly with their findings and comments. My secretary, Debby Warren, as usual, played an important role in helping me with the process of writing a book, which ranges from the tedious to the exhilarating.

As always, Angus Nesbit, a reference librarian at the University of Oregon School of Law, never questioned my calls for hundreds of sources, aiding me with legislative history and running down obscure newspaper sources. I'm also grateful for the assistance of librarians at the Walter Reuther and John F. Kennedy libraries.

My deepest thanks to Dolores Huerta and Richard Chávez for their insights adding to this book. While other voices have been silenced, Dolores and Richard march on for La Causa.

Part I

A Friendship Cut Short

CHAPTER ONE

Viva (John) Kennedy

I think that [Robert Kennedy and César Chávez] were kindred spirits before they met. They both recognized in the other the same values and the same hope for the country and hope for the [underprivileged].

—Ethel Kennedy[1]

Robert Kennedy and César Chávez first met in East Los Angeles in 1959.[2] There is nothing to indicate that their initial meeting was re-markable or that it sparked their inspiring friendship. That happened later, in 1966, when Kennedy went to central California as a U.S. sena-tor from New York to participate in Senate subcommittee hearings on farm labor. But their 1959 meeting was significant as it embodied their early but skillful efforts in the political arena, which set the stage for Chávez to campaign for Kennedy in the 1968 election. Chávez would return to Los Angeles in 1968 as a rural farm labor organizer, but his urban political organizing background among Mexican Americans in the barrio would boost Robert Kennedy to victory in California's primary that year, on an election night that represents both triumph and tragedy for the Mexican American experience.

Born in rural Arizona in 1927, Chávez went to California as a child and worked the fields picking fruits, vegetables, and cotton. So that he could help provide for his family, he quit school after the eighth grade. After serving in the Navy at seventeen in the final year of World War II, Chávez married and headed to northern California to work for a lumber company in the coastal redwoods. Not long after, Chávez and his wife Helen moved to the city—to the barrio known as *Sal Si Puedes* (translated, "get out if you can") in the California city of San Jose. While employed at a lumber mill there, Chávez was recruited to work on behalf of the Community Service Organization (CSO).

Formed in 1947 in East Los Angeles, the CSO was spurred in part by the defeat that year of Mexican American Edward Roybal in his campaign for the Los Angeles city council. Roybal's supporters started the CSO with the aid of Fred Ross, an organizer for the Chicago-based group Industrial Area Foundation, which sought to politically mobilize poor neighborhoods.[3] In addition to holding forums to discuss community problems and winning such community improvements as paved streets, sidewalks, traffic signals, recreational facilities, and clinics,[4] the CSO had a political bent through Ross, swiftly registering 40,000 new voters in East Los Angeles.[5] In the 1949 election, these newly minted Mexican American voters contributed to Roybal's election as the first Mexican American on the Los Angeles city council since 1881;[6] Roybal later became the first Mexican American representative elected to Congress from California. It was the CSO that took Ross to the *Sal Si Puedes* barrio in 1952 during his effort to establish a San Jose chapter. Chávez was helping a local priest address the problems of Mexican farm workers, and the priest pointed Ross to Chávez. The night of their first meeting, Chávez began work registering Mexican American voters in San Jose, laboring by day at the lumberyard and by night going door to door. Soon, Chávez was chairing the registration campaign in San Jose for CSO.

Most of these newly registered voters would vote Democrat. Scholars attribute this Democratic allegiance of Mexican American voters at the time to the New Deal administration of Franklin Delano Roosevelt in the 1930s and early 1940s, some of whose programs benefited them. Their loyalty was cemented by the thousands of Mexican Americans, like Chávez, who served in World War II under a Democratic president.[7] Perhaps fearing the impact of these new Mexican American registrants in San Jose, Republican operatives stalked the voting booths in the 1952 election, demanding that Mexican American voters confirm their citizenship.[8] With Chávez taking a leadership role, the CSO filed a complaint against the Republican Central Committee with federal authorities, who instructed the Republicans not to interfere with CSO's organizing.

To increase the eligible electorate, Chávez began helping Mexican immigrants obtain citizenship. César's involvement with the CSO led him to Oakland, where he organized a CSO chapter; to the San Joaquin Valley;

and to Oxnard on the California coast. By 1959, Chávez moved his family to East Los Angeles, when he was asked to come to Los Angeles to work at the CSO headquarters, located between downtown and East Los Angeles, and promoted to serve as CSO's national director.

At that time, 80 percent of the Mexican American population in the United States lived in urban areas such as Los Angeles, San Antonio, and Chicago.[9] Los Angeles County housed the largest Mexican population in the United States, starting the 1960s with 576,716 people and ending the decade with 1,228,593 Mexican residents. At the same time, the Anglo population in Los Angeles County actually decreased.[10] Anglos in Los Angeles fled the inner city for the suburbs, commuting to work on freeways that decimated neighborhoods throughout the increasingly Mexican communities east of downtown Los Angeles. Once home to substantial numbers of Anglos and Jewish Americans, the East Los Angeles area browned in the 1950s and 1960s as it became more Mexican, and more poor. Compounding the poverty of the barrio was the absence of political power of the Mexican American community in Los Angeles.[11] In addition to the challenges of galvanizing young, poor, immigrant voters, gerrymandered legislative districts fractured the barrio. Ensuring local, state, and federal underrepresentation, the California legislature in the early 1960s split East Los Angeles and the surrounding areas into nine assembly districts, seven Senate districts, and six congressional districts, so that no one district had more than 30 percent of its registered voters of Mexican American heritage.[12] From 1962 to 1985, no Mexican American or other Latino was elected to the city council or other citywide office in Los Angeles.[13]

Managing his brother John's 1960 presidential campaign, Robert Kennedy came to Los Angeles in late November or early December 1959 and met at two in the morning with César Chávez in César's capacity as director of the CSO. They discussed the CSO's voter registration drive among Mexican Americans. Kennedy's campaign staff pitched to Chávez a public relations approach to registering voters that relied on radio and newspaper publicity. But Chávez disagreed and contended the only way to register voters in the area was by going door to door: "So I was outlining a campaign where we would go to every Spanish-speaking door in the state, minimizing the radio and newspaper and all that, saying that that wasn't going to get them to vote, to register."[14] Robert Kennedy arrived late at the early-morning meeting and listened to Chávez explain his strategy to the campaign team. After listening, Kennedy intervened on Chávez's behalf and instructed his team, "Let him do it the way he's used to doing it. It's been effective."[15]

The 1960 national Democratic Party convention, held in Los Angeles, nominated Senator John F. Kennedy. California's Edward Roybal and two other Mexican American politicians from New Mexico and Texas wanted to enhance the involvement of Mexican Americans in the Kennedy campaign, and after the convention they spoke to campaign manager Robert Kennedy.[16] He approved their idea of outreach to the Mexican American community. Overseen by a Latino[17] law student from George Washington University, the outreach effort took the name Viva Kennedy. The Viva slogan actually came from the Nixon camp, which had rejected the idea of galvanizing the Latino population through an organizing "Viva" campaign.[18] Adopting the symbol of Senator John Kennedy's riding a burro while wearing an oversized sombrero emblazoned with the words *Viva Kennedy*, the Viva Kennedy effort launched by forming local clubs that answered to Robert Kennedy rather than to the state Democratic Party leadership.[19]

The Viva Kennedy clubs sought to connect John Kennedy to the Mexican American community through Kennedy's progressive politics, which were sympathetic to the poor. Other selling points included Kennedy's ethnic Irish heritage—Mexican American voters, plagued by racism such as signs in the Southwest reading "No Mexicans or Dogs Allowed,"[20] could appreciate the struggles of the Irish, who faced their own discriminatory signs on the East Coast, such as "No Irish Need Apply."[21] Further, Kennedy was a Catholic, as was an overwhelming percentage of the Mexican American population, and his wife spoke Spanish. As a biographer of the Viva Kennedy club campaign effort described:

> For Club leaders, [John] Kennedy's religious affiliation represented a cultural bridge to the Mexican American community. His Catholicism meant that he understood religious and cultural prejudices. It meant he understood the [funding] dilemma of Catholic schools.... And it meant that he valued family and tradition. The fact that his wife Jacqueline understood and spoke Spanish meant that Kennedy could communicate with Mexican Americans and understand their needs. With these points to sell, Mexican American reformers felt confident that they could get barrio residents to vote for him. The fact that he was simpatico [a nice guy] made it an easier sell.[22]

Organizers initiated Viva Kennedy clubs throughout the United States in about thirty states,[23] and reached out beyond Mexican Americans to Puerto Ricans, Cubans, and those from Central and South America. In California, the Viva Kennedy effort tapped into the existing organization of the Mexican American Political Association, formed in Fresno in spring 1959 and chaired by Edward Roybal. Roybal served as the liaison between the California clubs and the national Kennedy headquarters. Central to the Viva Kennedy effort was registering new Mexican American and other Latino voters, and the Chávez-led CSO helped to conduct this mission. By the time of the election, an estimated 140,000 Mexican Americans were newly registered to vote in California.[24] César Chávez saw the Viva Kennedy campaign primarily as a public relations tool, distinct from the hands-on organizers of the CSO, who were doing the real work of registering voters. As Chávez explained, the CSO was "cleared" of any accountability to the Viva Kennedy club infrastructure: "We don't want any of those guys telling us what to do. We do it ourselves. We're judged on whether we did fail or we didn't, but we don't want any committee or anything in between us."[25] Later, when *Time* magazine attributed the success of the drive to register Spanish-speaking voters to the Viva Kennedy organization, Chávez asked CSO organizer Dolores Huerta to protest this to Robert Kennedy. As Huerta recalls, she confronted Kennedy with the *Time* magazine in her hand, and Kennedy threw up his hands, saying "I know, I know."[26] Kennedy agreed that the story was a mistake and a few weeks later *Time* published a letter from Kennedy revealing "[t]he credit for this outstanding job of registration should go to the Community Service Organization, which for a number of years has been dedicated to this work among Spanish-speaking citizens of California."[27]

John Kennedy came to East Los Angeles in early November during his 1960 presidential campaign, speaking after dark at the East Los Angeles Junior College stadium, which seated 22,000 but on this occasion was filled beyond capacity with 25,000 listeners and an estimated 10,000 to 15,000 onlookers surrounding the stadium. Kennedy ate a Mexican lunch that day on Olvera Street—the historic old Mexico center of downtown—in Casa Avila, dating to 1818 and reputed to be the oldest building standing in Los Angeles.[28] As the *Los Angeles Times* reported the next day, Kennedy appealed to "new voters, to minority groups, and the working [person]."[29]

John Kennedy was elected in 1960 by the slimmest of margins—nationally only 114,673 votes, and with an electoral college margin of 303 to 219. Robert Kennedy told a Mexico City reporter that it was the "votes of Mexican Americans and other Latin Americans in the United States" that elected his brother.[30] John Kennedy attracted more than 85 percent of the national Mexican American vote, a bloc vote for the Democratic candidate.[31] Commentators credited the Viva Kennedy campaign with Kennedy's victory in at least three states (Illinois, New Mexico, and Texas). Kennedy carried 91 percent of the Mexican American vote in Texas. Although he received only 70 percent of the Mexican American vote in New Mexico, Kennedy won New Mexico by 2,000 votes even without securing a majority of Anglo votes.[32] Kennedy also prevailed in Illinois, another Viva Kennedy state with a large Mexican American community, by only 9,000 votes. Although Kennedy lost California to former California congressman and senator Richard Nixon, the strong turnout in his favor of Latinos (an estimated 85 percent favoring Kennedy) almost gave Kennedy the Golden State. Nationally, Latinos turned out to vote in record numbers in the 1960 election.[33]

Reflecting on the aftermath of the Kennedy victory, one Latino commentator summarized that "Kennedy's victory in November 1960 delighted Mexican Americans but brought little change to their communities."[34] Organizers of the Viva Kennedy campaign expected that Kennedy would make high-profile Latino appointments to his cabinet and to the judiciary, but appointments were few (two prominent Latinos did decline ambassadorships) and to minor posts.[35] Edward Roybal complained that Kennedy "failed almost completely to recognize Viva Kennedy leaders or supporters in patronage appointments."[36]

Chávez and Robert Kennedy first met in late 1959 when the campaign of Senator John Kennedy for president brought them together in Los Angeles. When they would meet again six years later in central California, President Kennedy would be dead from an assassin's bullet, Robert Kennedy would be a freshman senator from New York, and César Chávez would have left the East Los Angeles barrio for central California to pursue his life's work in rural Delano organizing farm workers.

CHAPTER TWO

Viva la Huelga[1]

*[Robert Kennedy] came to us and asked two questions.... "What do you want?
And how can I help?" That's why we loved him.*

—Dolores Huerta[2]

Although he grew up in the farm fields of Arizona and California, the
early 1960s found César Chávez living in the urban East Los Angeles
barrio while serving as director of the Community Service Organization
(CSO). But in March 1962, Chávez took a new direction, a return to his
rural roots among the farm workers.

At CSO's annual convention in March, Chávez broached an idea to the
membership of a pilot project to organize farm workers. His salary for the
year would be paid by the workers, rather than by CSO, through charging
dues. But the CSO membership voted down his proposal on the convention floor. According to biographers Susan Ferriss and Ricardo Sandoval,
"[a] majority of CSO members wanted to keep the focus on the growing
population of Chicanos who lived in cities—those who had left the field
work behind them."[3]

Chávez stuck to his conviction and resigned on the spot: "I have an announcement to make. I resign."[4] On his thirty-fifth birthday at the end of
March, he left CSO and the urban barrio and moved his family of eight
children to Delano, California. Chávez's wife's family lived there, as did his
brother Richard (a carpenter who headed the Delano CSO);[5] as a teenager
Chávez had resided at times in Delano, and he met his wife Helen in a
Delano malt shop.

Located some twenty-five miles north of Bakersfield, Delano was home
to about fourteen thousand people in the early 1960s.[6] An agricultural town,

its growers were white Yugoslavians, Italians, and Armenians, and their farm workers were from all backgrounds but tended to be either Filipino or Mexican American.[7] These workers were mostly migrant farm laborers, but Delano had a substantial year-round farm labor workforce—32 percent of its seven thousand field workers in 1968 for example[8]—and this facilitated union organizing.

Working in the fields of Delano with his wife Helen to make ends meet, Chávez set out to organize farm workers seeking dignity in their work and lives. Among those joining the struggle were Dolores Huerta, who later would serve as vice president of the United Farm Workers organization. In the early 1960s, Huerta was a schoolteacher and a lobbyist in Sacramento, California, for the CSO's legislative agenda. As Huerta remembered, "I quit the CSO because I couldn't stand seeing kids coming to class hungry and needing shoes. I thought I could do more by organizing farm workers than trying to teach their hungry children."[9]

César Chávez and Dolores Huerta christened their fledgling organization the National Farm Workers Association (NFWA), which they envisioned more as a social movement than as a union.[10] Its first formal meeting took place in September 1962 in Fresno, where they adopted the movement's symbol of a black Aztec eagle in a white circle.[11] Signing up farm workers, Chávez and his organizers provided death benefits to worker families as well as a credit union and other services, in exchange for modest dues. Chávez and Huerta targeted towns and farm labor camps between Stockton (near Sacramento) and Arvin (just south of Bakersfield), distributing registration cards to workers and forming committees in the towns and camps.[12] Initially, Chávez concentrated on organizing Mexican American workers, but later extended the campaign to other ethnic groups.

In September 1965, workers belonging to the Agricultural Workers Organizing Committee (AWOC), a Filipino farm labor union, launched a strike in Delano against grape growers. Unfair wages precipitated their strike—growers offered only $1.00 an hour for the grueling work, while paying $1.40 an hour in other locations. As Chicano historian Rodolfo Acuña recounts, "[t]he strike demands were simple: $1.40 an hour or 25¢ a box."[13] At the time, Delano grape pickers were earning about $2,400 a year, but the poverty line in 1965 for a family of four was $3,223.[14] Although it was still early in their plan of organization, Chávez and his NFWA members (mostly Mexican American) voted overwhelmingly out of solidarity to join the Filipino workers on strike.[15]

Their combined grape strike, later known as the Great Delano Grape Strike,[16] evolved into a protracted struggle that would tax the health of César Chávez and propel the cause of poor Mexican American farm workers into the national spotlight. The strike and its accompanying boycott would not succeed until all the Delano grape growers signed union contracts in the summer of 1970, long after Robert Kennedy would come to Delano to join the cause, and after an assassin's bullet in 1968 would end the life of the farm workers' most powerful political friend.

Following John Kennedy's assassination in 1963, his successor Lyndon Johnson was elected president in 1964. By the mid-1960s, the Mexican American community nationally numbered four to five million.[17] Capitalizing on this growing Mexican American population loyal to the Democratic Party, Johnson's 1964 campaign revived the Viva Kennedy organizing model restyled as Viva Johnson.[18] Republican candidate Barry Goldwater countered with "Amigos de Goldwater" and "Arriba Goldwater," and emphasized that he spoke Spanish and his running mate was Catholic, but Goldwater's record on civil rights and labor was far afield from the sentiments of the Latino community.[19] In California, the CSO that Chávez had left behind in Los Angeles continued its task of registering Latino voters, most of whom were expected to vote Democratic. In the relative quiet before the Delano grape strike, Chávez and his fledgling NFWA organization campaigned for Johnson in 1964, with their efforts again independent of the Viva (Johnson) clubs.[20]

Armando Rendón characterized the Mexican American vote for Johnson in 1964 as a "sympathy vote [for JFK] to a great extent," but "a massive vote no less, and one that held many hopes."[21] Johnson trounced Goldwater, receiving 61 percent of the national vote. Mexican Americans voted 90 percent for Johnson, and Puerto Ricans 86 percent, both resounding bloc votes. Still, the overwhelming victory margin meant that Latinos were discounted as a factor in the election, and the Viva Johnson infrastructure was dismantled after the election despite urgings that the Democratic Party retain its momentum in the Latino community with monthly newsletters to local Viva club leaders.[22]

After serving as attorney general during his brother's presidency and being passed over as Johnson's running mate in 1964, Robert Kennedy was sent by New York voters that year to the U.S. Senate. As a freshman senator in Congress, Kennedy sat on the Migratory Labor Subcommittee of the Senate Labor Committee. In that capacity, he soon reunited with César Chávez, this time in circumstances that forged a deep friendship that endured for the remainder of Kennedy's short life.

When Kennedy began his Senate term in 1965, farm workers were excluded from most of the basic protections that federal law accorded to other workers. Chávez's efforts to organize farm workers in the early 1960s were hampered by the exclusion of agricultural laborers from the federal National Labor Relations Act (NLRA). The NLRA protected employees in other industries in their unionizing effort by prohibiting employers' firing employees who unionized. Unrestrained by the NLRA, farm employers not only could fire employees who supported unions, but they also could interfere with efforts of others to unionize their employees, and refuse to bargain collectively with any union that represented its workers.[23] The federal Fair Labor Standards Act of 1938, which established a minimum wage, also excluded agricultural employees.[24] Child labor laws failed to protect farm worker children—Chávez himself worked the fields as a young boy. As a child in California, Chávez enrolled in at least thirty-six schools while his family migrated from farm to farm, until he left school after the eighth grade to help support his parents and siblings.[25]

Early on, in a 1965 hearing of the Senate Subcommittee on Migratory Labor, Robert Kennedy made clear his support for reforms protecting farm laborers. Appearing before that subcommittee, a senior lobbyist for the American Farm Bureau Federation opposed the pending reform package that would bring farm workers under the NLRA, strengthen child labor laws in agriculture, and extend minimum wage protection to farm workers. Kennedy blasted his testimony, commenting: "This is the first time I have heard you, so perhaps this comes as more of a shock to me; to be opposed to a minimum wage, to be opposed to legislation which would limit the use of children between the ages of 10 and 13 for working, to be opposed to collective bargaining [under the NLRA] completely … to oppose all that without some alternative makes the rest of the arguments you have senseless."[26]

The next year, 1966, the chairman of that Senate subcommittee, Democrat Harrison Williams, Jr. of New Jersey, reintroduced his farm labor reform package in the Senate. By that time, the AWOC/NFWA grape strike in Delano was under way and gaining national attention. In December 1965, the president of the United Auto Workers (UAW) union, Walter Reuther, and its western director, Paul Schrade, came to Delano with a national media following in order to lend their union's support to the grape strike.[27] They persuaded Senator Williams to hold hearings in California's farm country as an aid to the proposed reform legislation, and also to boost the grape strike. Williams scheduled hearings over three days in 1966—March 14 in Sacramento, March 15 in Visalia (located between Fresno and Delano), and March 16 in Delano—and also arranged for committee visits to farm labor camps and the grape picket lines.

That March, Kennedy was consumed in Congress with spiraling U.S. involvement in Vietnam. According to his Senate aide Peter Edelman, Kennedy was reluctant to leave Washington to attend the labor hearings, but Reuther persuaded him to participate. Kennedy's decision was politically risky—as Michael Harrington, author of the seminal work on poverty, *The Other America*, explained, "The grape growers of California are an extremely powerful group of people, and traditionally, many of the growers have been conservative Democrats rather than Republicans. Politically speaking, in California at that time, it was probably a stupid thing to do."[28]

The Senate hearings opened in Sacramento without Kennedy. Subcommittee chair Williams presided over testimony from grower and worker representatives. Williams explained that the committee chose California for hearings because it was the nation's "largest and most varied agricultural State."[29] Williams explained further: "We have also come to California to seek the causes and the background of the protracted strike in the grape vineyards in the Delano area—to see whether this bitter dispute stands as a symbol of the need to provide procedures in place of chaos."[30] Before the hearings, Williams commented that "the migrant worker lives and works under conditions that must be recognized for what they are—a national disgrace."[31] In political contrast to Williams, who was regarded widely as a champion of farm workers, California Republican senator George Murphy, a grower supporter, also attended the farm hearings.[32] César Chávez testified before these bookend senators on the opening day in a jammed hearing room at the state capitol, prefacing his testimony with the following observation:

[W]e are meeting, once again, to discuss the problems of the farmworker, and what might be done to correct these problems. Such meetings have been called for decades, and unfortunately things have not changed very much in spite of them. The same labor camps which were used 30 years ago at the time of the La Follette committee hearings are still housing our workers. The same exploitation of child labor, the same idea that farmworkers are a different breed of people—humble, happy, built close to the ground—still prevails.[33]

He articulated labor's demand: "What the farmworkers in our country are asking for is equality.... All that these [reform package] bills do is say that people who work on farms should have the same human rights as people who work in construction crews, or in factories, or in offices."[34] Chávez explained the economics of poverty that farm workers face:

[The] average farm worker in Delano has seven children, lives in a house which he rents for $55 a month, makes payments on a car, furniture, and to a finance company. Before the strike he worked eight months of the year [during picking seasons] at $1.10 an hour and his wife worked four months beside him, and on weekends and in the summer, his children worked too.... This man buys food at the same stores at the same prices that the farmer does.[35]

Growers uniformly denounced the proposed Williams reform package. Regarding wages, they testified that California growers offered the highest wages in the country and that wages could improve only through nonunion "individual relationships" between the growers and workers.[36] Minimum wage laws would "destroy incentive." Child labor restrictions would frustrate the "far-reaching educational benefits in allowing children to work [in the fields]."[37] The reform proposal to add farm workers to the unionizing protections of the NLRA drew sharp accusations from growers that the impetus for organizing was coming from "trouble-makers from the cities"[38] rather than from the farm workers themselves: "There is no strike among the Delano farm workers. The so-called strike is pure myth, manufactured out of nothing by outside agitators who are more interested in creating trouble in the United States than in the welfare of farm workers."[39] Growers also decried federal intervention in what they viewed as local problems: "Any regulation of labor relations covering farm labor should be done under

State law so that a State board can properly handle the multitude of local problems involved in production of farm crops."[40]

Robert Kennedy joined the hearings in Visalia on the afternoon of the second day, making him the third and final Senate committee member (of six committee members) to participate in the California hearings. Earlier that day, Republican George Murphy denounced as "shameful" a nearby farm labor housing camp (home to some of the striking Delano workers) that he toured with an entourage of fifty reporters; he urged its destruction and replacement with a federally financed project. The labor camp consisted of small, one-room tin shacks without toilets or water. That afternoon, Kennedy stated his support for improving farm worker housing, but suggested further that "a whole range of legislation is needed for farm workers."[41] Responding to grower opposition to including farm workers under the collective bargaining protections of the NLRA, Kennedy quipped: "If we can put a man on the moon by the end of the 1960s, it seems we should be able to work out such a simple problem for farm workers after 30 years of talking about it."[42]

Kennedy aide Peter Edelman remembers an encounter in the parking lot during a lunch recess between Kennedy and Chávez, their first since the Kennedy presidential campaign six years earlier, as a "riveting scene":

> The two men immediately bonded. Chavez, himself a child of poor farm workers, had a mystical quality. He was a very quiet man, short in stature, with a face that was as purely kind in its appearance as that of any human being I have ever seen. The two of them stood there talking, eye to eye, in a low conversational tone that was barely audible even to the first ring of people around them. A crowd gathered, two deep, then four deep, and finally ten or fifteen people deep. It went on maybe five minutes, maybe even ten. I don't know what they said to each other. I do know that when it was over they were friends for life.[43]

There was much to draw the two men together, some reasons immediately obvious and other alliances to emerge. Kennedy crusaded for causes of the underprivileged throughout his term in the Senate, and Chávez embodied the struggle for dignity for the forgotten, ravaged farm workers. They were both about the same age (Kennedy two and one half years older), both Catholic, and both committed to a nonviolence credo. Chávez was a disciple of Gandhi who later imperiled his health with a near month-long fast to stave off violence in the grape strike, and Kennedy tried to quell violence throughout his Senate career—on a later trip to Delano he told a crowd that "violence will bring no answer."[44] One Kennedy biographer summed up their bond: "For all their differences in background, the two men were rather alike: both short, shy, familial, devout, opponents of violence, with strong veins of melancholy and fatalism. Chavez, Kennedy believed, was doing for Spanish-speaking Americans what Martin Luther King had done for black Americans: giving them new convictions of pride and solidarity."[45]

The third and final day's Senate hearing occurred in Delano during the throes of the grape strike there. Kennedy addressed Delano grower contentions—that Chávez and the other union organizers were outside agitators and that their workers had no interest in union elections—by comparing union elections to democratic participation in America: "I've heard people say quite frankly down in Mississippi, 'You don't understand. Negroes don't want to vote.' I think you've got to give people an opportunity. Maybe they don't want to, but at least you've got to open the door to them. That's all I think members of the committee are suggesting, not that you should recognize one union over another or one better than another, or even that there should be any union at all."[46] Earlier, in the first day's testimony, Chávez drew the same comparison to the struggles of African Americans for a say in their destiny: "Ranchers in Delano say that the farmworkers are happy living the way they are—just like the southern plantation owner used to say about his Negroes. But our workers know what the Negro has done to achieve a vote, and they are working for the right to vote, believing that they too will succeed."[47]

That final hearings day in Delano, a confrontation between Kennedy and Sheriff Leroy Galyen of Kern County (which includes Delano) became legend among local Mexican Americans and cemented the budding friendship between Kennedy and Chávez.[48] The prior fall of 1965, Sheriff Galyen had issued a special directive against the striking farm workers in Delano, declaring that anyone who shouted from the roadside was disturbing the peace. The day after Galyen issued his directive, police arrested a striker who read from a famous Jack London essay, "Definition of a Strikebreaker," which describes strikebreaker scabs as having a "corkscrew soul" and a "tumor of rotten principles."[49] Two days later, Sheriff Galyen forbade strikers from using the word *huelga*, which means "strike" in Spanish. Earlier, the FBI had investigated the Delano strikers' use of that word, fearful it meant to revolt, but finding that it meant simply to strike or to leave a place behind vacant.[50] When the sheriff issued his new directive, several farm workers and Helen Chávez began shouting "huelga" toward strikebreakers. César Chávez was in Berkeley that day speaking to college students participating in the Free Speech Movement,[51] and students there took up the "huelga" cheer.[52] But back in Delano, police arrested Helen and forty-three other pickets who violated the sheriff's order, booking them into the county jail, where bail was set at $276 each—more than a month's salary at the time. Workers gathered at the jail to picket their arrest and sing songs while they were detained; Helen spent three days in the county jail merely for shouting "huelga."

Before these arrests, the Delano police department and the Kern County sheriff's office had conducted striker surveillance, compiling a dossier on about five thousand picketers with their photographs taken from the picket lines. Police would complete the file with information gathered by stopping pickets and asking questions such as their names and backgrounds.[53]

No doubt this frontier law enforcement of intimidation and the baseless arrest of his wife Helen riled Chávez. On the first day of the Senate hearings in Sacramento, Chávez told the senators (Williams and Murphy) that the Kern County lawmen were photographing and interrogating picketers while they marched peacefully on the road. Senator Williams commented to Chávez: "I don't understand by what authority you have to go through the inquisition and questioning and all that." Chávez replied: "At one point we made up our minds we had been harassed enough, and we refused to give them any information and refused to let them take our pictures after we had been subjected to this many, many times, and we told the inquiring officer from the Kern County Sheriff's Office that if he wanted more information from us or wanted to take our picture, he would first have to arrest us."[54]

Senator Murphy suggested inviting the sheriff to explain these actions, setting up the confrontation between Sheriff Galyen and former attorney general Kennedy in Delano two days later. Nearly one thousand spectators, many of them Mexican American, crowded into the hearing, held in the Delano high school auditorium. Over three hundred could not squeeze in and waited outside the auditorium.[55] The day was stiflingly hot and the auditorium was jammed—space had to be cleared for the growers who attended.[56]

Kennedy first questioned Galyen about the policy of photographing and naming each striker:

> KENNEDY: Do you take pictures of everybody in the city?
> SHERIFF GALYEN: Well, if he's on strike or something like that.[57]

Kennedy pressed on, leading his questioning into the territory of civil liberties and constitutional guarantees that Kennedy understood well as a former attorney general. The questioning soon reached the arrest the previous October of Helen and the other forty-three picketers:[58]

> GALYEN: [W]e had news from the inside, that there was going to be some cutting done if they didn't stop saying certain things, so I'm responsible to arrest them as well as anyone else.
> KENNEDY: What did you arrest them for?
> GALYEN: Why, if they got into a riot and started cutting up the people
> . . .
> KENNEDY: I'm not talking about that. Once you got into a riot, I understand that, but before, when they're just walking along, what did you arrest them for?
> GALYEN: Well, if I have a reason to believe that there's going to be a riot started, and somebody tells me there's going to be trouble if you don't stop them, it's my duty to stop them.
> KENNEDY: Then do you go out there and arrest them?
> GALYEN: Yes.
> . . .
> KENNEDY: What do you charge them with?
> GALYEN: Violation of—unlawful assembly.
> KENNEDY: I think that's most interesting. Who told you that they're going to riot?
> GALYEN: The men right out in the field that they were talking to said, "If you don't get them out of here, we're going to cut their hearts out." So rather than let them get cut, we removed the cause.[59]

Senator Murphy joined in questioning the sheriff:

> MURPHY: Do I understand you, Sheriff, that it's your opinion that it's better to take precautionary moves before the trouble starts, that this is in the best interest of the community and the peaceful interests of the citizens?

GALYEN: Who wants a big riot on his hands? And if you can stop it, why, let's stop it before it gets to that point. And I think you'll find all down the line that we've had wonderful cooperation between all of them, and the longer we went along, you'll find nobody say we beat anyone, or anything like that. This is not Selma, Ala[bama].

KENNEDY: ... This is a most interesting concept, I think, that you suddenly hear or you talk about the fact that somebody makes a report about somebody going to get out of order, perhaps violate the law, and you go and arrest them, and they haven't done anything wrong. How can you go arrest somebody if they haven't violated the law?

GALYEN: They're ready to violate the law. [60]

The auditorium crowd laughed in disbelief, as did Kennedy. At this point, Senator Murphy, either praising or, as he contended later, mocking the sheriff, interjected "I think it's a shame you weren't there before the Watts riots."[61] Then, Senator Williams called a recess for lunch, and Kennedy delivered his immortal scolding to hearty cheers from the overflow crowd:[62]

KENNEDY: Can I suggest in the interim period of time, the luncheon period of time, that the sheriff and the district attorney read the Constitution of the United States?

Chávez later conveyed the unusual tenor of Kennedy's support at the Senate hearings: "By the time the hearing ended Senator Kennedy was like a thousand percent behind us endorsing our efforts. There's no question—there was no dilly-dallying in our mind, his mind, or the grower's mind where he stood. That was what was so beautiful about it because usually what happens is you have a politician who's always trying to please both sides. Senator Kennedy just came right down to the issue."[63]

Kennedy had spent the morning of the Delano hearings with Chávez and the farm workers. After the Visalia hearing Kennedy flew to Los Angeles for dinner with singer Andy Williams. Chávez's aide and Peter Edelman met him at the airport in the morning, and the farm workers took Kennedy on a tour from the vineyards to the picket lines to the union's headquarters.[64] At the Filipino Hall, Kennedy declared his support for the farm worker struggle in Delano. Speaking with César Chávez at his side, Kennedy told the press: "We have come clearly to the conclusion that an ignored part of our population has been the farm workers. The farm workers have suffered over the last thirty years, and that has to be changed. It's not just a question of wages. It's a question of housing. It's a question of living conditions. It's a question of hope for the future."[65]

Kennedy even joined the striking farm workers on their picket line that morning, marching at a Di Giorgio Fruit Corporation ranch, a primary target of the grape strike given Di Giorgio's holdings at the time in California, which exceeded 13,000 acres of vineyards and fruit orchards.[66] As UAW official Paul Schrade described it:

[I] was marching in front of the DiGiorgio Ranch where there was this half-mile picketline of farm workers under the blue skies and in the wide open spaces of the San Joaquin Valley and Bob [Kennedy] came marching down the line shaking hands with all of the pickets. And you could hear coming from a distance these great voices shouting "Viva Kennedy" and "Kennedy por presidente" and it was a great time when you knew that friendship had been cemented and Bob wouldn't forget; that the farmworkers wouldn't forget. It really was very important towards building the movement.[67]

Kennedy's enthusiastic embrace of the grape picket struggle that day surprised many, including Chávez:

Even then, I had an idea he was going to be a candidate for the Presidency, and I was concerned for him because he endorsed us so straightforwardly, without straddling the line. This was a time when everybody was against us; the only people for us were ourselves. I was sitting next to Dolores Huerta [in the Senate hearings], and we both had the same thought—that he didn't have to go that far. Instead of that awful feeling against politicians who don't commit themselves, we felt protective.[68]

Paul Schrade summed up Kennedy's statements at the Delano hearing and his expressions in support of the grape strike later that day: "I'd never seen any Democrat, much less a Republican, do that before."[69]

Media gave the Senate labor hearings prominent coverage, prompting several Californians to send Kennedy letters suggesting that farm workers, not growers, were overreaching, or criticizing Kennedy's questioning of the sheriff. One writer from Delano contended that "[w]e are fostering a nation of parasites" and that Democrats "who believe in free enterprise" should abandon the Democratic Party.[70] Comments critical of Kennedy included: "Surely Mr. Senator as the brother of our late President you should not want an officer of the law to wait until somebody is killed before he takes any action to prevent this.... You sounded more like some little school boy than a U.S. Senator and Former Atty. General."[71] Chávez, however, was appreciative of Kennedy's strong showing of support and wrote Kennedy in late March shortly after the hearings:

> This is, from my point of view, one of the first times that farm workers and their advocates have ever participated as equals in hearings devoted to their own problems....
>
> [We] deeply appreciate the strong and provocative lines of questioning which you used to elicit important information from many witnesses....
>
> I am sure you share my pleasure in seeing so many labor, church, and ethnic leaders speaking more strongly than ever about the rights of farm workers. I pray that we will have the strength to help ourselves and to make wise use of the help of others in gaining our freedom and our cherished rights as Americans. I hope that you will continue to have a strong concern for the farm workers in New York State, in California, and elsewhere. Our movement is new, but it will grow. We will be pressing Washington for equal protection of the law, and I am hoping that you will always be counted among our staunch advocates.
>
> Again, my sincere thanks to you.[72]

The friendship that emerged during the Senate farm worker hearings in California ultimately paid both men spiritual and even political dividends. Kennedy's presence at the hearings drew national media attention to the grape strike.[73] It spurred Chávez's efforts to raise funds to support the strikers,[74] and boosted morale of the farm workers who had been picketing for six months at the time of the hearings. Chávez reflected: "He gave us credibility. We were being murdered. Literally. So when he came and championed our cause, he made us credible. He helped stop the cops from beating the hell out of us."[75] Elsewhere, Chávez remembered, "No one was taking any notice of what we were doing. Then Robert Kennedy came out to see us. He joined our picket lines. That was unheard of. Once he took an interest, lots of other people started coming, offering help."[76]

Throughout his early organizing career, Chávez was dogged with allegations that he was a Communist. During the administrations of both

Johnson and Nixon, the FBI shadowed Chávez, searching for evidence of Communist or subversive influence in his unionizing efforts.[77] As governor of California, Ronald Reagan blatantly attacked Chávez as a Communist, calling Chávez and his organizers "classic Communists" who are "a danger to American society," and warning that "loud-mouth Chávez must be punished."[78] After the Delano hearing, reporters asked Kennedy whether the strike leaders were Communists. Kennedy responded "No, they are not Communists, they're struggling for their rights." Kennedy brought unique credibility to this declaration—he was widely regarded as an anti-Communist figure since his role as assistant counsel in the Senate investigations led by Senator Joseph McCarthy. Moreover, Kennedy often lashed out at Communist ideals and practices, remarking in various speeches:

> The challenge which international communism hurls against the rule of law is very great.[79]
>
> Yes, we have our problems in Alabama [in ensuring civil rights for blacks], but to be blunt, we are not shooting old women and young children in the back as Communists are doing in Berlin.... Can anybody equate the disturbance in Alabama last spring with the death by starvation of hundreds and hundreds of thousands of Chinese peasants under a farm commune system which has failed?[80]

Chávez reflected later on Kennedy's remark to the Delano reporters dispelling the notion of Communism in the farm worker movement: "So he really helped us, and things began to change."[81] Chávez also recalled: "I think it was the turning point in the vicious campaign on the 'Red-baiting' issue and us. He turned it completely around, completely destroyed it, tore it apart. They kept trying for another year, but after that ... people just wouldn't believe them any more."[82]

Shortly after the hearings, a New York constituent wrote Kennedy about a John Birch Society magazine that included a photo of Kennedy in Delano with the caption "Kennedy defends Reds," prompting the constituent to ask "What is your relationship to and with this Delano [farm worker] group? Could it be true that decent citizens of that area are being led by communist-trained members?"[83] Kennedy replied: "[At the Senate hearings] I came to the conclusion that the strikers are fighting for the very legitimate goals of union organization and collective bargaining, opportunities all workers should have if they want them. We also did not find any evidence of communist infiltration among the strikers, contrary to the accusations of the John Birch Society."[84]

Commencing the day after the Delano hearings, Chávez led the farm workers on a *peregrinación*—a pilgrimage—covering 350 miles on foot from Delano to Sacramento, where the hearings had opened. While Chávez was at the state capitol seeking to garner legislative and public attention for the farm worker cause, Kennedy was back in Washington, D.C. There he embraced the Williams farm labor reform package, and some progress was made in Congress that year. The Williams package proposed to include farm workers within the federal minimum wage protections, initially at $1.15 an hour, 10 cents an hour less than other workers. At the Senate hearings, many California growers opposed this protection, contending they already paid their workers more than the proposed minimum wage. By contrast, California governor Pat Brown believed the proposed federal farm worker wage was too low, and urged that farm workers receive the same $1.25 minimum wage as other workers.[85] Following the Senate hearings, Congress enacted the Fair Labor Standards Amendments of 1966, which extended a minimum wage to agricultural workers.[86] Still, this coverage came with significant exceptions—including the condition that a farm employ the equivalent of seven full-time workers (five hundred "man-days" a quarter) before the minimum wage applied, which in the 1970s meant that only about 35 percent of farm workers were covered. Further, agricultural employees were left unprotected by federal overtime pay benefits. By the early 1970s, the minimum wage for farm workers increased to $1.30 an hour, but other workers were guaranteed $1.60. Labor market economics also failed the farm workers. By 1971, the composite farm wage rate was $1.48 an hour, but the average manufacturing wage was $3.77 an hour.[87]

Williams's proposal to include farm workers in the National Labor Relations Act (NLRA) died in Congress, and has not been enacted since. At the Senate hearings in California, growers contended that extending the collective bargaining and other union-friendly protections in the NLRA to farm workers would "give to the union a monopoly over agricultural labor so that the unions could effectively control the food supply to the nation."[88] Further, inclusion would result in "compulsory unionization of agricultural labor" because farmers were uniquely vulnerable to harvest-time labor strikes.[89] But Kennedy took up the call for inclusion of farm workers, arguing in a Senate speech in June 1966 that:

If ever there were a classic case for bringing farm workers under the collective bargaining provisions of the National Labor Relations Act, this is certainly it. The lack of legally constituted, orderly procedures upon which labor and management may rely created chaos in this situation. And if, as seems inevitable, the union movement among farm workers is going to spread, the chaos also will spread unless we enact legislation to extend the rights and obligations of our national collective bargaining laws to the farm industry.[90]

Among the issues on which Kennedy and Chávez communicated after the 1966 Senate hearings was this proposed reform of the NLRA. In early January 1968, during what Chávez framed in a letter to Kennedy as "the winter of our discontent," caused by the now-multiyear strike's sapping morale, Chávez inquired about the chances for passage of NLRA reform: "At times like this I cannot help but wish for the speedy passage of the extension of the National Labor Relations Act [to farm workers]. How does it look for 1968? Will agricultural labor be included in the Act? ... Thank you again for your help to us in the past; may your interest and devotion to social justice grow with the years."[91] Kennedy responded: "I think we have a good chance of getting that legislation passed this year. There seems to be movement and concern about it in both Houses, and so I am cautiously optimistic."[92]

Much of the correspondence between Kennedy and Chávez after the California hearings concerned the union's struggle with the Di Giorgio Corporation, an agri-giant that counted a 4,700-acre ranch in Delano among its holdings. The Di Giorgio company resisted unionization of its field workers, and in one bloody incident during spring 1966, Di Giorgio guards confronted union organizers trying to talk to company workers. As Chávez detailed in a telegram to Kennedy: "We call upon you to assist us in establishing some protection for Delano NFWA pickets. Di Giorgio employee security guard threatened girl picket with a gun. Then set upon our pickets beating them with billy clubs. One picket [was] seriously injured needing ten stitches in the head from blow."[93] Kennedy also heard about this grower's violence from a priest who visited his aide Peter Edelman in Washington. Kennedy responded to Chávez:

There is, of course, no excuse whatsoever for this kind of brutal behavior on the part of security guards and for police failure to take action in response to it.

I am bringing this matter to the attention of the proper authorities and asking them to look into it with a view to ensuring the law is properly and fairly enforced.[94]

Chávez retaliated peaceably against Di Giorgio by declaring a boycott against the company's products, including its juice brand TreeSweet and its canned foods under the S&W label.[95] In June 1966, Chávez wrote Kennedy about the legality of federal government purchases of Di Giorgio products covered under the boycott. Kennedy replied that federal regulations did not prohibit the Defense Department from purchasing nonunion products.[96] That June, the Di Giorgio company held a union election contested by Chávez and won by the Teamsters union. Senators Kennedy and Williams, chair of the Senate Subcommittee on Migratory Labor, sent a telegram to Di Giorgio demanding that it delay negotiation with the Teamsters pending an investigation of charges of coercion and improper conduct in the election.[97] Di Giorgio ultimately agreed to hold new elections, which the Chávez-led union won.[98]

In addition to the other intersections in their lives, Chávez and Kennedy were linked by their struggles with the Teamsters union and its corrupt and brutal tactics. Not until the mid-1970s would the Teamsters retreat from representing field workers, after a decade-long battle in which Teamsters goons assaulted organizers for Chávez while the Teamsters union entered into sweetheart contracts with growers who sold out their employees for minor concessions to avoid dealing with the more tenacious Chávez union.[99] Robert Kennedy too had a storied history of confrontation with the Teamsters union, particularly its mercurial and criminal leader, Jimmy Hoffa. During Kennedy's stint with a Senate investigations committee in the late 1950s, including two years as its chief counsel, Kennedy and his staff indicted 201 Teamsters officers and associates, securing 126 convictions.[100] Kennedy's enforcement efforts against Jimmy Hoffa for corruption and Hoffa's alignment with organized crime continued throughout Kennedy's tenure as U.S. attorney general. In his book detailing his early efforts to derail Hoffa, *The Enemy Within*, Kennedy identified Hoffa as one of a handful of labor leaders who betrayed their trust.[101] Kennedy also described Hoffa as embodying "absolute evilness"[102] and as running the Teamsters not as a "bona fide union," but as a "conspiracy of evil."[103] Further, Kennedy accused Hoffa of rigging his own election and making a "travesty" of democratic procedure, as well as conducting often illicit relationships with employers that contradicted the interests of his union employees.[104] For his turn, Hoffa referred to Kennedy as a "spoiled rich kid."[105]

In the Di Giorgio elections won by the United Farm Workers Organizing Committee (UFWOC), the Teamsters union suggested that the Chávez-led UFWOC was Communist oriented—circulating copies of a John Birch pamphlet that made Communist allegations against the union and yelling "Go back to Russia" to the UFWOC supporters.[106] Countering the Teamsters tactics, the UFWOC handed out excerpts from Robert Kennedy's *The Enemy Within,* in which he excoriated Hoffa and the Teamsters.[107] Finally convicted on federal charges of jury tampering and, in a separate trial, mail and wire fraud and conspiracy in the misappropriation of union pension funds, Hoffa was imprisoned from 1967 until President Nixon granted him clemency on Christmas Eve 1971. The Teamsters union supported Nixon, handing Nixon his only major union endorsement in 1972; one writer even contends that FBI records reveal that Nixon received campaign contributions in the 1968 election from the Teamsters in exchange for the eventual presidential pardon of Hoffa.[108] Despite his campaign against Hoffa and other Teamsters leaders, Kennedy was a proponent of organized labor, calling the labor movement "the backbone of a democracy"[109] and supporting such labor leaders as Walter Reuther and Chávez.

Following the California Senate hearings, Kennedy also aided Chávez's farm worker union in its strike and boycott against the Giumarra Vineyards Corporation. The union's lawyer informed Kennedy that Giumarra was eluding the boycott against it by falsely labeling its grapes with other growers' labels. The union took the position that under the federal Truth in Packaging Act administered by the Food and Drug Administration, consumers have a right to know the true source of products in order to discern whether they are purchasing a struck product.[110] Kennedy intervened and an FDA official reported to Kennedy in November 1967 that Giumarra was indeed using labels of other companies on boxes packed in its vineyards, and that the FDA was taking steps to promptly correct the mislabeling.[111]

Kennedy even helped Chávez and the union with fund-raising—in spring 1967 Kennedy and Chávez met in Marin County at a fund-raising event for a farm worker health clinic that raised nearly $10,000. In his May 17,

1967, letter thanking Kennedy for his appearance, Chávez wrote that the farm workers had the "highest esteem" for the Kennedy name.[112]

According to Kennedy's aide Peter Edelman, from his meeting with Chávez in the parking lot during the Senate labor hearings in March 1966, "Kennedy was the farmworkers union's best friend in Washington."[113] For Kennedy, too, his friendship with Chávez would pay political dividends when his visit to Delano in 1968 would help launch a presidential campaign in which Chávez and Mexican American voters would play a crucial role. As one commentator described the friendship that emerged in 1966 and its mutual returns:

> For the next two years, it was almost impossible to think of Chavez except in conjunction with Robert Kennedy.... Kennedy's real concern for the farm workers helped soften his image as a self-serving keeper of his brother's flame and in turn plugged Chavez into the power outlets of Washington and New York. For the first time Chavez became fashionable, a national figure registering on the nation's moral thermometer. Robert Kennedy and Cesar Chavez—the names seemed wired into the same circuitry, the one a spokesman, the other a symbol for the constituency of the dispossessed.[114]

CHAPTER THREE

César's Fast and Deeds of Love

Social justice for the dignity of man cannot be won at the price of human life.

—César Chávez[1]

Robert Kennedy came to Delano when no one else came.... He approached us with love; as people, not as subjects for study—as Anglos usually had done—as equals not as objects of curiosity. He helped the oppressed. His were Hechos de Amor. Deeds of love.

—César Chávez[2]

At the time of the Senate labor hearings in March 1966, Chávez led the Mexican American–dominated labor organization called the National Farm Workers Association (NFWA). Concurrent with the NFWA efforts, the Agricultural Workers Organizing Committee (AWOC) represented Filipino workers in the Delano labor strike. To increase its clout, the NFWA membership decided to merge with the AWOC in the summer of 1966. Both groups became the United Farm Workers Organizing Committee (UFWOC), a name shortened in 1972 to the United Farm Workers (UFW) when the union became a full affiliate of the AFL-CIO national union. Upon the merger in 1966, the executive board of Mexican American and Filipino leaders selected Chávez to direct the new organization, the UFWOC.[3]

As the Delano grape strike wore on into 1967 and early 1968, tensions erupted and strikers increasingly strayed from Chávez's directive of nonviolence. A few sabotaged the growers by scattering nails on roads and destroying water irrigation pumps. There were suspicious fires in grape-packing sheds.[4] Chávez expelled union members who provoked fights on the picket lines, and chastised those who questioned the commitment to nonviolence. He contended that "no union movement is worth the death of one farmworker or his child or one grower...."[5] But as incidents mounted—in one instance, the Kern County district attorney announced in February 1968 that he was considering charges against union members for destruction of property—Chávez launched his most memorable and dramatic response—a fast until the union membership disavowed violence. As Chávez put it, "I think my biggest success in life was being able to go without food for twenty-five days [in 1968]. I don't think I could top that."[6]

Drawing inspiration from Gandhi, who fasted for twenty-one days in 1924 to protest violence between Hindus and Muslims, Chávez began his fast on February 15, 1968, initially subsisting on drinking cola, but switching on the fourth day to just water. The union released a statement that "[t]he fast is an act of penance, recalling farm workers to the nonviolent roots of their movement."[7] Thousands of farm workers came to join Chávez to pray, sing, and build shrines. One account described the scene as:

> a fascinating and awesome spectacle to view. By the second week of the fast a sprawling tent city had sprung up around the little service station at forty acres [the union-owned property where Chávez took up residence during his fast]. Farm workers from all over California came to live in the tents and share in the event.... [T]he deliberate pace, the quiet voices, the huddled figures, the sharing of food and drink [among the workers]—all these gave the impression of serious religious vigil.[8]

As one commentator concluded, "The irony of the fast [for nonviolence] was that it turned out to be the greatest organizing tool in the history of the labor movement—at least in this country."[9] National media flocked to Delano, amidst absurd allegations from nervous growers that Chávez's fast was fabricated and that he was eating takeout milk shakes and sandwiches from local restaurants.[10]

On the thirteenth day of his fast, Chávez was summoned to the Kern County courthouse to face a contempt charge alleging he violated a court order restricting the number and positioning of picketers. Over three thousand farm workers greeted the weakened Chávez at the courthouse, and the contempt charges were dropped.

Chávez read from two books during his fast—the Bible and a book on Gandhi.[11] Every evening during his ordeal Chávez participated in a Catholic mass. By the end of February, nearly one thousand people were joining the daily services, with almost two thousand for Sunday service.[12] Robert Kennedy was kept current on Chávez's fast by an aide. Many farm workers, knowing of their friendship, wrote Kennedy to express concern over Chávez's deteriorating condition. One letter implored:

> [W]e have a problem that is disturbing us greatly, our leader César Chávez has gone on a hunger fast to bring the issue of nonviolence across to the people, not only in organizing our union, but nonviolence in general.…
>
> We feel that if you come it would cause worldwide attention to the subject of nonviolence and therefore persuade César to discontinue his hunger fast.
>
> We would appreciate it from the bottom of our heart.[13]

Concerns about Chávez's health prompted Kennedy to wire Chávez asking him to consider the consequences for the farm worker movement if his health failed because of the fast.[14] Kennedy also sent Chávez a letter that same day in late February, expressing his "support and concern for [Chávez] at this difficult time" and adding, "Again, let me say how concerned all of your friends are about you now. You know, of course, that we stand ready to help you in any way that we can at any time."[15]

In the final five days of his fast, Chávez agreed to take a few ounces of bouillon and unsweetened grapefruit juice after being warned he faced permanent kidney damage.[16] He also began taking carbohydrate pills to reduce the uric acid that threatened his kidneys. Chávez's weight had dropped from 175 pounds to 140 pounds, and he relented: "Finally, I was convinced that we could end the fast, that it had gone on long enough to put across our ideas on nonviolence. Besides, there was the concern [for my health] expressed by many, but very strongly by my family."[17]

Chávez decided to break his fast, but wanted his friend Kennedy present for the occasion. Kennedy had a speech scheduled in Iowa, and decided to fly to Delano by charter plane the next day. Kennedy's friend in California, Edwin Guthman, recounted his advice to Kennedy that visiting Chávez offered no political gain: "I don't think it will make much difference. Those who don't agree with you won't like it. The people who will appreciate it are already with you. It's a long way out here. Why do you want to haul your tail across the country on a Sunday just to go to Delano?" Kennedy replied, "Well, I guess because I like Cesar."[18]

On Sunday, March 10, 1968, the *Los Angeles Times* reported that Chávez planned to end his twenty-five-day fast that day, and that thousands of farm workers were gathering in Delano. In Monday's edition, his celebratory ending of the fast made the front page of the *Times,* with the headline "Chavez Breaks Fast at Mass Attended by Kennedy, 6000 [supporters]."[19]

Kennedy was accompanied on his charter plane trip to Delano by Paul Schrade, a United Auto Workers official who presented Chávez with a $50,000 check from the UAW that day "to carry on the building program at the Forty Acres"—toward construction of the union headquarters there, and pledged the continued payment of $5,000 a month toward the success of the grape strike. Kennedy reached Delano on Sunday, March 10, and greeted Chávez where he had stayed throughout his fast—in a tiny room on a small bed inside the service station on the humble union-owned property known as Forty Acres that would eventually blossom into the union's headquarters. On arrival, Kennedy queried of Schrade, "[w]hat do you say to a man who's on a fast?"[20] After a brief greeting, the men journeyed to Delano's Memorial Park for a formal mass and ceremony. When they arrived at the park, six thousand to perhaps eight thousand or more farm workers and supporters waited to greet them, flanking a processional path. Aides escorted the weakened Chávez, who clung to their shoulders as they propped him up. The crowd gave Kennedy a wildly enthusiastic greeting, chanting "Viva Kennedy." Dolores Huerta described Kennedy's arrival at the park:

> It was absolute bedlam. When we got out of the car, all of the photographers closed in on us, interviewing the Senator. Then he started walking, and I have never experienced a scene like that in my life. People just started pushing in. He would start shaking hands.... People were coming up to him, and they would grab him and hug him and kiss him on the mouth! And, you know, [they would say] "Un gran hombre"—great man, Kennedy—"Un gran hombre!" People would grab him, and his hands were all scratched up. When he sat down in front of me, his hands were all bloodied....[21]

Interviewed by media at the park, Kennedy remarked on the powerlessness of Mexican American farm workers:

[S]o many of our farm workers, particularly the Mexican Americans and others of minority groups ... have not had the protection of the laws as exist in so many other elements of society. ... What we need is some federal legislation which will be comparable to the legislation that we passed in the 1930s for other workers in this country. And the fact is that we haven't done that and the result has been that the farm workers have suffered ... and grown much more slowly economically than any other segment of our society. It is terribly unfair ... and very unjust. ... [But farm workers are a] relatively uninfluential group in the country. They're poor, they don't have many spokesmen in Washington. They don't have many people fighting for them. There's nobody that's terribly interested in them or in their problem.[22]

In a roped-off area in front of the truck trailer platform that served as an altar, Kennedy sat next to Chávez, with Helen Chávez at his right; Chávez's seventy-five-year-old mother sat at her son's left, holding his hand while the now-frail Chávez sat with his legs wrapped in a blanket. She gave Chávez occasional sips of water as he sat slumped in an upholstered chair throughout the mass at the foot of the altar. Someone had pinned a "Huelga" button on Kennedy's lapel, bearing the union's eagle symbol. The mass began with a prayer in Hebrew, followed by a Protestant sermon and a Catholic ritual.[23] Kennedy and Chávez held hands at times during the mass while praying. Following mass, Kennedy and Chávez partook in a ceremonial breaking of bread. About three hundred loaves of Mexican *semita* bread (known as poor man's bread) were baked in Fresno for the occasion and then blessed by a priest at the ceremony.[24] Priests distributed the bread loaves through the huge crowd. As the bread was passed, Kennedy took some, and gave a piece to Chávez as national news cameras popped. Because the throng blocked the ABC news camera, one of their crew members approached Kennedy with the question, "Senator, this is perhaps the most ridiculous remark I've ever made in all my life. Would you mind giving Cesar another piece of bread so we can get a picture?" Kennedy replied, "No. In fact he should have a lot of bread now," and handed him another piece.[25]

Chávez had prepared a statement for the crowd, but was too weak to read it himself.[26] Chávez explained in his opening lines: "my heart is so full and my body too weak to be able to say what I feel."[27] So after the breaking of bread, a reverend read Chávez's remarks in English, and a union official read them in Spanish. Chávez's heroic words thanked his supporters and Kennedy: "We should all express our thanks to Senator Kennedy for his constant work on behalf of the poor, for his personal encouragement to me, and for taking the time to break bread with us today."[28] He then remarked about the purpose of the fast ("It was a fast for nonviolence and a call to sacrifice"), and the unity of the union family: "We are gathered here today not so much to observe the end of the fast but because we are a family bound together in a common struggle for justice. We are a union family, celebrating our unity and the nonviolent nature of our movement."[29] The conclusion of his prepared statement is the most memorable part, striking the chord of greatness:

> Our struggle is not easy. Those who oppose our cause are rich and powerful and they have many allies in high places. We are poor. Our allies are few. But we have something the rich do not own. We have our own bodies and spirits and the justice of our cause as our weapons.
>
> When we are really honest with ourselves we must admit that our lives are all that we really have. So, it is how we use our lives that determines what kind of men we are. It is my deepest belief that only by giving our lives do we find life. I am convinced that the truest act of courage, the strongest act of manliness is to sacrifice ourselves for others in a totally nonviolent struggle for justice.
>
> To be a man is to suffer for others. God help us be men![30]

Kennedy then mounted the platform truck, and after Dolores Huerta's introduction he addressed the crowd:

> This is an historic occasion for all of you. It's an historic occasion I think for the whole country. We come out here to honor César Chávez. You come here as members of his union to honor him as your leader. I come here as an American citizen to honor him for what he's done, not just for you, not just for this state, but for all of the United States of America.... We here in the United States [are] so lucky and fortunate to have produced a man so committed to justice, to compassion, to honesty, to truth, and to service for all humanity. And that's César Chávez....
>
> You're not the first farm workers to organize, but the first to fight and the first to triumph over all odds without proper protection from the federal law.... The victories are yours because you won them ... not outsiders, you

won them for yourselves.... And therefore no one can come in and take it away from you....

So when your children start to grow up, and they go on to school, and they go on to college, and they go on to better jobs, they will know as you will know, that you paved the way ... and that you made it possible for them to lead a better life....

And you are serving under ... a leader of this union who is committed to the principle of nonviolence. That's so important to any success that you are going to have in the future.... If there's anything that we've learned during the 1960s ... [it] is that violence is not the answer to our problems. Let no one say that violence is the courageous way, that violence is the short route.... Because violence will bring no answer, it will bring no answer to your union, it will bring no answer to your people, it will bring no answer to us here in the United States as a people. And that's why I come here to honor César Chávez for what he's done and for what he stands for. How desperately you and the people of this country, of our country, need people like him today.

So as ... you continue your efforts, let all of those who are the employers in this area, and all across America, understand and respect you....

Kennedy spoke also about needed legal reforms. In the interim between the 1966 Senate hearings and that early 1968 Sunday in Delano, Congress had extended a minimum wage to farm workers. However, farm workers remained unprotected in their union organizing under the National Labor Relations Act, and Kennedy urged their inclusion:

We in the government, we also have a responsibility. We must have a federal law ... which gives farm union members protection. We must have a law which permits farm workers to engage in collective bargaining. We must give farm workers the same rights, the same justice that we gave to all other workers thirty years ago. Another area in which we need federal action is that we need more adequate regulation of green card workers to prevent green card workers' being brought into this area and being used as strikebreakers. And we must have equal protection of the laws for all of our people. This is written into the Fourteenth Amendment of the Constitution but it must be enforced here in California and all across the United States. Further, the California labor code, the federal immigration laws, the federal labor and department regulations, these are laws and these are rules and regulations which are supposed to protect all of you. They must be enforced from now on.

Kennedy concluded:

> So I come here today to honor a great American, César Chávez. And beyond that I have come here today to honor all of you for the long and the patient commitment that you have made to this great struggle for justice. And I come here today to say that we will fight together to achieve for you and with you, the aspirations of every American—a decent wage, a decent house, a decent school for your children, and a chance for yourselves and for your children in coming generations. That I pledge to you. You stand for justice and I am proud to stand with you....
>
> ¡Viva La Causa! ¡Viva César Chávez! ¡Viva La Causa! Viva all of you. Bye. Adiós.[31]

Kennedy linked arms with Dolores Huerta on stage to audience cries of "Viva Kennedy" and the chorus of the famous union song *Solidarity Forever.* After his remarks, Kennedy had to fight his way through the crowd back to the car waiting for him. But once he got into the car, Kennedy jumped out and onto its roof for an encore, and began speaking to the throng. At times, Kennedy attempted to speak Spanish, including shouting *Huelga!,* which he pronounced *Hool-ga!* in his Boston Irish accent, to the crowd's delight. Kennedy peppered his earlier remarks with Spanish too, opening his speech with a hearty "Buenas tardes [good afternoon]." At one point during his speech, after attempting to pronounce more Spanish, Kennedy looked down from the platform altar and asked Chávez, "Am I destroying the language? Should I translate that into Spanish?"[32] Chávez's brother Richard remembered Kennedy's efforts to speak Spanish: "Everybody just loved him for it. They just went wild."[33]

Chávez summed up the occasion: "It was a great day."[34] Regarding the depth of the farm worker affection for Kennedy, Chávez explained it was "a phenomenon that can't be explained.... It's that line that you very seldom cross—I've never seen a politician cross that line and I don't think that I'll ever live to see another public figure [do so]."[35]

Back in Washington, D.C., Kennedy received several angry letters from Californians and even his New York constituents questioning his bond in California with Chávez. One writer from Fresno declared the Chávez fast a "fraud" to gain sympathy for the union. A telegram to Kennedy from Merced, California, stated "Chauvez [sic] is a California problem. Your assistance is not needed." A writer from Alhambra, California, conveyed that the writer was terribly upset at Kennedy for interfering with California's farm "problems": "Our State pays our farm worker's [sic] more than any other state in the nation.... What gives you the idea we need you out here. So far we do not have the spectacle of our Calif. Senator's [sic] running to N.Y. State trying to solve problem's [sic]. Your politicing [sic] is'nt [sic] appreciated here at all.... I am just as Irish as you are and am Damned MAD."[36]

Another writer from California accused Kennedy of "carpetbagging" in California and of ignoring the fact that California farm workers had no desire to unionize. Rather, he contended that Kennedy was misinformed by "talking to troublemakers like Ceasar [sic] Chavez and the militant clergy who follow him."[37] A New York constituent commented on the "barber shop discussion today" centering on newspaper pictures of Kennedy and Chávez, questioning why Kennedy was "image creating in California with Cesar Chavez, instead of representing his New York constituents in Washington, D.C."[38]

Kennedy responded to critics of his visit to California with a form letter explaining that:

> I was in California because the problems which migrant farm workers face are not, as you suggest, a California problem, but a national concern. They are the lowest paid, least protected group of workers in our economy. In addition, I have specific legislative responsibilities in regard to farm problems. I am a member of the Senate Subcommittee on Migratory Labor, and pursuant to that responsibility, I have visited a number of migrant worker camps throughout the country in connection with specific legislative proposals now before our Committee.

To his New York barbershop critic, Kennedy added a tribute to Chávez in his response: "I went to California to honor one of the great and heroic figures of our time—Cesar Chavez. His nonviolent struggle for the rights of the migrant worker is an achievement which will afford Americans of Mexican descent the full participation in our society which they deserve."[39]

CHAPTER FOUR

Viva (Bobby) Kennedy

[Because Mexican Americans saw the Catholic Robert Kennedy] as sort of the minority kind of person himself ... with Senator Robert Kennedy it was like he was ours.

—César Chávez[1]

[Farm workers felt] they didn't have to act any different in front of him or talk to [Kennedy] differently. [They could] just talk to him like anybody else.

—Richard Chávez[2]

The Delano experience and the adulation he received there appeared to help inspire Kennedy to commit to run for president against the incumbent Democrat Lyndon Johnson. At the time of Kennedy's visit to Delano in early March 1968, speculation was widespread that he was poised to join the presidential race. While in Delano, Kennedy inquired, "Well, how goes the boycott, Cesar?" Chávez replied, "How goes running for president, Bob?" and both men laughed.[3] After the mass and bread-breaking to end the hunger fast, people crowded around Kennedy and urged him to run for president. Chávez remembered:

[H]e had a heck of a time getting from where we were sitting to the car. The crowd was pushing and surging, and when he got there, he didn't get in, the way the people were reacting, he wanted to stand there and shake their hands and talk to them. Everybody was afraid of so many people pushing like that, and when finally Jim Drake got him inside, the people were saying through the windows, "Aren't you going to run? Why don't you run? Please run!"[4]

In a car headed to the airport, Kennedy is said to have remarked to a passenger, "You know, I might just do that."[5] On the plane ride from Delano, Kennedy informed an aide, "I'm going to do it. I've got to find a way to get McCarthy out. But I'm going to do it anyway."[6] The Tuesday after the Sunday mass in Delano, Democratic senator Eugene McCarthy made an unexpectedly strong showing in the New Hampshire primary, dispelling the possibility he would withdraw from a race with President Johnson. A few days later, on March 16, only six days after the Delano mass ending Chávez's fast, Kennedy officially entered the race, explaining:

> I do not run for the presidency merely to oppose any man but to propose new policies....
>
> I run to seek new policies—policies to end the bloodshed in Vietnam and in our cities, policies to close the gaps that now exist between black and white, between rich and poor, between young and old, in this country and around the rest of the world.
>
> I run for the presidency because I want the Democratic Party and the United States of America to stand for hope instead of despair, for reconciliation of men instead of the growing risk of world war.
>
> I run now because it is now unmistakably clear that we can change these disastrous, divisive policies only by changing the men who are now making them. For the reality of recent events in Vietnam has been glossed over with illusions.
>
> The Report of the Riot Commission has been largely ignored.
>
> The crisis in gold, the crisis in our cities, the crisis in our farms and in our ghettos have all been met with too little and too late.[7]

Almost immediately, the Kennedy team started assembling potential delegates to the Democratic National Convention. They asked Chávez to serve as one of the delegates, but given the affiliation of the United Farm Workers Organizing Committee union with the powerful AFL-CIO union, he was concerned about alienating AFL-CIO president George Meany, a Johnson supporter. Paul Schrade, western director of the United Auto Workers and a friend of Kennedy and Chávez, called to secure Chávez's agreement to join the delegation. Kennedy also called Chávez that night, Tuesday, March 19. But when Schrade and Kennedy compared notes after their calls, Kennedy lamented that "Cesar sounded so sick and weak from the fast, I didn't have the heart to ask him to do it."[8] Schrade promptly called Chávez again and told him about Kennedy's reluctance to request him to serve.[9] Chávez agreed to ask the union membership to approve his service as a delegate. About eighty-five union officers met within hours and unanimously approved Chávez's participation, as well as the union's oversight of a voter registration campaign.[10] Answering concern about the AFL-CIO's support for Johnson, Chávez told the membership that "we had our own political decisions to make."[11] As the farm worker newspaper *El Malcriado* reported, "The unanimous vote marked the first time in history that a presidential candidate asked a farm worker to serve in such a capacity."[12] Chávez asked nothing in return from Kennedy in directing the full resources of the union briefly toward his presidential campaign: "I knew it would not be honorable to ask for something in return. With most politicians this would have been all right, but not with this man who had already helped us so much."[13]

Chávez and the farm workers union went swiftly to work for Kennedy. As Chávez explained, the union "literally stopped the strike, for that time."[14] Drawing on his valuable experience registering California voters for the CSO in the 1950s and early 1960s,[15] Chávez orchestrated a voter registration drive. The union leadership split the meaningful rural counties as well as the assembly districts of Los Angeles among them, and set out to register voters. According to several reports, Chávez and the union registered thousands of new voters, most of them Mexican Americans; one report states the number of voters newly registered as over 200,000.[16]

Of equal importance was ensuring that Latino and other voters favored Kennedy and would turn out to vote. Despite his weakened condition from his recent twenty-five-day fast, Chávez embarked on a whirlwind speaking tour for nineteen days in support of Kennedy, focusing on farm worker communities and on universities to reach the student vote.[17] Chávez recalled his university speaking tour:

> Those universities were all solid [for] McCarthy. But I would come in there and the students were very respectful. They didn't abuse me. I would talk about why farm workers want Kennedy. I went to Berkeley and there must have been about four thousand people there and I got there and I spoke for about thirty minutes and answered questions for about an hour. And we changed people.... We went to Stanford and to almost all universities.[18]

When campus hecklers asked him where Kennedy was when McCarthy was stumping in New Hampshire, Chávez replied "He was walking with me in Delano!"[19]

Chávez also went to "every county where there are Spanish-speaking people."[20] As Chávez remembered, "I made a swing, speaking to farm workers, making as many as six appearances a day all over the state, places like Soledad and Salinas and Stockton. We called rallies, and it seemed like the whole town attended."[21] In these towns, Chávez and the union workers took straw ballot voting polls. The Fresno poll, for example, yielded 583 votes for Kennedy, 1 additional ballot for Kennedy with Chávez as vice president, 4 votes for Johnson, 6 for McCarthy, and 1 each for Reagan and Nelson Rockefeller.[22]

Chávez's voter registration drive and efforts for Kennedy were particularly intense in Delano and in East Los Angeles. In Delano, the farm workers assigned 175 men to cover its 26 precincts. About 250 other union representatives shuttled between rural Delano and the urban East Los Angeles barrio. Chávez and his organizers lived out of suitcases and slept on the floor of an East Los Angeles church in sleeping bags without a place to shower and in conditions that Chávez found "miserable."[23] As Chávez recalled, "We set up telephone and walking committees, and the last thing we did was organize thousands of little kids to leaflet people."[24] Comparing the Mexican American push for Robert Kennedy to the 1960s campaign for his slain brother, Chávez calculated, "For every man working for John Kennedy we must have had about fifty men working for Bobby."[25] Chávez described the voter mobilization effort in the East Los Angeles barrio:

[W]e organized by precincts.... We got there about two weeks before and we assigned the Assembly districts. In each Assembly district we had one leader and that Assembly district was broken down and then broken down again until our guys were in charge of five precincts each. Then they, in turn, organized those five precincts to get at least one person for each block to work. We had a tight organization. It was a machine. We just turned it on and produced. But we had a good candidate and we had a lot of discipline, a lot of work.[26]

Chávez described how his farm workers gained the participation of residents in Los Angeles by going door to door for volunteers:

They knew about us and about the [farm worker] cause and so it made it so easy.... We used to say, "I'm from Delano with the farm workers." "Oh, the farm workers!" Just like that. "Yes," in Spanish. And we'd say, "We're going to ask you to work for Kennedy." "Oh, wonderful. Sure. Sure." We used to open more doors [that way] ... I don't think as long as we live, we'll ever get that combination again on a political election.[27]

The union organizers went beyond just rallying Mexican American voters, reaching white college students and also organizing in the black communities in South Central Los Angeles using the same techniques relied on in the Mexican American barrio.

The farm workers union financed much of its political efforts for Kennedy from worker donations, with Chávez telling them: "You've got to give of your time and your heart and your money, and you've got to give us money right now because these things cost money. You want to elect him? Put up.... And they came through."[28] Although the union did not pay its organizers wages for their campaign efforts, the union spent considerable sums on car rentals, gas, telephones, and food during the brief Kennedy campaign, and the union successfully raised thousands of dollars from the farm workers to offset these costs.

Chávez played a sizable role in political advertising targeting the Mexican American community. A campaign leaflet from the United Farm Workers Organizing Committee included a quote from Chávez: "To achieve justice and bring peace to this troubled land, we need a wise and courageous man. We feel that man is Senator Robert F. Kennedy."[29] A letter from Chávez graced a bilingual Kennedy campaign brochure targeting Latino voters:

Senator Robert F. Kennedy is a man whose many selfless acts on behalf of struggling farm workers have been expressions of love through practical deeds.

Senator Kennedy came at a time when our cause was very hard pressed and we were surrounded by powerful enemies who did not hesitate to viciously attack anyone who was courageous enough to help us. He did not stop to ask whether it would be politically wise for him to come. We have learned, sadly, that many persons who hold high political office feel that it is not "good politics" to become too closely identified with farm workers because it would antagonize rich land owners who have tremendous political and economic power....

But Senator Kennedy did not bother himself with such fears, nor did he stop to worry about the color of our skin ... or what languages we speak....

We know from our own experience that he cares, he understands and he acts with compassion and courage....

We are proud to support Senator Robert Kennedy for President.[30]

The Mexican American community responded to Chávez's entreaties. As he characterized them, the Mexican American votes cast for Kennedy were a product of "respect, admiration, [and] love."[31]

Concurrent with the efforts of the farm workers union and Chávez, the Mexican American Political Association (MAPA) and revived Viva Kennedy clubs aided the campaign bid. Bert Corona, leader of the Viva Kennedy effort, recalled, "[Kennedy] was intensely interested in mexicanos and supportive of our goals in a nonpatronizing fashion.... Bobby touched our souls."[32] Viva Kennedy offices sprung up around the country, with over one hundred in California and others located throughout the Southwest, Northwest, and Midwest.[33] There was some disagreement in the California-based MAPA organization over whether it should endorse McCarthy or Kennedy, with Johnson disfavored because of his positions on farm worker reform and the war. In McCarthy's favor, he had criticized the Vietnam War before Kennedy, and had long supported farm worker reforms. Still, McCarthy was seen as appealing to college students and suburban liberal whites, not poor communities of color. And Kennedy had embraced the farm worker cause by coming to Delano. Following debate two-thirds of the MAPA leadership voted to support Kennedy.[34]

Although the Viva Kennedy organizations developed their own campaign material targeting the Latino vote, Latino issues were part of Kennedy's mainstream campaign. For example, one mainstream pamphlet produced by the Kennedy national campaign headquarters featured a cover picture of Kennedy with a Latino boy, and its text addressed the campaign issues of poverty, Vietnam, and fair wages for farm workers, each with particular relevance to the Latino community. By contrast to the support it claimed Kennedy held for farm worker reform legislation, the pamphlet contended that Johnson "turned a deaf ear" to reform.[35] Reflecting the concerns of

Mexican Americans, Chávez similarly had scolded Johnson by letter, "God's blessing on your work during the year," but "unfulfilled promises are a poor substitute for food, wages, and justice."[36]

Only two weeks after Kennedy entered the race, President Johnson announced he would not run for reelection, leaving a two-man race at the time for the Democratic nomination between McCarthy and Kennedy. With Johnson and his hawkish attitude toward the war gone, Kennedy focused more on issues of poverty and race. In a speech on April 11, 1968, at Michigan State University, Kennedy addressed these issues of inequality that weren't simply black and white:

> [I]f we try to look through the eyes of the young slum-dweller—the Negro, and the Puerto Rican, and the Mexican American—the world is a dark and hopeless place indeed....
>
> [L]et us stop thinking of the poor ... as liabilities. Let us see them for what they are: valuable resources, as people whose work can be directed to all these tasks to be done within our cities, and within the nation....[37]

From the beginning of his eighty-one-day campaign in 1968, the California primary on June 4 loomed of crucial importance to Kennedy. Given his enormous popularity in New York, if Kennedy could win California's delegates, those two states alone would give him 28 percent of the votes needed for the Democratic nomination.[38] He stumped often in California, giving particular attention to communities of Mexican Americans and African Americans. Early in the campaign, on March 24, he spoke to a Mexican American crowd on Olvera Street near downtown Los Angeles, praising César Chávez:

> Two weeks ago, I came to California to pay homage to one of the great living Americans: César Chávez. For more than two years from his base in the grape fields of California, César Chávez has been sending the rest of America a message.
>
> The message says that Americans of Mexican descent were walking taller than ever before. The message says that dignity is not something awarded coldly in a welfare office. The message says that dignity is something a man attains with his mind, with the labor of his body, with his belief in himself.[39]

In the same speech, Kennedy spoke to national unity across classes and color:

> I come here because America is a divided nation. I come here because America has become a nation which will spend $36 billion this year on the far side of the earth in Vietnam, and somehow cannot raise money for a school lunch program....
>
> This week an American of Mexican descent, Raul Rojas, fights for the featherweight championship of the world. I wish him my best but this country must insure that Mexican Americans do not have to bleed for a living....
>
> Together we can do all of this. United we are a nation. Divided we are nothing.[40]

Campaigning in northern California, Kennedy rode a motorcade through San Francisco to the Mexican American Mission District, met there by throngs that rivaled the Delano farm workers in their enthusiasm. He spoke to over seven thousand people, most of them Mexican Americans, at St. James Park in San Jose—another ecstatic crowd.[41] In the days before the California primary, Kennedy embarked on a train tour of the San Joaquin Valley, giving speeches to largely Mexican American audiences from the caboose of an old-fashioned train journeying from Fresno to Sacramento. Kennedy told supporters at the Fresno rail stop, "I don't think we have to accept the gap that exists between races and age groups."[42] Kennedy's speeches on the rail tour addressed the entry into the campaign of Vice President Hubert Humphrey, and continued to focus on solutions to end the Vietnam War and provide employment and hope for residents of racially troubled cities. Kennedy campaigned in the East Los Angeles barrio, on one occasion taking a convertible motorcade from Long Beach fifteen miles up through Watts to the streets of East Los Angeles, which were jammed with thousands of exuberant Mexican Americans shouting "Viva Kennedy!"[43] As one reporter described the atmosphere in East Los Angeles, "The spectacle included small children racing alongside the senator's car as if trailing a pied piper."[44]

By then, McCarthy's remark while campaigning in Oregon that his supporters were the "better educated" had angered African American and Mexican American leaders in California and enhanced Kennedy's appeal there.[45] On Election Day at the California primary, these groups turned out in record numbers. César Chávez recalled that "We worked right up to the last minute on Kennedy's campaign. It was just like organizing a strike—hectic."[46] Farm worker representatives walked the streets of East Los Angeles from nine in the morning until night, talking to voters and handing out leaflets.[47] On Election Day, they went door to door in East Los Angeles with the message, "This is the day Cesar says to vote for Robert Kennedy."[48] Mexican American voters responded. In some Mexican American precincts voter turnout that day was an amazing 100 percent, most or all voting for Kennedy.[49]

CHAPTER FIVE

One Night in America

A shot rang out in the night
Just when everything seemed right
Another headline written down in America....

A quiet voice is singing something to me
An age old song about the home of the brave
In this land here of the free
One time one night in America

—Los Lobos, "One Time, One Night"

June 4, 1968, was election day for the California primary. That night was perhaps the biggest triumph and tragedy in the history of the Mexican American experience.

Latino voters played a key role in the election of John Kennedy in 1960, but his campaign was not shaped around issues particular to the Latino community. Robert Kennedy's campaign, by contrast, focused on Latino issues—both rural and urban, with his campaign emphasizing extending federal protections to farm workers and ameliorating urban poverty in the black ghettos and brown barrios.

Latino issues would surface again in national campaigns, but in the form of anti-immigrant and anti-Mexican sentiment that infused such xenophobic platforms as Republican candidate Pat Buchanan's call in the 1996 and 2000 presidential campaigns for an immigration "time out" and Republican candidate Bob Dole's anti–Spanish language rhetoric in the 1996 campaign. After Robert Kennedy's 1968 campaign, farm worker issues and the needs of urban Mexican Americans and other Latinos would return to the margins of U.S. politics.

Urban and rural Latinos rarely unite. Following Robert Kennedy's assassination, urban Mexican Americans resumed their burgeoning Chicano Movement, which eventually came to alienate César Chávez when it advocated nationalism and separatism, as reflected by such developments as a Mexican American political party—La Raza Unida. César Chávez and the farm worker struggle were not central to the Chicano Movement, which had a more urban orientation. But the night of the 1968 California primary was a triumph for urban-rural unity in the Mexican American community, with rural farm workers responsible for galvanizing urban Mexican American voters to support a candidate with visions for a better world in both cities and rural America.

The California primary also was a triumph for the role of Mexican American voters in a national campaign. For the first time ever, some East Los Angeles precincts had a 100 percent voter turnout.[1] Overall, fourteen out of fifteen Mexican American voters in California favored Kennedy that day.[2] Bert Corona, state chairman of the Mexican American Political Association, called the farm worker union's vote drive for Kennedy the turning point in Chicano politics, demonstrating the potential political force of the barrio.[3] The farm worker newspaper *El Malcriado* opined that "It appeared that farm workers are at last developing a political muscle which must be reckoned with."[4]

The friendship between César Chávez and Robert Kennedy brought a grassroots Latino organizer and his issues for betterment of the Latino community into the near inner circle of a prominent national politician, an unprecedented and since unmatched moment of opportunity.

César Chávez and Robert Kennedy stood poised to bridge the gap between Anglos, particularly Anglo immigrant groups, and Mexican Americans. Kennedy's admiration for Chávez brought national attention to the farm worker struggle, and Chávez's affection for Kennedy united the interests of Anglos and Mexican Americans.

But, as the African American community had lost its champion in Martin Luther King, Jr. earlier that year, so too would the Mexican American and Latino community suffer a tragic, irreplaceable loss of its own that election night.

Coming off his primary defeat in Oregon, Kennedy needed to prevail in California to restore momentum to his campaign and reap the rich harvest of California's delegate count. In mid-April of 1968, polls showed McCarthy running 2 to 1 in front of Kennedy in California's liberal middle-class districts.[5] By contrast to Oregon, which had few minority voters, California's electorate was diverse even then—at the time Mexican Americans constituted 10 percent of California's population, and African Americans 7 percent.[6] With this substantial minority population, California was poised to deliver a victory to Kennedy if these voters overcame the anticipated votes for McCarthy in middle-class Anglo neighborhoods.

The polls closed at 8:00 p.m. on Tuesday, June 4, and by 8:25 the first returns had McCarthy ahead 49 percent to Kennedy's 40 percent, but all of these returns came from outside the Kennedy stronghold of Los Angeles County, which alone held 38 percent of the state's total voter registration.[7] The unprecedented voter turnout by Mexican and African Americans in Los Angeles ultimately proved sufficient to deliver Kennedy the victory.

Kennedy established headquarters at the Ambassador Hotel in Los Angeles. A few days before the primary Chávez asked Kennedy's campaign aide whether he could bring his union volunteers to the election night celebration, along with a mariachi band. The aide waited in front of the hotel for Chávez, who arrived with two hundred Mexican American workers and the mariachi band in tow.[8] Chávez had spent Election Day campaigning from a truck, urging votes for Kennedy while the mariachi band aboard played. Chávez's traveling election bandwagon went through the barrio and also the black neighborhoods of Los Angeles, before heading to the Ambassador Hotel after the polls closed that night. Chávez and the musicians did not arrive until around 10:00 p.m.[9]

Kennedy reached the hotel earlier, at 7:15 p.m., and retired to a fifth-floor suite. César Chávez, Dolores Huerta, and Kennedy's other friends, family, and reporters gathered in room 516 across the hall from the Kennedy suite to watch the election returns. Those present included Milton Berle, John Glenn, George Plimpton, and Rosey Grier.[10] Kennedy's other supporters and the farm workers celebrated in the Embassy Ballroom downstairs, waiting for Kennedy's address.

The ballroom crowd of fifteen hundred volunteers alternated chanting "We want Kennedy" and "We want Chávez."[11] Chávez recalled he was "embarrassed" by their calls and left the hotel before Kennedy made his

late-night address to the crowd. Chávez also remembered that he "must
have sensed something wrong. I was happy until the time I got to the
Ambassador, and then I began to feel melancholy."[12] Further, Chávez was
still weak from his monumental hunger fast just weeks before the primary
night ("I left early because I was so damned tired"),[13] and his painful back
was hurting; later, his back would force his hospitalization. Near midnight,
Kennedy's victory was assured and Kennedy began assembling his platform
party to address the throng in the ballroom. Kennedy wanted Chávez to
escort him downstairs and to stand on the platform with him, and was
disappointed to hear that Chávez had left. His aide asked Dolores Huerta
to escort Kennedy downstairs, and they chatted on the way down. Huerta
told Kennedy she was glad the California campaign was over and that Kennedy had won, to which Kennedy replied, "I'm very grateful for all of the
work that you've done for me. To César and all of you." When Huerta told
him that in four precincts in East Los Angeles 100 percent of the voters
had turned out, Kennedy hugged her.[14]

Kennedy gave his last public address with Dolores Huerta, her head
wrapped in a red scarf emblazoned with the farm union's rising eagle, and
his wife, Ethel, at his side. Kennedy gave credit and thanks to Chávez,
Huerta, and the Mexican American community:

> I want to thank César Chávez, who was here a little earlier. And Bert Corona
> who also worked with him, and all of those Mexican Americans who were
> supporters of mine. And Dolores Huerta, who is an old friend of mine.... I
> want to thank all friends in the black community who made such an effort
> in this campaign, with such a high percentage voting today. I think it really
> made a major difference for me.

Kennedy spoke to the emerging consensus for his candidacy:

> I am very grateful for the votes that I received—that all of you worked for
> ... in the agricultural areas of the state, as well as in the cities ... as well as
> in the suburbs. I think it indicates quite clearly what we can do here in the
> United States. The vote here in the state of California, the vote in the state
> of South Dakota: Here in the most urban state of any of the states of our
> union, and South Dakota, the most rural state of any of the states of our
> union. We were able to win them both [on the same day].
>
> I think we can end the divisions within the United States. What I think
> is quite clear is that we can work together in the last analysis. And that what

has been going on with the United States over the period of the last three years ... the violence, the disenchantment with our society, the divisions, whether it's between blacks and whites, between the poor and the more affluent, or between age groups, or over the war in Vietnam—that we can start to work together again. We are a great country, an unselfish country, and a compassionate country. And I intend to make that my basis for running over the period of the next few months.[15]

After Kennedy's speech, Dolores Huerta followed him off the podium and Kennedy went through the hotel kitchen toward a room with an expectant press waiting. Kennedy was shot in the kitchen while reaching for the hand of Juan Romero, a Mexican American dishwasher.[16] Also shot was Paul Schrade, the United Auto Workers official who had worked so closely with the farm workers and Chávez, but he recovered from his wound. Dolores Huerta was walking behind Kennedy with his wife Ethel when the shooting began. As Dolores recalled, "I was only a few steps behind senator Kennedy.... Suddenly I heard the shots and everything became confusion. Someone pushed me against the wall to protect me."[17] The gunman was a Palestinian immigrant, but onlookers thought initially from his appearance that he was Mexican. One onlooker recalled, "My God, he looks like a Mexican. Oh Bob! Oh Cesar! After all you've done! Shot down by a Mexican!"[18] The Mexican dishwasher whose hand Kennedy had been reaching to shake knelt by him and prayed after placing a set of rosary beads from his pocket into Kennedy's hand.[19] Kennedy died a little more than twenty-four hours after he lay bleeding on the Ambassador Hotel kitchen floor.

By the time he passed, the final tally in the California primary gave him 46 percent of the vote (1,472,166 votes) to McCarthy's 42 percent (1,322,608). McCarthy carried suburban areas of Los Angeles and San Francisco, as well as the city of San Diego. Kennedy fared well in Central Valley counties, where the farm worker movement took root, but elsewhere in rural areas did poorly.[20] His victory came from Los Angeles, where African American and Mexican American voters turned out in record numbers to support him. The media attributed his victory to these voters, one journalist concluding that "Mexican Americans contributed most of the slender margin by which Kennedy beat McCarthy in California."[21] Chávez acknowledged later, "We played a major role in getting his victory in California."[22]

The rural and urban Mexican American community mourned Kennedy's death. Chávez and the farm workers returned by bus and a caravan of cars to Delano Wednesday morning. Back in Delano, Chávez talked to the union's doctor and nurse about Kennedy's injuries and chances for survival. Their disheartening opinion prepared Chávez for the news that came in the middle of that night when Kennedy died.[23] That Thursday, Delano farm workers mourned and held a memorial evening mass attended by over fifteen hundred farm workers.[24] Among urban Mexican Americans, a mass in Kennedy's honor at the East Los Angeles Junior College Stadium followed a candlelight procession through the streets of East Los Angeles. The director of the Community Service Organization, which Chávez had once led, lamented that day: "Every time anyone speaks out to champion any worthwhile causes for the Spanish-speaking community, he is either knocked down or smeared. Bobby Kennedy has been more vocal and seemed to grasp the situation in the Mexican American community more and more. It was very encouraging ... and then, last night, another blow."[25]

Chávez captured the loss in the Mexican American community on Kennedy's death: "It was so senseless, so useless! We felt it closer than most people because we were so involved with him. I was convinced he would have gotten the nomination, and I was pretty sure he could have won. Kennedy was by far the real force for change, and he was willing to take in the poor, and make the poor part of his campaign. It was a tremendous setback. A vacuum was created when he died."[26]

Kennedy's funeral mass was held Saturday, June 8, at St. Patrick's Cathedral in Manhattan, before 2,300 invited guests.[27] Chávez was one of forty-nine honorary pallbearers in addition to the thirteen active pallbearers that included Kennedy's brother Ted and his son Joseph.[28] By the time Chávez and Dolores Huerta arrived at the cathedral, there were no seats left, so they stood, along with the few farm workers that came with them. As Kennedy's legislative aide remembered, "He didn't realize where he was standing, but he was standing directly in front of the whole section of Congressmen, blocking their view. You know, he didn't do it deliberately, but it was just such a nice touch."[29]

Part II

The Dream of Dignity Survives

CHAPTER SIX

Aftermath

César always told us, on most politicians you have a two-year warranty. But not Bobby. In Bobby's world there were no lesser people.

—Dolores Huerta[1]

He [Robert Kennedy] was the last hope for the Chicano.... I don't mean him, personally, but the whole white liberal bit, it's dead now. McCarthy lost tonight, too. It doesn't matter who killed him; liberals choke at violence. You watch and see. This will insure the election of ... Nixon.

—Oscar "Zeta" Acosta, *The Revolt of the Cockroach People*[2]

We farm workers have labored with a new determination in recent months, because there was a beacon which guided us much as the lighthouse guides the sailor on a stormy night.

That beacon was Kennedy—a beacon of hope for the farm worker. Who, except him, had come to the bottom of the pit to bring hope and encouragement to the farm worker? It was he who gave us new spirit.

It was he who said there was a place in the social order for farm workers, and that there would be new laws to help us gain entry into this great society and so-called democracy.

It was he who told us he would work for these laws, and that promise was more than anyone else had ever given us....

May our friend Rest in Peace....

—*El Malcriado* (UFWOC publication), June 15, 1968[3]

With Kennedy gone, the Democratic Party nomination went to vice president and former Minnesota senator Hubert Humphrey. The United Farm Workers Organizing Committee (UFWOC) voted to endorse Humphrey in his race against Republican candidate Richard Nixon, with 98 percent of the membership favoring Humphrey over Nixon.[4] Although the farm workers union worked on Humphrey's behalf, its effort failed to match its outpouring of energy and resources for Kennedy. As Chávez recalled: "The spirit wasn't there ... the spirit was empty. [Union supporters went to the polls] only because we were so afraid of Nixon. So it was Nixon that we were voting against and not for Humphrey."[5]

Humphrey, for his part, expressed unconditional commitment to the farm worker cause. When President Johnson was still in the race, Humphrey had asked Latino leader Bert Corona for Latino support of Johnson in the 1968 race. To Corona's rejoinder that Johnson would need to support the farm worker struggle, Humphrey replied, "We can't do that."[6] But on his own, Humphrey soon embraced many of the concerns of urban and rural Latinos. Humphrey pledged programs to aid the urban barrios, and in August endorsed the national grape boycott that the UFWOC had instituted to augment its grape strike. While campaigning in San Francisco's heavily Latino Mission District in September, Humphrey wore a UFWOC button and promised in his speech: "The worker in the fields is entitled to all protection, ... and when I'm president, he'll have those rights, make no mistake about it."[7] In a summer 1968 editorial to the *New York Times*, Humphrey endorsed including farm workers under the organizing protections of the National Labor Relations Act. In a letter to Chávez on August 1, 1968, Humphrey acknowledged his appreciation for Chávez's meeting with him in Los Angeles in late July to discuss farm worker needs. Humphrey wished Chávez success with the national boycott effort and declared unconditionally: "I want to make it clear that I do endorse your efforts and I hope you will feel free to use that endorsement and the contents of this letter in any way you feel will best serve 'La Causa' [the farm worker movement]."[8]

Nixon sporadically courted the Latino vote in 1968. He addressed a rally in San Antonio and remarked that Mexican Americans were not rioting or breaking the law, an allusion to his "law and order" campaign message and an implication that African Americans rather than Mexicans were to blame for the urban unrest that needed to be checked.[9] Nixon coupled his "law and order" campaign with an appeal for "states' rights," another potentially race-charged platform, this one to keep the federal government from enforcing civil rights mandates imposed on reluctant states, particularly southern ones.[10] Although both Humphrey and McCarthy endorsed the farm worker grape boycott, Nixon denounced it.[11] The UFWOC union and the Mexican American Political Association (MAPA) produced campaign literature with the slogan "No Deje Que Nixon Quite Lo Que Usted Ha Ganado" ("Don't Let Nixon Take Away What You've Won"), as well as a *corrido* (ballad) of Richard Nixon: "You have swallowed scab grapes / And now you're choking on them . . . / When the elections are here . . . mexicanos / Will have no mercy."[12] A campaign publication of the AFL-CIO and MAPA showed Nixon proudly holding a large bundle of grapes with the caption, "Nixon shows more real tenderness for the grapes he holds than he ever showed for farm workers!"[13] The leaflet also reprinted a newspaper article with Nixon's boast "I will continue to eat California grapes and drink the product of these grapes whenever I can."

During the presidential campaign in September 1968, a UFWOC official wrote to Nixon addressing his condemnation of the grape boycott:

> You have the right to do this as a friend of the large growers of California. What is perplexing is your apparent ignorance of basic facts about labor law. You claim that farm workers are covered by the National Labor Relations Act. They are not. It is for this reason alone that strikers are forced to go to consumers for help. . . .
>
> You claim that farm workers are engaged in an illegal boycott—that it is somehow illegal for farm workers to inform the public of their plight and ask the consumer to buy no grapes. Are you saying that freedom of speech has become illegal? . . .
>
> You have a right to disregard the boycott. But this slander is unforgivable and we respectfully request an apology which can be made public.[14]

Nixon had contended that "We have laws on the books to protect [farm] workers who wish to organize."[15] But contrary to Nixon's assertion, these federal laws do not encompass farm workers. Further, Nixon opined that the "secondary boycott of California grapes is clearly illegal," and should be condemned "with the same firmness we condemn any other form of law breaking." Again, because the federal National Labor Relations Act does not encompass farm workers, it did not prohibit their secondary boycott of wine and other products containing grapes, or of supermarkets selling grapes.

As election day approached, Humphrey recreated Kennedy's motorcade route through the ghetto and barrio districts of Los Angeles, riding past celebratory crowds in an open convertible. But Humphrey couldn't overcome Nixon's home state advantage in California and lost the state by a narrow margin. Nationally, Nixon won a plurality of votes, taking 43 percent to Humphrey's 42.7 percent with the anti–civil rights candidate George Wallace garnering 13.6 percent of the vote and handing the election to Nixon.[16] Although the black and Latino votes did not overcome Nixon in California, their votes helped Humphrey to win Texas by fewer than 40,000 votes; observers speculated that a shift of only 5 percent of the Mexican American vote in Texas would have delivered that state to Nixon.[17] Nationally, estimates ran that Nixon received no better than 12 percent of the African American vote,[18] no more than 10 percent of the Mexican American vote, and no more than 15 percent of the Puerto Rican vote.[19] Still, Mexican American turnout was low after Robert Kennedy's assassination, with Mexican Americans casting far fewer votes than they did in the 1960 Viva Kennedy election.[20]

Chávez was overcome with sadness after Robert Kennedy's death. Nixon's presidency aggravated the loss when his administration targeted the farm workers union for hostile federal action and reversed any influence the union had enjoyed in prior years within the executive branch.[21] Chávez saw no comparison of Nixon to Robert Kennedy, remarking that after Nixon was elected "we saw an immediate change, hostile and not caring. The Executive Department ceased completely to involve us in anything. We were completely shut off."[22] In early 1970, Chávez contrasted with some regret the "disinterested" Johnson administration to Nixon's White House, which was "actively working against us."[23] Chávez confided after Kennedy's death that "I have no taste for politics in my heart."[24] But his alliance with Robert Kennedy had brought Chávez into the inner circle of influence within the Democratic Party as a representative of the Mexican American vote. Wielding that clout, Chávez continued to serve an important role in Democratic politics, even delivering the nominating speech for California governor Edmund "Jerry" Brown at the 1976 Democratic National Convention in New York City (but Jimmy Carter won the nomination).[25]

Shortly after his brother's death, Senator Ted Kennedy asked Chávez and others to consider how best to honor Robert Kennedy's memory in the form of a living memorial. In a letter to Ted Kennedy in late June 1968, Chávez outlined a proposal for political mobilization of the poor. He prefaced his proposal by acknowledging Kennedy's special relationship with the poor: "I cannot speak for the other states but never in California have I seen evidence of so much faith and hope in what your brother stood for; even more so than when we worked for your brother, John. And unless something positive and effective is done, the faith that the poor had in what your brother represented will fade and hope will turn to despair."[26]

Chávez's letter went on to explain that the poor cannot help themselves because they are unorganized and disenfranchised: "They neither speak with power and cannot effect change first of all in their own lives and then for the country as a whole. What we propose as a living memorial is something which meets one of the most basic needs of the poor, i.e., the power of the vote."

Chávez proposed nonpartisan voter registration centers in areas where the poor reside. Further, to empower the immigrant populations of non-citizen poor, he proposed citizenship classes to help resident aliens become citizens and register to vote. In late summer 1968, Ted Kennedy informed Chávez that the Kennedy family was establishing the Robert F. Kennedy Living Memorial as a vehicle to carry out proposals to aid the wide range of constituent groups and interests, both national and international, that had inspired Kennedy.[27] Rather than targeting a specific proposal or interest, the memorial would serve as an ongoing "catalyst in the solution of pressing public problems" that would help form new, independent, local organizations to carry out its project goals. Named to the fifty-six-member board of trustees were Chávez; leaders in the African American community such as Julian Bond, Charles Evers, and Coretta Scott King; labor leaders such as Paul Schrade; and a raft of politicians and Kennedy friends and family.[28]

By this time in the fall of 1968, Chávez was bedridden from severe back pain, resulting in his hospitalization for twenty days. Not until after the November presidential election did Chávez find relief—when former president Kennedy's personal physician visited Chávez and diagnosed and treated his spinal problem.[29] Shortly after Robert Kennedy's death, his sister Patricia Kennedy Lawson edited a collection of remembrances of Kennedy, with Chávez contributing his recollections of Kennedy's 1968 visit to Delano. In her letter to Chávez thanking him for his contribution, Patricia Kennedy Lawson handwrote a postscript: "My brother cared so much about your cause so I only hope everything you and he hoped for turns out!"[30] Chávez responded four months later in March 1969, apologizing for the delay caused by his health problems, and acknowledging that it was "a difficult and saddening experience to recollect and write about your brother. It is still a painful experience for me and millions of farm workers and poor of this country who saw in him a ray of hope."[31]

CHAPTER SEVEN

Viva la Causa: Rural Latinos and
the Farm Worker Movement

All my life, I have been driven by one dream, one goal, one vision: to overthrow
a farm labor system in this nation which treats farmworkers as if they were not
important human beings. Farmworkers are not agricultural implements. They
are not beasts of burden to be used and discarded.

—César Chávez[1]

It's not just a question of wages. It's ... a basic question of hope for the future.
—Robert Kennedy[2]

A lot of [Americans] think that fruits and vegetables grow right there on the
supermarket shelf. They have no idea how the fruits and vegetables get there.
—Richard Chávez[3]

Latinos entered the national political consciousness through the Chávez-
led farm labor struggle in the 1960s and beyond. The rural roots of the
farm worker campaign held the potential to complement the struggles for
dignity in the urban barrio. Chávez captured this urban and rural connection among Latinos in his address to the Commonwealth Club of San
Francisco in 1984:

All Hispanics—urban and rural, young and old—are connected to the farm
workers' experience. We had all lived through the fields, or our parents had.
We shared that common humiliation. How could we progress as a people,
even if we lived in the cities, while the farm workers—men and women of
our color—were condemned to a life without pride? How could we progress

as a people while the farm workers—who symbolized our history in this land—were denied self-respect? How could our people believe that their children could become lawyers and doctors and judges and business people while this shame, this injustice was permitted to continue?[4]

The year 1968 found the United Farm Workers Organizing Committee (UFWOC) union in a regulatory vacuum that in some ways worked to its benefit but in other ways harmed the fledgling union. Enacted by Congress in 1935, the National Labor Relations Act (NLRA) protected the organizational rights of employees. From its inception, the NLRA excluded agricultural employees, leaving growers the freedom to fire or discriminate against farm workers who unionized, to interfere with efforts to unionize their employees, and to refuse to bargain collectively with a union representing its employees.[5] This exclusion likely stemmed from the strength of the grower lobby rather than from any inherent incompatibility of farming with the protections of the act. But their exclusion from the NLRA did free farm workers and unions from the limitations on union activity added to the NLRA by the 1947 Taft-Hartley and 1959 Landrum-Griffin Acts. As so amended, the NLRA restricted secondary boycotts (such as picketing an innocent employer hoping to cause it to cease doing business with the employer with which the union is struggling). Once the UFWOC union adopted the secondary boycott of supermarkets selling grapes as crucial leverage in its dealing with growers, the secondary boycott ban under the NLRA became undesirable for farm labor organizers.[6] As César Chávez stated, "the boycott . . . is the *only* way we can organize."[7] Therefore, although he testified before a House subcommittee as late as spring 1967 urging inclusion of agricultural labor in the NLRA,[8] Chávez came to oppose adding farm workers to the NLRA without at the same time excluding them from its secondary boycott restrictions. As Chávez reasoned, the 1947 amendment to prohibit secondary boycotts came only after the industrial unions had enjoyed a twelve-year period following the enactment of the NLRA in 1935 in which to gain strength: "We, too, need our decent period of time to grow strong under the life-giving sun of a public policy which affirmatively favors the growth of farm unionism . . . [and] has proved beneficial to the nation in the past when unions were weak and industry strong."[9]

In the late 1960s, the UFWOC initiated its most famous boycotts, rooted in its efforts to organize table grape workers—the national (and even international) grape boycott that encompassed all California table grapes and later the secondary boycott of supermarkets selling grapes. The California table grape boycott began in August 1967 as a strike against Bakersfield-based Giumarra Vineyards, California's largest grape grower. A nationwide boycott of Giumarra grapes complemented the strike.[10] Because this grower evaded the boycott by marketing its grapes under labels of other vineyards, the UFWOC widened its boycott in January 1968 to include all table grape growers. By the spring of 1969, the union began boycotting supermarkets—a secondary boycott—particularly the Safeway chain, which marketed 20 percent of the Giumarra grapes. Through its targeting of grocery chains, the union was using tactics prohibited by the NLRA for covered workers, but legitimate for excluded farm workers.

In the 1968 presidential campaign, Robert Kennedy, Eugene McCarthy, George McGovern, and Hubert Humphrey all endorsed the national grape boycott, while then California governor Ronald Reagan and Republican presidential candidate Richard Nixon denounced it.[11] Accompanying Nixon on a campaign tour in September 1968, Reagan condemned the boycott as illegal and immoral, and called the striking farm workers "barbarians."[12] Nixon ate grapes at campaign rallies and labeled the boycott illegal, contending it should be put down "with the same firmness we condemn illegal strikes, illegal lockouts, or any other form of lawbreaking."[13] Acting swiftly after the election, the Nixon administration eased the boycott for growers by directing the Department of Defense to sharply increase its grape purchasing—grapes shipped to the military in Vietnam increased between 1968 and 1969 from 555,000 to 2,167,000 pounds.[14]

After Nixon appointed a conservative Republican as general counsel of the National Labor Relations Board (NLRB), the NLRB took the legal position that while the UFWOC union was unprotected under the NLRA, the union was nevertheless subject to its ban on secondary boycotts. The NLRA secondary boycott ban applies to those labor organizations in which covered employees participate. Although agricultural laborers are excluded from the act, the NLRB argued that by striking packinghouses and boycotting wine, the UFWOC union was trying to organize workers in those industries subject to the act. Implementing this theory, the NLRB sought to enjoin the farm union's secondary supermarket boycott under the NLRA. Chávez fumed that under Nixon's presidency the NLRB legal counsel "was stretching the meaning of the federal law very far to get us."[15]

Ultimately, the NLRB dropped its court challenge in exchange for the UFWOC's pledge to abandon its wine boycott and any effort to organize nonagricultural workers or involve them on picket lines.[16]

Although Nixon administration proposals were introduced in Congress to amend the NLRA to directly encompass farm workers and thus prohibit UFWOC secondary boycotts, no such amendment was forthcoming. Growers had better success in a few states—Arizona, Idaho, and Kansas—which passed strict laws governing farm workers. Enacted in 1972, the Arizona law outlawed secondary boycotts and harvest-time strikes.[17] Arizona's Republican governor signed the bill within an hour of its passage, prompting Chávez and the farm workers union (which became the United Farm Workers [UFW] in 1972) to launch an unsuccessful recall campaign against him.[18] To counter this trend of antiunion legislation, Chávez undertook a twenty-four-day fast. Recalling his historic fast in Delano in early 1968 in which he broke bread with Robert Kennedy, Chávez's 1972 fast culminated in Arizona following a march through the streets of Phoenix to a memorial mass for his departed friend Robert Kennedy. Accompanied by more than 5,000 supporters, Chávez ended his fast with Communion bread, as he had done in Delano.[19]

By 1973, the Safeway grocery store chain invoked the new Arizona antiunion law in court to enjoin a UFW secondary boycott that utilized picketing and distributing handbills at Arizona Safeway stores urging customers not to patronize Safeway.[20] The UFW was embroiled in a long-standing territorial dispute with the Teamsters union in the lettuce and grape fields, and was hoping to induce growers to hold union elections rather than hire Teamsters members.[21]

In California, growers sponsored a ballot initiative in 1972 (Proposition 22) to outlaw secondary boycotting. The UFW portrayed the initiative as an unconstitutional assault on its free speech rights, contending that under Proposition 22 farm workers could be jailed simply for saying "Boycott Lettuce." Voters soundly defeated the California initiative 58 to 42 percent, suggesting that at the time public sentiment still sided with the farm worker organizers. By the summer of 1975, however, its struggle with the Teamsters union had left the UFW only a few contracts with grape growers while the Teamsters dominated the California agricultural industry. Newly elected Democratic governor Jerry Brown, a friend of the UFW, orchestrated compromise legislation among the growers, the UFW, and the Teamsters, resulting in the 1975 California Agricultural Relations Act. That act permits secondary boycotting aimed at requesting that the public cease purchasing a particular product of the primary employer (for example, a request not to purchase a grower's grapes from a Safeway store). Further, although it outlawed a secondary boycott encouraging the public to boycott the entire business of the secondary employer (for example, a boycott of an entire Safeway store), it permitted even such a comprehensive secondary boycott when the labor union is certified to represent the primary employer's workers. Thus, a union that wins an election and gains status as a certified union can use the comprehensive secondary boycott as leverage to gain a favorable collective bargaining agreement.[22] By 1974, however, the UFW decided to discontinue storewide boycotting and concentrate on secondary boycotts of specific products.[23]

Of equal importance, the California Act required, among other things, that bargaining representatives would be elected by secret ballot and certified before they could negotiate bargaining agreements with employers.[24] At the time the California Act took effect, UFW membership had declined from a peak of 40,000 farm workers to only 10,000. But under the new election provisions, the invigorated UFW won 198 elections in the months following the act's passage to the Teamsters' 115 election victories.[25] With this success, the UFW was able to negotiate an end to its territorial dispute with the Teamsters, allowing the UFW to organize farm workers and the Teamsters to pursue cannery workers and truck drivers.[26]

Throughout the union's battles in the fields and the courtrooms over forty years, the Kennedy family supported the Chávez union. For example, in fall 1970 a California court enjoined the UFWOC from "[u]rging, encouraging, or recommending, or asking any other persons to urge, encourage or recommend, that any customer [of lettuce producer Bud Antle] boycott [Antle's] agricultural products, or that persons patronizing [Antle's] customers or stores purchasing from [Antle's] customers refrain from purchasing [Antle's] products, or purchase products produced by others rather than the products of [Antle]." The injunction stemmed from the lettuce worker battle with the Teamsters that led the UFWOC to boycott all non-UFWOC lettuce, including lettuce from the Bud Antle company. Chávez was jailed in Salinas, California, for failing to comply with the court's order. Ethel Kennedy, Robert's widow, visited Chávez in jail on December 6, 1970, and celebrated a candlelight mass with over two thousand Chávez supporters on her arrival. As national television captured the event, an angry John Birch Society and antiunion crowd of about two hundred challenged her visit, yelling "Ethel go home" and "Reds go home"[27] and carrying signs reading "Reds, Lettuce Alone," "Chappaquiddick Now Salinas," and "Kennedys are Jailbirds."[28] After visiting with Chávez, Ethel Kennedy remarked to the UAW's Paul Schrade that "you really throw some weird parties here in California."[29] A few days later, Coretta Scott King, widow of Martin Luther King, also visited Chávez. On Christmas Eve, twenty days after Chávez was jailed, the California Supreme Court ordered his release pending its review of the injunction,[30] and four months later the court ruled that the Antle boycott injunction violated the union's free speech rights.[31]

Eventually, grower use of pesticides in grapes led to another grape boycott, spanning from 1985 to 2000. At age sixty-one, Chávez undertook a lengthy and dangerous water-only fast in summer 1988 to protest pesticides. Two weeks into the pesticide fast, three children of Robert Kennedy visited Chávez and helped publicize the link between crop pesticides and farm worker cancer and other health problems. Following a press conference with the Kennedys that garnered national press coverage, the Kennedy children marched outside a local supermarket that sold table grapes.[32] After fasting for thirty-six days, Chávez broke his fast with a mass in Delano attended by eight thousand supporters and several Hollywood celebrities. Among those present were Ethel Kennedy and some of her children—Ethel took the role of her late husband and gave Chávez *semita* bread to end his fast.[33]

Ethel Kennedy was back in Delano for Chávez's funeral, after he died suddenly in April 1993 while testifying for the UFW in a decade-long court battle in Yuma, Arizona. A lettuce grower sought money damages against the UFW for the union's mailings to consumers and grocers accusing the grower of using child labor and toxic pesticides. Ironically, this same megagrower now owned the Arizona farmland the Chávez family had lost in the Great Depression. An earlier trial resulted in a jury verdict against the union of $5.4 million, an annihilating blow. But an Arizona appeals court overturned the verdict because it improperly extended Arizona's 1972 law prohibiting secondary boycotts to the farm union's protest in California and other states that permit secondary boycotts.[34] During retrial of the grower's separate claim for wrongful interference with its business relations, Chávez died in his sleep at the age of sixty-six while staying at a friend's house near Yuma.[35]

In the funeral procession through Delano, Ethel Kennedy held the hand of Chávez's widow, Helen, and Kennedy's sons took turns as pallbearers of Chávez's simple pine coffin, made by his brother Richard.[36] Conducting the mass in both English and Spanish, Roman Catholic cardinal Roger Mahony called Chávez "a special prophet for the world's farm workers."[37] Farm workers had now lost two of their strongest allies, too soon.

From its heyday of surging membership after the 1975 California Act, the UFW endured several legal battles in the 1980s and 1990s[38] as well as internal struggles and the impediment to negotiating with growers posed by increased undocumented immigration.[39] In the early 1980s, UFW membership was 60,000 to 90,000, but membership had decreased at the time of Chávez's death in 1993 to 5,000.[40] Precipitated by undocumented labor and the farm crisis of the 1980s, farm wages declined in the 1980s 50 percent faster than manufacturing wage rates did.[41] Seasonal farm workers' real wages fell 10 percent in the 1990s.[42] In the 2000s, the average life expectancy of a farm worker was an abysmal 48 years at a time when the average U.S. expectancy had increased to 77.6 years,[43] and in 1997 a farm worker's average yearly income was only $9,828.[44] Farm workers are plagued with inadequate housing and other hallmarks of poverty.

As conditions deteriorate, union membership continues to slide, mirroring the national trend among all workers prompted by such national and international influences as employer union-busting strategies, continued immigration, globalization, and technology. By 2005, the UFW included only about 8,000 to 9,000 workers in its union,[45] a mere 10 percent of its high watermark in the mid-1970s through the early 1980s. Further, the UFW did not have any Central California Valley grape growers among its labor contracts. The UFW slide mirrored the decline in the agricultural sector, which in 2005 saw a scant 2 percent of California's approximately 450,000 field laborers represented by a union. Unions have lost favor in other employment sectors. Overall, in 2006, only about 12 percent of the U.S. workforce belonged to unions, down steadily from 12.5 percent in 2005 and 13.4 percent in 2001, and down substantially from 20.1 percent membership in 1983.[46] The numbers are even lower when looking at the private employment sector, where only 7.4 percent of workers were unionized in 2006, and lowest-wage workers, with fewer than 1 percent union organized.[47] Union membership in the United States peaked in the mid-1950s, when 35 percent of U.S. workers were protected by union contracts.[48]

Rather than looking to the national and international roots of decline in unions across the United States, a four-day investigative series ("UFW: A Broken Contract") published in January 2006 by the *Los Angeles Times* laid blame for the evident slumping fortunes of U.S. farm workers on the doorstep of the United Farm Workers union. The *Times* assumed to know what was best for farm workers and accused the union of straying from its roots of organizing farm workers by focusing instead on fund-raising, on organizing workers in other industries, and on such entrepreneurial endeavors "far from the fields" as the ownership of Spanish-language radio stations. More broadly, the paper traced blame to César Chávez, whom it accused of eventually steering the UFW away from its "core mission of organizing farmworkers," now a mere "afterthought," toward the creation of a larger ethnic-based social movement.[49] Already reeling from the larger forces that devastated the prospects for farm labor organizing, this series threw the last shovelfuls of dirt on the legacy of César Chávez and the optimism of the past when change in the fields and beyond seemed possible.

By the time of Chávez's death in 1993, the farm worker movement had already passed from public consciousness. Few knew of the grape boycott in place, prompted by the risks of pesticides to consumers and the farm workers. Today, when Latinos are in the media or public discussion, the topic is the threat posed to the U.S. culture and economy by undocumented immigrants, not the threat posed to Mexican Americans and Mexican workers by subhuman farm labor conditions. In this nativist environment, little progress can be expected for worker and immigrant rights. As one commentator lamented in 1998:

> There was a time, back in the middle of the 1960s, when many who worried about the fate in America of migrant agricultural workers had good reason for optimism.... But the migrant agricultural workers who then seemed on their way at least to some political and economic and social progress ... are, arguably, worse off now.... Cesar Chavez is dead.... We have no national political figures like Robert Kennedy, who went out of his way to visit migrant communities to learn of the fate of those who lived in them.[50]

CHAPTER EIGHT

Viva la Raza: Urban Latinos and the Chicano Movement

Every man who comes to the picket line is our brother, immediately, regardless of color.

—César Chávez[1]

Historian Ignacio García documented the Viva Kennedy campaign at the start of the 1960s that prompted Mexican Americans throughout California, the Southwest, and the upper Midwest to form Viva Kennedy clubs in aid of John Kennedy's 1960 presidential campaign.[2] As García observed, Mexican American activists had not yet looked within the barrio for inspiration for their reformist ideals—their 1960 dream was in search of Camelot, not a separatist Aztlán.[3]

During the 1960s, César Chávez's farm labor movement was a class-based struggle that aimed beyond the Mexican American community in attracting membership and support. Among the workers represented by Chávez were Filipinos and Anglos; moreover, Anglo supporters of the farm workers union included the Kennedys as well as Hollywood entertainment notables such as Steve Allen. The farm labor struggle engaged a broad coalition but with its rural foundation did not resonate as much with urban youth.[4] By contrast, urban Mexican American youth in large part propelled the so-called Chicano Movement that emerged in the late 1960s.

The Chicano Movement was an urban-based awakening of activists and youth channeled through such events as protests of urban school conditions and the Vietnam War, and by the political uprising that formed a separatist

Chicano political party. The movement was marked by a nationalist orientation toward self-determination and anti-assimilationism that sometimes was hostile toward Anglos. For example, the movement's manifesto from 1969, "El Plan Espiritual de Aztlán," declared:

> Brotherhood unites us, and love for our brothers makes us a people whose time has come and who struggles against the foreigner "gabacho" [Anglo] who exploits our riches and destroys our culture.... We are a bronze people with a bronze culture. Before the world, before all of North America, before all our brothers in the bronze continent, we are a nation, we are a union of free pueblos, we are Aztlan....
>
> Nationalism as the key of organization transcends all religious, political, class, and economic factions or boundaries. Nationalism is the common denominator that all members of La Raza [the Mexican race] can agree upon.[5]

By the late 1960s, Mexican Americans made up 67 percent of California's farm workers, with only 12 percent of the farm labor force Anglos.[6] In leading the United Farm Workers union, Chávez often invoked Mexican American influences—for example, the union flag portrayed an Aztec eagle, the farm worker theme song was *De Colores,* a religious song in Spanish, and the union's rallying calls were in Spanish: "¡Viva La Huelga [strike]!," "¡Viva La Causa [the movement for farm worker justice]!" and "¡Sí Se Puede [we can do it]!" Still, Chávez lamented about the budding nationalism of the Chicano Movement in contrast to the colorblind aspirations of the farm labor struggle:

> [I]f we wanted civil rights for us, then we certainly had to respect the rights of blacks, Jews, and other minorities.... That's why today we oppose some of this La Raza business [in the Chicano Movement] so much. When La Raza means or implies racism, we don't support it. But if it means our struggle, our dignity, or our cultural roots, then we're for it.... [W]e can't be against racism on the one hand and for it on the other....
>
> [At the time of my earlier involvement with the Community Service Organization,] the constitution of most [barrio-based] groups said members had to be Mexican, but our [union] constitution had no color, race, religion or any other restrictions, and we stuck to it."[7]

Expressing his movement goals in broader terms than the struggles of just Mexican American workers, Chávez also questioned: "La Raza? Why be racist? Our belief is to help everyone, not just one race. Humanity is our belief."[8]

Harboring fear that nationalism eventually would splinter opportunities for coalition as well as fracture the Mexican American community itself, Chávez explained: "I hear about *la raza* more and more. Some people don't look at it as racism, but when you say *la raza*, you are saying an anti-gringo thing, and our fear is that it won't stop there. Today it's anti-gringo, tomorrow it will be anti-Negro, and the day after it will be anti-Filipino, anti–Puerto Rican. And then it will be anti–poor-Mexican, and anti–darker-skinned Mexican."[9]

Chávez faced the pressures of nationalism in his own movement—particularly when the Mexican American–dominated union he led, the National Farm Workers Association, united in 1966 with the Filipino union, the Agricultural Workers Organizing Committee, to form a single union with greater clout. Chávez held his ground that Filipinos must be represented in union leadership, despite some Mexican Americans who were ready to leave the union in protest. As one author explained, Chávez from the beginning "had not thought of La Causa as a movement that would be motivated primarily by appeals to race or nationality."[10]

The Chicano Movement peaked between 1968 and 1973.[11] Although I do not contend that the assassination of Robert Kennedy prompted the heyday of the Chicano Movement, I nonetheless suggest that some of the nationalism that emerged in that movement was a reaction to the sentiment that the potential for Mexican Americans to find Camelot with other Americans died with Kennedy in 1968. This change in attitude was captured best in a memorial procession for Kennedy at dusk through the streets of East Los Angeles. Members of the Brown Berets, a Chicano youth group described unflatteringly by the *Los Angeles Times* as "militant," marched in the procession and sang "We Shall Overcome." As night overtook the marchers on their way to the East Los Angeles Junior College Stadium, Brown Beret members lit flaming torches to guide the journey. At the Stadium mass, leader of the Brown Berets David Sánchez lamented "It is a time of real mourning. He was our last hope. There will be no more outside help for us."[12] While serving a jail term in early 1968 for unlawful assembly, Sánchez struck chords of nationalist contempt, warning the Brown Berets to avoid "Anglos," and commanding "Do not talk to the [Anglo] enemy, for he is either a dog or a devil."[13]

Despite the potential for coalition with African Americans, at times the Chicano Movement excluded black participation as well. For example, in announcing that Martin Luther King, Jr. was invited to attend his land rights convention, Chicano Movement icon Reies López Tijerina cautioned "[W]e are only going to admit the Negroes when Martin Luther King speaks. After that they have to get out, because the convention belongs to our *raza*."[14]

A defining episode of the Chicano Movement was the 1968 school "blowouts" in East Los Angeles. By that time, almost every East Los Angeles resident was Mexican American—87 percent bore Spanish surnames and of those an estimated 95 percent were Mexican American.[15] In early March 1968, thousands of mostly Mexican American students walked out of Garfield, Roosevelt, Lincoln, and other barrio high schools, voicing demands that included bilingual education, more Mexican teachers, and reduced class sizes.[16] In the same days that Chávez fasted in rural Delano to aid the struggle of farm worker equality, Chicano students were leading their own urban strike against inequality in the classrooms. While in California to celebrate the end of Chávez's fast in March 1968, Robert Kennedy bridged these urban and rural struggles of Mexican Americans by meeting in East Los Angeles with the student leaders of the blowouts and expressing his support for their cause: "He knew all about the walkouts.... He had a list of our demands ... and he told us that he supported everything that we did."[17]

Kennedy's embrace of the organizers of the East Los Angeles school blowouts in 1968 reflected his imperatives of educating youth effectively and creating opportunities for them. It is unclear, however, what tools the federal government could wield in relieving the conditions that led to the blowout. The impetus for school reforms was a grassroots movement intended to assert community control over localized issues of cultural competency and educational funding, and federal law would have little influence here. Further, the concurrent move to establish Chicano Studies programs and Mexican American support networks at colleges was far removed from federal prerogatives. But the federal government played a role in bilingual education, funding these programs in legislation cosponsored by Robert Kennedy, and presidential leadership intersected with the Chicano Movement in other respects such as the war in Vietnam and economic programs and policies for the inner cities.

As the Chicano Movement blossomed, student activism followed a nationalist path, evidenced best by the genesis of the above-quoted "Plan Espiritual de Aztlán" at the Chicano Youth Liberation Conference, held in March 1969 in Denver, and the production of the blueprint for college Chicano Studies programs, "El Plan de Santa Barbara," drawn at a conference held in Santa Barbara in April 1969.[18] Historian Juan Gómez Quiñones asserted the significance of the Denver student conference as signaling "a break at a national level from the assimilationist 'Mexican American' consciousness and politics of the previous decades,"[19] instead substituting a new nationalist ideology. Similarly, the "Plan de Santa Barbara" expressed an anti-assimilationist ideology for the Chicano community by stating: "Cultural nationalism is a means of total Chicano liberation."[20]

In addition to the nationalism that marked the Chicano Movement, the occasional punctuations of violence that accompanied events loosely grouped within the movement were contrary to principles espoused by Chávez and the farm labor movement. Although there was no organized agenda of violence in the Chicano Movement, its galvanizing document, "El Plan Espiritual de Aztlán," invoked a Malcolm X–like message of community defense in advocating "[s]elf defense against the occupying forces of the oppressors at every school, every available man, woman, and child." The Brown Beret group also mirrored the philosophy of Black Power leaders by calling for use of "any and all means necessary . . . to resolve the frustrations of our people."[21] Among the episodes of violence that erupted in the movement were those of the fringe group Chicano Liberation Front that took credit for bombing government targets in Los Angeles in 1971, and the land grant movement, led in New Mexico by Reies López Tijerina, that triggered the kidnapping of law enforcement officers and later a jailhouse shooting in a failed effort to make an armed citizen's arrest of a reticent district attorney.[22] Rioting also flared occasionally in East Los Angeles in 1970 and 1971, leading to several confrontations with local police. As a Los Angeles television station editorialized critically about one of these episodes:

> About a thousand angry youth, perhaps inflamed by [antiwar] rally speeches, certainly frustrated by the ghetto conditions in which they live, turned to meaningless destruction and violence. . . .

The Mexican American community is a vitally important part of our Southern California society. But such immature displays by a minority of the citizens there are major obstacles in keeping it from gaining the position of respect it deserves.[23]

As discussed previously, Chávez adhered steadfastly to the nonviolence principles of Gandhi. Robert Kennedy also preached a nonviolent ethos, declaring flatly that "violence will bring no answer" while addressing farm workers at the end of Chávez's 1968 hunger fast. In his 1967 book *To Seek a Newer World*, Kennedy similarly condemned violence as a means of social change:

> [Urban violence] is the most destructive and self-defeating of attempts. This is no revolution. The word means to seize power, but the advocates of violence are not going to overthrow the American government; when Rap Brown threatens "to burn America down," he is not a revolutionary, he is an anarchist. The end is not a better life for Negroes, but a devastated America; as William Pfaff has said, "a program of death, not life." So it has already proven, all over the face of America.[24]

Although it is hard to pinpoint its precise date of birth,[25] the late 1960s and particularly the early 1970s saw the rise (and rapid fall) of La Raza Unida (the united race) Party, another defining facet of the Chicano Movement. La Raza Unida is said to be the first political party to have represented a single ethnic group,[26] as its membership was almost exclusively Mexican American. Although evolving over time and varying locally in California, Texas, and the other states of its presence, La Raza Unida's party platform tended to advocate national health care, immediate withdrawal from Vietnam (where Latino soldiers were dying in disproportionate numbers), bilingual/bicultural education, abolition of the death penalty, and reform of the tax system, including repealing regressive sales taxes.[27] La Raza Unida Party counted successes primarily in Texas, where it achieved local victories, gained control of the Crystal City school board, and placed two members on the five-member Crystal City council.[28] In two other Texas towns, La Raza Unida party members won election to the mayor's office.[29]

Conflicts emerged quickly within La Raza Unida Party over its nationalism and its relationship to the Democratic and Republican parties. At a 1972 party conference in California, for example, membership rejected a proposal to convert La Raza Unida into a multiracial "people's party."[30] Generally the party's positions followed themes of anti-assimilationism and self-determination.[31] At La Raza Unida's national convention in 1972, party organizer Rodolfo "Corky" Gonzales (the former head of the 1960 Viva Kennedy Club in Colorado)[32] reflected the distance from the two national mainstream parties in describing them as "a monster with two heads [Republican and Democrat] that feed from the same trough."[33] In late December 1969, a co-organizer of the party, José Angel Gutiérrez, declared that "Democrats and the Republicans are all alike. They are all Gringos ... neither party has ever delivered for the Chicano ... both parties have promised a hell of a lot, but neither has delivered. Now we as Chicanos are calling their bluff.... [T]he only viable alternative is to look into political strategies which will yield maximum benefits for la Raza."[34]

The northern California chapter of La Raza Unida ultimately passed a motion that "La Raza Unida will not support any candidate of the Democratic or Republican Party or any individual who supports these parties."[35] The tension of whether La Raza Unida would function as a bona fide third party or instead would lend its support to mainstream party candidates who best served its platform existed throughout La Raza Unida's brief political life in the early 1970s. Representing this tension was the uneasy relationship between La Raza Unida and César Chávez. Chávez had a history of alliance with the Democratic Party, highlighted by his support of Robert Kennedy but also evidenced by his endorsement of other local, state, and national Democratic candidates, such as George McGovern's 1972 presidential campaign. Further, Chávez had distanced himself from the nationalistic advocacy of the Chicano Movement. To the organizers of La Raza Unida, then, Chávez must have represented the old guard assimilationist Mexican American with close ties to the Democratic Party "monster."

The strained relationship between Chávez and La Raza Unida party leadership became national news during the late summer 1972 campaign for the presidency between incumbent Nixon and Democrat George McGovern. Holding the party's national convention in El Paso in early September 1972, La Raza party leaders invited Chávez, along with Nixon and McGovern, to address the convention; none ultimately attended. Party leaders imposed conditions on Chávez that led him to decline; among them was that Chávez could only discuss the Chicano Movement and not

McGovern's candidacy.[36] The *Washington Post* reported that "La Raza Unida Party leadership apparently has severed its loose ties with farm labor leader Cesar Chavez over Chavez's announced support for presidential candidate George McGovern and over his longtime connection with the Democratic Party."[37] One party leader attacked Chávez, singling out his alleged failure to assist young Chicanos, while others in the party accused Chávez of being a "one-issue" leader more relevant to the rural labor struggle than the more comprehensive Chicano Movement.[38]

Democratic Party leaders were attacked along with Chávez. During the 1972 presidential campaign, La Raza Unida members heckled Senator Edward Kennedy when he came to an East Los Angeles College rally for McGovern. They carried signs such as "Kennedy and McGovern are carpetbaggers and political pimps," "What have we gained from the Democrats?" and "Raza, sí, Kennedy no."[39] As author Tony Castro opined:

> It is significant that the brother of President Kennedy and Robert Kennedy, both of whom had been revered and elevated to a kind of sainthood by Mexican Americans, should be so harshly treated by even a small segment of that same minority group. For if anyone represented the unfulfilled hopes of the Chicanos during the past dozen years [the 1960s and early 1970s], it was the Kennedys, whose own tragedy had served only to magnify the despair and frustrations of the Chicanos and others who had attached their own aspirations to the promise the Kennedys extended.[40]

La Raza Unida Party criticism of Chávez reflected the growing divide between the causes of urban and rural Latinos, particularly within the Mexican American community. Nixon's campaign exploited the rift, with Nixon's top Latino campaigner contending that Chávez represented only the small percentage of Mexican Americans who were field workers, and challenging Chávez: "He speaks for only 5 percent of the Spanish-speaking people in the country. I'm concerned about the other 95 percent. He's not. I'm concerned about the Mexican Americans in East Los Angeles and other urban areas. When has he ever done anything for the urban Mexican American?"[41]

Chávez avenged the hostility directed at him by La Raza Unida Party organizers by helping to defeat La Raza Unida candidates in Los Angeles in the 1970s. Dolores Huerta explained the union's position as stemming from the acceptance of money by La Raza Unida candidates from the Nixon campaign in order to attack the farm workers union.[42] McGovern also accused La Raza Unida of accepting money from Republicans in exchange for its neutrality in the 1972 race.[43] A McGovern representative contended that Nixon promised Crystal City, Texas, officials a medical clinic in exchange for votes.[44] Nixon campaign strategy documents boldly suggested that the Republicans assist the nationalist Mexican American party in order to pull votes from the Democrats.[45] Allegations of support from the Nixon campaign are not surprising given that at the time that La Raza Unida was formed as a predominantly Mexican American party, 85 percent of Mexican American voters were registered as Democrats. The Republican Party clearly stood to gain the most from La Raza Unida votes that likely otherwise would have gone to Democratic candidates. Still, La Raza Unida posed no real sustained threat to the Democratic Party, "declining rapidly"[46] after 1973 from its internal power struggles, having managed only a few years of localized political viability from perhaps 1970 until 1973.

The Chicano Movement faded as the Chicano political party flickered out. By the mid-1970s, the Vietnam War finally ended, La Raza Unida Party lost favor, and New Mexico land movement icon Reies López Tijerina was jailed, all contributing to derailment of the struggle. As the urban-based Chicano Movement lost momentum, so too did the rural organizing of farm workers. Ironically, as the Chicano Movement and the farm worker La Causa movement separated over such fault lines as urban nationalism and Chávez's support for the Democratic Party, the lack of cohesion accelerated their declines. The urban-rural Latino divide became even more pronounced in the 1980s. Perhaps, though, in the mid-1990s, California's divisive anti-immigrant initiative, Proposition 187, helped to restore a galvanizing pro-immigrant and pro–farm worker consciousness among Latinos that helped unite urban and rural interests. By that time, undocumented Latino workers dominated the agricultural workforce, and were the target of this backlash initiative attacking their health and education. Many urban Latinos came to realize that no matter how separated they were from their migrant worker backgrounds of past generations, the voting public viewed all Latinos as a work force to be exploited, then discarded if they caused trouble, needed services, or tried to forge a culture or community in the United States. This consciousness connecting the urban Latino to the rural farm worker offers the possibility of political unity on issues of crucial relevance to Latinos—immigration, health care, fair labor laws, education, recognition of culture, and the other building blocks of community and dignity that later chapters explore.

CHAPTER NINE

Vietnam and Mexican Americans:
Patriotism and Protest

Our resistance to [Vietnam], and all war, stems from a deep faith in non-violence.

—César Chávez[1]

One of the two key issues in the 1968 presidential campaign, along with the economic crisis and consequent unrest in the inner cities and the rural United States, that drew Robert Kennedy into that race, was the mounting bloodshed in Vietnam. Although publicly César Chávez did not denounce the war at the time, he opposed it privately and eventually added his voice to those seeking an end to U.S. involvement. Both men held a deep spiritual and moral commitment to nonviolence, and Kennedy's outspoken criticism of the Johnson administration policies escalating the war must have heartened Chávez. As discussed below, Chávez's initial public reluctance may have stemmed from several causes, including the foremost business of organizing the farm workers and managing the grape strike and boycott, as well as the diversity of positions on the war within the Mexican American community—contrary to stereotype most Latinos are deeply patriotic and many Mexican American farm workers and city dwellers supported U.S. participation in Vietnam. Responding to dovish college student volunteers in the labor movement who reported incredulously to Chávez that the workers they were helping to organize supported the war, Chávez replied that "farm workers are ordinary people, not saints."[2] At the same time, Mexican American opposition to the war gathered steam and became part of the Chicano Movement experience in the late 1960s and early 1970s, culminating in the tragic "Chicano Moratorium" in August 1970 in East Los Angeles. There, a stirring 20,000- to 30,000-person antiwar march and gathering at a local park devolved into police-demonstrator confrontations. Police killed three persons, including two (a fifteen-year-old and a prominent Mexican American reporter for the *Los Angeles Times*) with tear gas canisters fired into them.[3]

The Vietnam War hit the Mexican American community disproportionately hard, as it did for African Americans. On the campaign trail in 1968, Robert Kennedy decried the imbalance in the war—telling students at Idaho State University that college student deferments should be abolished: "We must realize that the system from which we have sent a disproportionate number of Negroes, Mexican Americans, and Indians to fight in Vietnam is a faulty one."[4] Low-income youth were more than twice as likely to fight in Vietnam than the children of middle- or upper-class families, in part due to the military deferment of full-time college students that survived until 1970 (and the extended deferral for graduate students that ended in 1967).[5] Illustrating the discrepancy in impact of these deferments, consider that at the time of their effect, despite the burgeoning Mexican American population in Los Angeles, only 70 Mexican Americans attended UCLA when its campus enrollment was 26,000.[6] Overall, an estimated 83,000 Latinos served in Vietnam.[7] These soldiers of color ended up on the more dangerous front lines of combat, and the casualty rate for Mexican American soldiers was over 50 percent higher than the percentage population of Mexican Americans in the United States;[8] the discrepancy existed too for African Americans, who accounted for 24 percent of all combat deaths in 1965.[9] That year, Martin Luther King, Jr. spoke boldly against the war well before Kennedy or Chávez did, but as one commentator observed, backlash from the Anglo community, including *New York Times* editorial page writers, caused King to "bac[k] away from the issue for eighteen months, until the conflict had grown huge and King identified it as the principal obstacle to domestic reform."[10] As King prophesized, the Vietnam War effort ultimately crippled the federal government's commitment to President Johnson's War on Poverty and other domestic programs that aided the Latino and black communities and other impoverished groups. In 1966, the United States spent $22 billion on the war and less than $2 billion fighting poverty.[11] Robert Kennedy captured the hurtful economics of war in his 1967 book *To Seek a Newer World*: "The [Vietnam] war is also diverting resources that might have been used to help eliminate American poverty, improve the education of our children, enhance the quality of our national life—perhaps even to save the nation from internal violence and chaos."[12]

César Chávez's distaste for violence in the farm worker struggle extended to the war in Vietnam. Episodes of violence in the grape strike precipitated Chávez's Delano fast in early 1968, but one union official writing to Robert Kennedy in March 1968 portrayed the fast in broader terms: "He is doing this to let everyone in the country know that we can accomplish many things without violence not only in organizing our Farm Worker Union, but else where including Vietnam, and Civil Rights Movements."[13] Still, in the initial years of the Vietnam War, Chávez avoided publicly stating his personal opposition to the war. In addition to those circumstances mentioned above, the emerging violence within the antiwar movement itself may have tempered any early public proclamations by Chávez against the war. Expressing his concern over the contradictions in the antiwar movement, Chávez remarked, "The real paradox here is that the people who advocate peace in Vietnam advocate violence in this country. Inconceivable; I don't understand it."[14]

Although he at first disdained public statements, Chávez exposed his personal opposition to the war in his conversation with Paul Schrade over Robert Kennedy's candidacy for president in 1968. Schrade recalled that Chávez's support for Kennedy encompassed not only the farm worker struggle but the war: "[W]e agreed that Kennedy was the only presidential candidate who could and would end the war against the people of Vietnam.... Cesar, who strongly opposed all violence, was horrified by this terrible war that was forcing American workers and their sons to kill peasants in a distant land and to die there without cause."[15]

After Kennedy's assassination, Chávez articulated his opposition to the war in a 1970 letter to organizers of the Chicano Moratorium rally. Although he declined to attend this Chicano antiwar march in East Los Angeles, his letter expressed a moral objection to violence:

It is now clear to me that the war in Vietnam is gutting the soul of our nation. Of course, we know the war to be wrong and unjustifiable, but today we see that it has destroyed the moral fiber of the people.

Our resistance to this, and all war, stems from a deep faith in nonviolence. We have to acknowledge that violent warfare between opposing groups—be it over issues of labor or race [in the Civil Rights Movements]—is not justifiable. Violence is like acid—it corrodes the movements dedicated to justice.[16]

By the early 1970s, Chávez was voicing public opposition to the war, speaking in May 1971 at an antiwar rally at Exposition Park in Los Angeles,[17] and testifying that year in his son Fernando's trial in Fresno for refusing the draft, in which César detailed the lessons he taught his children against using violence to resolve disputes.[18] Later, Chávez blasted Nixon's hawkish policies in an early 1973 letter to the president:

> The greatest leaders of history have led and taught by what they do more than by what they say. You are teaching us by the example of your deeds to seek comfort and privilege and to solve our hardest problems by violence (and then more violence, if necessary). You should not be surprised if your countrymen follow your example in their own daily lives.
>
> It does not have to be this way! Americans would respond to a different example. At our best we want to care about human suffering, to work for justice and to solve our personal and social problems by nonviolent means.
>
> Open your heart to the poor of Vietnam and the world, Mr. President. Stop the war and work for justice. If you will lead in this direction, Americans will follow.[19]

In 2007, the United States was mired in another foreign conflict with mounting U.S. and civilian casualties. As with the Vietnam War, the War in Iraq exacted a toll on the Latino population—as of early 2007, 332 Latino soldiers in the U.S. Army had died there, representing 11 percent of the casualties and out of proportion to the percentage of Latinos (less than 9 percent) in the U.S. armed forces.[20] Latinos were overrepresented in the lower, more dangerous ranks of the military, and their numbers in the military were increasing given the bleak economic opportunity for young Latinos in the United States, the burgeoning youth of the Latino population, and even the prospects for accelerated citizenship for noncitizen Latinos in the military.[21] Overall, Latinos were somewhat less supportive of the War in Iraq than the general public; still, a PEW Hispanic Center study in spring 2004 found registered Latino voters equally split in their opinion on whether the United States made the right decision to use military force in Iraq.[22] For Latinos and the general voting public, their views on the war may have played a significant role in the 2004 presidential election. Of the 51 percent of U.S. voters approving the decision to invade Iraq, 85 percent voted for Bush, while of the 45 percent of voters expressing disapproval, 87 percent voted for Democratic candidate Kerry, who decried Bush's initiation and handling of the war.[23] In the 2007 vote on the congressional resolution opposing Bush's proposal to send additional troops to Iraq, Latino House representatives voted down party lines, with all Latino Democrats approving the resolution and all Latino Republicans rejecting it. By early 2007, a CNN poll disclosed a compelling dichotomy between Democrats and Republicans in their opposition to the war, with over 90 percent of Democrats opposing U.S. intervention and only 24 percent of Republicans opposing the war. This partisan divide was missing during the Vietnam War—despite overall opposition in numbers similar to the Iraq War, Democrats and Republicans opposed the war in nearly equal percentages, likely reflecting that the war was waged under both Democratic (Johnson) and Republican (Nixon) regimes.[24]

Robert Kennedy's public position on the Vietnam War had parallels to Kerry's stance on Iraq in the 2004 election, which called for building Iraqi security forces to shoulder the load of a sustainable democracy. Kennedy favored giving the South Vietnamese more responsibility in the conflict, as well as halting bombing while pursuing a negotiated peace. But neither Kerry nor Kennedy advocated an immediate and complete withdrawal of U.S. forces.[25] In the 1968 campaign, Nixon too pledged to get the United States out of Vietnam,[26] but under Nixon's leadership the war dragged on for another seven years into the presidency of Gerald Ford, with two-thirds of the war casualties coming after 1968.[27] Privately, Robert Kennedy was said to have voiced the intention to withdraw immediately from the war.[28] Answering a commentator's posthumous question to Kennedy's close friends of what Kennedy would have accomplished as president, César Chávez confirmed that sentiment: "He would have ended the Vietnam War right away."[29]

CHAPTER TEN

Latinos and Poverty

History will judge societies and governments—and their institutions—not by how big they are or how well they serve the rich and the powerful, but by how effectively they respond to the needs of the poor and the helpless.

—César Chávez[1]

Our ideal of America is a nation in which justice is done; and therefore, the continued existence of injustice—of unnecessary, inexcusable poverty in this most favored of nations—this knowledge erodes our ideal of America, our basic sense of who and what we are. It is, in the deepest sense of the word, demoralizing—to all of us.

—Robert Kennedy[2]

At the start of the 1968 presidential campaign, two issues dominated public attention—the war in Vietnam, and the domestic issue of urban unrest, particularly among African Americans in the inner city.[3] President Johnson's so-called War on Poverty was falling short of meaningful change in urban ghettos and barrios as the Vietnam War siphoned the domestic program budget. Launched in 1964 as an attack on the causes of poverty, the War on Poverty soon was victimized by the war-torn economy. By 1966, the budget for the Office of Economic Opportunity, which coordinated the federal antipoverty effort, was cut by nearly 25 percent, and funding for community action programs that brought antipoverty programs to the Southwest barrios was cut by a third.[4]

Not limited to African American ghettos, demoralization took hold in the barrios of Los Angeles in the 1960s. As Robert Kennedy observed on the campaign trail in 1968, "We have here in California a million Mexican

Americans whose poverty is even greater than that of many of the black people."[5] The *Los Angeles Times* reported in a 1966 story, "Revolt in the Barrios: Social Ferment Stirs Mexican Americans," that "high unemployment, low incomes, menial jobs and substandard housing" remain "'a way of life' in much of the barrios."[6] A special census released in early 1966 revealed that the economic status in Los Angeles of both Mexican Americans and African Americans had deteriorated in the preceding five years, "in sharp contrast to Anglos."[7] East Los Angeles median family income in 1965 was only $5,106.[8] A 1965 report on "Hard-Core Unemployment and Poverty in Los Angeles" suggested that residents in the barrios faced unemployment and poverty and exhibited "demoralization."[9] In his 1967 article "Crisis in Our Cities," Robert Kennedy captured their despair: "If we try to look through the eyes of the young slum dweller—the Negro, the Puerto Rican, and the Mexican American—the world is a dark and hopeless place."[10]

Urban riots scarring African American slums in the mid-1960s, such as the infamous Watts riot of 1965 and riots in the summer of 1967 that killed twenty-seven people in Newark and forty-three in Detroit, were slower to reach the Mexican American barrios.[11] But violence ultimately plagued their community in the 1970–1971 "East L.A. Riots," which stemmed from frustration with the effects of the Vietnam War on Mexican Americans and with incidents of police brutality. In East Los Angeles, a mass antiwar protest in 1970 devolved into chaos when police ended the rally; among other victims police killed innocent Rubén Salazar, a columnist for the *Los Angeles Times,* who was hit in the head by a tear gas canister fired into the tavern where he sat drinking a beer after covering the rally. Protests against police brutality in the East L.A. barrio led to other outbursts of violence, such as on January 31, 1971, when police shot at rioting Mexican Americans, killing one and wounding thirty-five.[12]

Inexorably tied to urban barrio poverty were the hardships faced by the rural farm workers who Chávez tried to organize in the 1960s. A 1967 report of the President's National Advisory Commission on Rural Poverty observed that because poor rural Americans were migrating by the millions to cities seeking better jobs, it is "impossible to obliterate urban poverty without removing its rural causes."[13]

Although they eventually bonded as friends, Chávez and Kennedy came from sharply contrasting backgrounds of urban/suburban wealth and rural poverty. At the time of Robert Kennedy's birth, his family lived in an affluent suburb of Boston, but they moved to New York City when he was two. By the time Robert was four, in 1929, his parents had purchased a country estate in a nearby New York City suburb, complete with cottages for the chauffeur and gardener, for the then princely sum of a quarter of a million dollars. Its palatial grounds featured a swimming pool and formal gardens. Eventually, Bobby also could winter at the family's oceanfront compound in Palm Beach, Florida.[14]

Chávez was born in rural Arizona, two years after Kennedy's birth. As the Kennedy family prospered during the Great Depression through shrewd stock dealings,[15] the Chávez family was less fortunate. Their hardscrabble farm in the Arizona desert was foreclosed in the 1930s for past-due property and water taxes. Hoping to raise money to save the farm, the Chávez family traveled to California as migrant farm workers, foraging wild mustard greens for food and living in a rickety shack. Chávez and his family spent most of his childhood in the California fields picking fruits and vegetables. They never had much; in the winter of 1939 the family lived in a "soggy tent,"[16] or worse yet at other times they lived under a tree with a piece of canvas overhead or in the family car.[17] Assuming the role of the family breadwinner when his father was injured, Chávez was forced to quit school after the eighth grade.[18] By contrast, Kennedy attended prestigious prep schools in England, Rhode Island, and Massachusetts,[19] ultimately graduating from Harvard and the University of Virginia law school.

Representing the interests of the poor came naturally for Chávez. He dedicated his life to establishing dignity for the poor rural farm worker, living humbly throughout his life. At the time of the 1960s grape strike, Chávez, his wife, and their eight children lived in a tiny two-bedroom house on a $10 a week union salary and food from the union communal kitchen.[20] Late in his life, he earned $5,000 a year at a time when other union heads made six-figure salaries. Chávez did not believe he could accept a large income while the farm workers endured poverty, so he lived on a subsistence salary.[21] When Chávez died he did not own a home or a car, and had few personal possessions.[22] Although Chávez championed several farm worker causes, including controlling pesticides in the fields, the greatest achievement of the farm workers union was the fruition of its 1960s grape boycott when growers signed union contracts in the summer of 1970. These contracts gave workers a pay raise to $1.80 per hour and created a worker benefits plan, called the Robert F. Kennedy Memorial Plan, into which growers contributed ten cents an hour to a health and welfare fund. The health plan included doctor visits, family and maternity care, and medicine, the first such plan in the history of U.S. agriculture.[23]

Robert Kennedy too embraced the cause of the poor and oppressed with sincerity and vision. As Chávez said, "He could see things through the eyes of the poor.... It was like he was ours."[24] Dolores Huerta concurred in praising Kennedy, commenting "Do you know why the poor loved those millionaires, John Kennedy and Robert Kennedy? It was their attitude.... Robert didn't come to us and tell us what was good for us. He came to us and asked us two questions. All he said was 'What do you want? And how can I help?' That's why we loved him."[25]

Kennedy was affected by the urban and rural poverty that he witnessed. As a freshman New York senator, Kennedy visited Harlem tenements and Brooklyn slums, where he met a disfigured Puerto Rican girl whose mother explained that "rats had bitten her face off when she was a little baby."[26] As part of his Senate duties, Kennedy also toured migrant labor camps, including one in rural upstate New York, finding migrants living in insect-infested shacks, abandoned buses, and even a chicken coop.[27] Kennedy captured this national disgrace of rural poverty:

> [I]n the hills and hollows of [the] Appalachians ... [t]hey eat bread and gravy and sometimes beans; and as one of them says, when another child is born, "we just add a little water to the gravy." ...
>
> And there are others: on the back roads of Mississippi, where thousands of children slowly starve their lives away, their minds damaged beyond repair by the age of four or five; in the camps of migrant workers, a half million nomads virtually unprotected by collective bargaining or social security, minimum wage or workmen's compensation, exposed to the caprice of fate and the cruelty of their fellow man alike; and on Indian reservations where the unemployment rate is 80 percent.[28]

Kennedy's plan to combat poverty focused on job creation, tax incentives, and public/private partnerships. Kennedy saw the welfare system as inadequate to meet the needs of America's poor—in most states welfare payments were "not enough for bare subsistence" and welfare aided less than a fourth of the poor.[29] Although he argued against a 1967 proposal in the Senate to freeze welfare payments, calling it "the most punitive measure in the history of the country,"[30] Kennedy often criticized welfare as destroying the self-respect of those who would much prefer jobs to handouts. Speaking to a mostly Mexican American audience on Olvera Street in Los Angeles during his 1968 presidential campaign, Kennedy remarked: "I come here because I believe that it is the business of government to allow free men to live in dignity. How can a man retain his dignity when a welfare system shames him? I believe that men would rather work at disagreeable jobs than accept the humiliation of a handout."[31]

Kennedy stated elsewhere, "How can we pay men to sit at home? ... The priority here is jobs."[32] He wrote in *To Seek a Newer World*: "Of all our failures in dealing with the problems of the poor, the greatest is the failure to provide jobs. Here is an aspect of our cities' problems almost untouched by Federal action. No government program now operating gives any substantial promise of meeting the problem of unemployment in the inner city, and thus of any way to avoid the inefficient, wastefully expensive, degrading and self-defeating system of welfare."[33] Kennedy relied on statistics showing that unemployment in what he called "the ghettos of poverty"—citing African Americans in Cleveland's Hough neighborhood, Mexican Americans in East Los Angeles, Appalachian whites in Chicago, Puerto Ricans in East Harlem, and Indians on reservations—was over three times the national unemployment rate.[34]

Among the means available to provide jobs, Kennedy saw public employment as a last resort, but he cosponsored a bill in fall 1967 to create 1.2 million jobs through public service employment in schools, hospitals, libraries, neighborhood health clinics, and municipal service agencies. Kennedy believed that developing these new jobs in urban poverty zones would stimulate job creation in private-service sectors, such as restaurants and clothing stores, to satisfy the needs of the new wage earners. But by 1967,[35] the Vietnam War was siphoning any monies for new and existing social programs and the Johnson administration successfully opposed Kennedy's employment measure.[36]

To revitalize the ghettos and barrios, Kennedy called upon the resources of private enterprise and capital in partnership with government. Government would supply tax incentives and subsidized loans to attract private industry to the slums. Citing the incentives already in the tax system, such as those for charitable contributions, those encouraging private investment through lower capital gains tax rates, and those stimulating oil production through depletion allowances, Kennedy offered two bills in summer 1967 to provide industry an incentive to invest in the U.S. ghettos. As he explained: "The first would provide tax credits, accelerated depreciation, and extra deductions against payroll for firms willing to locate new industry in or near areas of low income and create at least twenty new jobs, of which two-thirds or more would be filled by residents of the area involved. The second would provide comparable benefits, as well as low-interest loans, for firms constructing low-rent housing in these same areas."[37]

Again, opposition from the Johnson administration killed the bills, although when he was assassinated Kennedy was preparing to reintroduce these proposals.[38]

Kennedy put his vision for public/private revitalization partnerships into practice in what he called the Bedford-Stuyvesant experiment, in a Brooklyn suburb of the same name that in 1967 was home to the second-largest black ghetto in the country.[39] Although this experiment to attract jobs into the ghetto lured only one major corporation (IBM) to Bedford-Stuyvesant, creating four hundred jobs, the community development corporation that Kennedy initiated there still survives and became "the model for thousands of inner-city community development corporations around the country."[40]

At the same time that Kennedy focused attention on creating jobs and hope in urban slums, he was drawn to the struggles of migrant farm workers and of rural poverty. As Kennedy noted in *To Seek a Newer World*, "over a third of the nation's poor live in rural areas."[41] After his participation in the Senate subcommittee hearings in California in 1966, Kennedy actively supported the cause of Chávez and the farm workers union for inclusion of farm workers within the union organizing protections of the National Labor Relations Act. Not limiting his campaign against rural poverty to the California farm workers, Kennedy held Senate hearings on rural poverty throughout the country, including in Mississippi and upstate New York in 1967, and in Kentucky in early 1968.

Kennedy's alliance with Chávez and the farm workers was consistent with his emphasis on creating jobs rather than building the welfare system. The farm workers union never championed welfare as a replacement for jobs. Instead, Chávez focused on securing fair pay and safe working conditions for the workers earning poverty wages doing dangerous, crippling work. Testifying at the 1966 Senate hearings in California, Chávez lamented: "I believe that all Americans should want this for every American—equality, the opportunity to earn a living wage, and not charity. But what has happened to the farmworker is very strange. He usually gets special attention to attack the symptoms of his poverty. But he never gets anything that will destroy the roots of his poverty."[42] Robert Kennedy too grasped the need for more than mere full, but underpaid, employment: "We need jobs, dignified employment at decent pay."[43]

Robert Kennedy's aborted presidential dreams ended perhaps the last sustained chance for impoverished groups to gain federal protection and favor. After Robert Kennedy's assassination, Johnson's War on Poverty program floundered. Although Johnson's successor Richard Nixon proposed welfare reform (never enacted) to provide a guaranteed income to all needy families, and signed several laws expanding welfare programs, Nixon was hostile to the Johnson poverty programs and tried to abolish the Office of Economic Opportunity. Johnson had established the OEO through legislation, situating the OEO in the Executive Office and calling its director his "personal chief of staff for the war against poverty."[44] Although during Democrat Jimmy Carter's administration, from 1976 to 1980, Latino children benefited from significant reductions in their poverty rates,[45] this was not the case during the subsequent presidency of Ronald Reagan, who was openly hostile to the concept of welfare, ushered in a new era of welfare policy that placed blame on recipients as lazy and dependent, focused on the burden of poverty programs on working taxpayers,[46] racialized welfare by fostering images of recipients as all people of color,[47] and shifted responsibility for welfare programs to the states,[48] which often were hostile to welfare. Under the Clinton administration, welfare came under further attack, particularly welfare programs that benefited Latinos. Clinton trumpeted the vicious Personal Responsibility and Work Opportunity Reconciliation Act of 1996, which bolstered existing federal law barring undocumented immigrants from most federal public services by ending their eligibility for immunizations and school lunch programs. Further, the 1996 act barred most documented but noncitizen immigrants, a significant number of whom are Latino, from eligibility for such federal benefits as Aid to Families with Dependent Children, food stamps, Medicaid, and Social Security.[49] Peter

Edelman, a top official in the Department of Health and Human Services, and former aide to Senator Robert Kennedy, resigned from the Clinton administration in protest because Clinton signed this antiwelfare law.

In his remarks on signing the 1996 act, Clinton quoted Robert Kennedy: "Work is the meaning of what this country is all about.... We need it as individuals. We need to sense it in our fellow citizens. And we need it as a society and as a people."[50] Clinton remarked, "He was right then, and it's right now."[51] The 1996 act carried out Clinton's vision of personal responsibility by devolving responsibility for welfare to the states, placing a five-year lifetime limit on welfare benefits, and requiring the family head to be employed within two years. But Clinton omitted the humane component of Kennedy's plan to establish dignity for all Americans, first by jobs, but with a safety net for those unable to work. As Kennedy had urged in an official statement on the urban crisis just days before his assassination: "Having moved toward real employment [once his job creation proposals were adopted], we must also move toward an adequate system of assistance for those who cannot work. That system must, as I have proposed, be automatic, be based solely on need, have national minimum standards, and contain incentives to work for those who become able to work."[52]

By the 2004 presidential election, U.S. attention had shifted away from the poor to the upper and middle classes. John Kerry's 2004 campaign platform in book form, cowritten with vice presidential candidate John Edwards, *Our Plan for America: Stronger at Home, Respected in the World*, lauded the "best measure of our nation's progress" as "the condition of America's great middle class."[53] Meanwhile, President Bush focused his attention on economic plans to trickle down wealth to the lower class by improving the fortunes of the rich. Neither candidate addressed the squalor of migrant farm workers, or the despair in urban barrios or ghettos—after 1968 these issues disappeared from the political landscape.

In 2007, however, the Latino poor, and the poor in the United States generally, remained parched, and Hurricane Katrina exposed the deep swaths of poverty in U.S. urban and rural landscapes. Into the new century, 12.7 percent (about 37 million) of the U.S. population remained below poverty level, with the poverty rate rising in 2004 for the fourth year in a row since Bush took office[54] before leveling off in 2005. Further, the federally determined line of poverty (in 2005, an annual income of $19,971 or less for a family of four!) is an unrealistically low indicator of the earnings needed to survive, and the actual number of poor in the United States is much greater than the official number.[55] Latinos remain disproportionately poor—in 2005, the poverty rate for Latinos was 21.8 percent, while the Anglo poverty rate was only 8.3 percent.[56] Latino unemployment has run higher than for Anglos since statistics were first kept in 1973—for example, 7.7 percent to 5.2 percent in 2003.[57] Although a vibrant construction industry closed the gap for Latinos in 2006 to just 0.6 percent, the smallest gap ever recorded, the home construction bust in 2007 promised to restore the usual disparity.[58] As New Mexico governor Bill Richardson detailed in 2004, there were 1.5 million Latinos unemployed, with over 18 million of an estimated 41 million Latinos nationwide unprotected by health insurance.[59] A 2004 Pew Hispanic Center report revealed that in addition to an income gap, Latino (and African American) households suffer an even more pronounced wealth (asset ownership) gap in comparison with Anglos.[60]

Agricultural workers—substantially a Latino population—arguably are worse off today than they were in the 1960s. A journalist concluded in 2005 that it is "rare to find a farm worker whose annual income breaks $10,000 a year."[61] Further, "[v]irtually no workers have health insurance or paid vacations."[62] In 2000, only 15 percent of migrant and seasonal farm workers had health insurance.[63] A federal report published in 2005 found that the average U.S. farm worker family income ranged from only $15,000 to $17,499 a year, and that 30 percent of farm workers had family incomes below federal poverty guidelines.[64] Migrant farm workers, the vast majority of them of Mexican origin, are even worse off—in 2000 the median income for migrant and seasonal farm workers was a scant $6,250 a year.[65] Recently, an economist explained that "twenty-five years ago, a worker made 12, 13, 14 cents for a bin of oranges. Today that same bin pays maybe 15 or 16 cents—in spite of 250 percent inflation."[66]

Latinos are a diverse group spread out along the political spectrum. Cuban Americans as a group tend to vote Republican, Puerto Ricans tend to vote overwhelmingly Democratic, and Mexican Americans, the largest subgroup of Latinos by far, used to vote overwhelmingly Democratic but now vote in significant numbers (although typically not a majority) for Republican candidates. Of the factors that signal voting for Democrats or Republicans among Latinos, the most compelling may be class. As is the case for voters generally, the likelihood of Latinos voting Republican increases with income. A 2004 Pew Hispanic Center national survey determined that of Latino registered voters reporting an annual household income under $30,000, 33 percent identified as Democrats, 41 percent as Independents, and only 19 percent as Republicans.[67] Of registered Latino voters making over $50,000 a year, 44 percent identified as Republican (the largest percentage identification with any of the parties in any of the income groups surveyed), 34 percent as Democrat, and 23 percent as Independent. The income/party identification correlation carried over into the voting booth. According to a Republican Party pollster, in the 2000 election Bush won 31 percent of the vote of Latinos earning less than $30,000, but 46 percent of those earning more than $75,000 a year.[68] In the 2003 California recall election, in which 40 percent of Latinos overall voted for Republicans Arnold Schwarzenegger or Tom McClintock, Latino Democrat Cruz Bustamante garnered 60 percent of the vote of Latinos earning under $40,000 but less than a majority of Latino voters making more than $40,000. Although Latinos are disproportionately poor, the potential for Democratic-leaning poorer Latinos to dominate Latino voting ranks is diluted by the dismal voting participation of poor Latinos[69] and of poor voters generally. A 1996 study of U.S. voting behavior determined that although only 41 percent of those voters of any background with income less than $9,999 voted, participation rates increased steadily for each income group, reaching 76 percent for those with incomes over $75,000.[70] The 2000 presidential election confirmed this pattern, with three-quarters of those with family incomes over $75,000 voting and only 38 percent of those with household incomes under $10,000 voting.[71]

The developing political schism between Latino voters along the fault line of class suggests the need for consideration of an interethnic/racial coalition organized around issues of poverty. Robert Kennedy nurtured the seedlings of this poverty coalition in his candidacy for president. Previously, in his successful campaign for Senate in New York, Kennedy fashioned a coalition of blacks and Puerto Ricans, as well as ethnic groups such as Jews and Italians.[72] Kennedy gained 90 percent of the African American vote and 70 percent of the Catholic vote in his Senate race.[73] As Kennedy suggested privately during the Indiana state presidential primary in 1968:

I've come to the conclusion that poverty is closer to the root of the problem than color. I think there has to be a new kind of coalition to keep the

Democratic Party going, and to keep the country together.... We need to write off the unions and the South now, and replace them with Negroes, blue-collar whites, and the kids. If we can do that, we've got a chance to do something. We have to convince the Negroes and poor whites that they have common interests. If we can reconcile those two hostile groups, and then add the kids, you can really turn this country around.[74]

Uniting African American and working-class white voters was challenging in 1968, perhaps more in 1968 than today. Newly minted civil rights laws and War on Poverty programs were sometimes seen as intended for and benefiting only blacks. At the same time, urban unrest in the ghettos challenged the supposed law and order sensibilities of working-class whites.[75]

Kennedy encountered these potential divides while campaigning for the presidency in Indiana. Among black voters his campaign preached an antipoverty message as well as one to combat racial injustice. To white audiences he relied on his reputation as former U.S. attorney general not to tolerate lawlessness and he promised to punish "lawbreakers," which this audience might read as rebellious blacks.[76] Accounts of the Indiana primary outcome differ as to whether Kennedy was able to forge the coalition he hoped for. Kennedy received 42.3 percent of the vote, with Senator McCarthy gaining 27 percent and Indiana governor Roger Branigan 30.7 percent. Kennedy took the black vote in bloc (86 percent), but also did well among white Catholic working-class voters (particularly the Irish and Polish) in the industrial cities. In a Polish blue-collar precinct, Kennedy received 241 votes to McCarthy's 86; in a black precinct 341 to 11, and in a racially mixed, lower-middle-class neighborhood precinct, Kennedy prevailed 113 to 68.[77] One commentator contended, however, that Kennedy's plurality victory was due mostly to black voters, that Kennedy had won only eleven of seventy "white" precincts, and that the existence of any poverty coalition for Kennedy was a "spin."[78] Another commentator called the coalition in Indiana a "misconception" and pointed out that Kennedy lost 59 of the 70 white precincts in urban Gary, Indiana, while garnering 80 percent of the black vote there.[79] Gary at the time was "sharply divided" in population between blacks and lower- to middle-class whites. Overall, Kennedy received only 34 percent of the white vote in these 70 precincts, leading that commentator to suggest that the lesson of Gary "was that the more personally involved the white voters were with the racial struggle, the more they identified Kennedy with the black side of it, and turned to his opponents as an outlet for their protest."[80] But Kennedy's victory in the Anglo-dominated state of Kansas lent support to Kennedy's antipoverty coalition claim, particularly given his victory in Kansas counties with heavy concentrations of German and Polish voters.[81]

Kennedy hoped to attract the youth vote to his coalition, but he polled poorly in the colleges. A mock presidential poll for all party candidates conducted by *Time* magazine in May 1968 on the campuses of Berkeley, Stanford, and nationally showed Kennedy receiving only 17 percent of the Berkeley student vote to McCarthy's 48, 13 percent of the Stanford vote to McCarthy's 56, and nationally 21 percent of campus support to McCarthy's 28 percent and Nixon's 19 percent.[82] Kennedy also showed poorly with college-educated voters—Indiana opinion polls gave McCarthy a 44 to 18 percent margin over Kennedy among these voters.[83] Ultimately, Kennedy finished last in the Indiana primary among professionals, drawing only 24 percent of their vote.[84] Indeed, during the campaign McCarthy boasted that "the better-educated people vote for us."[85]

Kennedy's appeal among working-class voters, particularly ethnic Irish and Italian Catholics, apparently did not extend to the white middle class. Kennedy's experience in Oregon illustrated his vulnerability among middle-class white voters. McCarthy triumphed there over Kennedy, garnering 44.7 percent of the primary vote to Kennedy's 38.8 percent.[86] Devoid at the time of any significant minority population (one observer estimated only about 20,000 African Americans in the state[87] and in total minorities made up only 2 percent of its population)[88] and greeting Kennedy with all-white, middle-class audiences, Oregon prompted Kennedy to lament that "[t]his ain't my group."[89] Explaining his subsequent loss in the California primary, McCarthy suggested "We've made our real test in Oregon, where there were no bloc votes."[90]

In the California primary, Kennedy added the state's substantial Mexican American population to his coalition of African Americans and working-class whites. Still, the vote was close, 1,402,911 for Kennedy and 1,267,608 for McCarthy,[91] and Kennedy did poorly in the agricultural districts, aside from the Central Valley, where César Chávez had the most influence, and poorly "in the north, and in smaller cities and suburbs."[92] McCarthy carried the suburbs of Los Angeles and San Francisco, and the more conservative San Diego.[93] Overall Kennedy carried only eighteen California counties to McCarthy's thirty-eight, but it was the Los Angeles area that swept Kennedy to victory—the incredible turnout of African Americans and Mexican Americans there helped Kennedy gain a margin over McCarthy in Los Angeles County of over 120,000 votes.[94] Thus, it was his coalition of Mexican Americans, African Americans, and the Anglo working poor that made the difference, but only in a state with considerable numbers of these constituents. As one commentator concluded: "In placing his power behind [the poor's] aspirations, especially those of the blacks, [Kennedy] alienated a large segment of the comfortable middle class. If blacks and Mexican Americans were his margin of victory in California, the voters he frightened were his margin of defeat in Oregon and his source of weakness throughout the country."[95]

Among the few successful antipoverty or class-based coalitions in recent U.S. history was the farm labor movement led by César Chávez and Dolores Huerta. As Chávez once observed: "We have many ethnic groups in our union. Mexican Americans, Negroes, Filipinos, Portuguese, Puerto Ricans, Arabs, and ... a few Jews. And we work side by side and there is no real difference."[96] The farm union's policy statement "The Plan of Delano," published the day after the 1966 Senate hearings in California, relied on interracial unity in building an antipoverty coalition:

> We shall unite. We have learned the meaning of UNITY. We know why these United States are just that—united. The strength of the poor is also in union. We know that the poverty of the Mexican or Filipino worker in California is the same as that of all farm workers across the country, the Negroes and poor whites, the Puerto Ricans, Japanese, the Arabians; in short, all of these races that comprise the oppressed minorities of the United States. The majority of the people on our Pilgrimage are of Mexican descent, but the triumph of our race depends on a national association of all farm workers. The ranchers want to keep us divided in order to keep us weak.... We must use the only strength that we have, the force of our numbers. The ranchers are few; we are many. UNITED WE SHALL STAND.[97]

The farm labor movement constituency extended beyond the multiethnic composition of its workers, to include backing from religious leaders, urban Latinos, labor leaders such as Walter Reuther—the Anglo president of the United Auto Workers—college students, and even wealthy liberals and entertainers such as comedian Steve Allen.[98] Reuther marched with Chávez in Delano during the grape strike, and donated significant sums to the farm worker cause. For example, at the end of Chávez's dramatic fast in early 1968, the UAW presented Chávez with $50,000 toward construction of the union's headquarters.

Generally, though, efforts to mobilize an effective class-based coalition have fallen short of expectations. Martin Luther King, Jr., too, became an advocate for the poor of all backgrounds. By late 1967, shortly before his assassination in early 1968, King had launched (apparently at the suggestion of Robert Kennedy) the Poor People's Campaign. He sought to enlist rural and urban poor of all ethnic backgrounds in a crusade for their economic rights with a platform that encompassed full employment and a guaranteed minimum annual income.[99] But King's Poor People's Campaign fractured shortly after his murder.

In the 1960s, the campus organization Students for a Democratic Society (SDS) initiated a campaign in low-income inner-city neighborhoods hoping to build there "an interracial movement of the poor" through community organizing.[100] Known as the Economic Research and Action Project, the effort sent young white, mostly middle-class organizers to low-income neighborhoods to mobilize residents to address problems such as unemployment and housing conditions. By 1968 these community projects had disbanded, falling victim to several pressures, including growing black nationalism in the 1960s that questioned the role of white organizers of blacks and also imperiled black/white coalitions. For example, at a 1967 meeting of two of the SDS-organized community groups aligned to address police brutality, one predominantly white and the other black, members of the black group made derogatory comments about whites (such as "white trash").[101] At the same time, poor white residents harbored negative views toward blacks. One commentator suggested an additional structural impediment to any interracial coalition among the poor: "The reality of de facto residential segregation in urban America and the employment advantages enjoyed by white southern migrants relative to blacks militated against a common consciousness or political coalition among low-income whites and blacks."[102]

Jesse Jackson's Rainbow Coalition in his 1984 and 1988 campaigns for the Democratic presidential nomination consisted of groups Jackson saw as neglected by the Reagan administration, encompassing the poor of all ethnic backgrounds, as well as women and minority groups.[103] Although Jackson ultimately failed to secure the nomination, his vote among Democrats did improve from 18.5 percent in 1984 to 29.7 percent in the 1988 primaries.[104] In 1988, Jackson won 30 percent of the Latino vote and 12 percent of Anglo votes, even drawing near 40 percent of the Anglo vote in Michigan's primary and 38 percent of the vote overall in Oregon, with its nearly all-Anglo population at the time.[105]

In today's sociopolitical climate, groups situated to form a coalition for an antipoverty agenda include some Latinos, particularly recent immigrants, African Americans, Native Americans, some Asian Americans, some white groups such as Jewish Americans, and Catholics. Sprinkle in some Hollywood upper crust and college students, and the recipe for an antipoverty coalition takes shape.

Issues that would coalesce an antipoverty coalition are multifold, but center on the connected goals of economic progress and educational development. One galvanizing issue related to economic advancement, if not survival,[106] is the minimum wage. As one commentator revealed, a $1 raise in the minimum wage in 2001 would have entitled more than 10 million workers (8.7 percent of the workforce) to a raise, with Latinos and African Americans in particular benefiting.[107] Although many states have minimum wage laws, conservative legislators tend to resist increases (California's Governor Schwarzenegger vetoed an increase in 2004 before he relented in 2006 and raised the minimum wage there), and workers in all but fourteen states as of early 2005 were protected only by the outdated federal wage floor, which remained unchanged for years and, when adjusted for inflation, is 40 percent lower than the federal rate in 1968.[108] At the time of publication in 2007, the newly Democratic Congress had managed to gain approval of a federal minimum wage increase inserted into the legislation funding war in Iraq. Earlier, in 2004, Senator Ted Kennedy proposed the same incremental raise finally approved in 2007 to increase the federal floor by $2.10 an hour total, from $5.15 (where it had stood since September 1997!) to $7.25. In arguing for his plan in 2004, Ted Kennedy challenged "I believe that anyone who works 40 hours a week, 52 weeks a year should not live in poverty in the richest country in the world."[109] Robert Kennedy's focus on job creation in the 1960s is vital today, but must include the component of decent wages to help hard-working families escape the indignity of poverty and welfare. In her best seller *Nickel and Dimed,*

Barbara Ehrenreich poignantly exposed the shortcomings of our current system, which forces welfare recipients into the workplace but leaves them unprotected from underpaid jobs that provide employment but keep them mired in or near poverty. Still, national surveys give hope to the political prospects of ensuring fair wages if politicians have sufficient courage to buck their wealthy campaign donors—a 2000 poll revealed that 94 percent of Americans agree that "people who work full-time should be able to earn enough to keep their families out of poverty,"[110] and another poll found that 85 percent of Americans support increasing the minimum wage.[111] Upon passage in 2007 of the increase he had sought for years, Ted Kennedy remarked: "The minimum wage has been stuck at $5.15 an hour for more than 10 years, but now—finally—Americans across the country will get the raise they need and deserve. Certainly, the increase we've passed today is only the first of many steps we must take to address the problems of poverty and inequality."[112]

Universal health care insurance is a critical component of an antipoverty coalition platform. Health insurance acutely concerns Latinos, as more Latinos lack health care insurance than any other ethnic group—a staggering 62 percent of Latino adults aged nineteen to sixty-four were uninsured at some point during 2005.[113] Embracing an unfulfilled idea that dates to Harry Truman, Robert Kennedy urged adoption of universal health care in his 1968 presidential campaign: "I think this nation is willing to make the effort necessary for an effective system of care. We have the resources to do it—we have the will to do it—and we are going to do it if I am the next President of the United States."[114]

Among the goals of an antipoverty coalition would be restructuring the financing of public education, which currently ensures that children from segregated urban neighborhoods will confront underfunded public schools. Education initiatives such as the proposed federal Dream Act would open doors to immigrants seeking the American dream by extending to the undocumented the same college tuition as other state resident youth.

Yet, in 2007, daunting structural impediments existed to the antipoverty political coalition that both Robert Kennedy and César Chávez strove to engineer. Recent immigrants who were not yet citizens, both documented noncitizens and the undocumented, often occupied the lowest-paid jobs with the fewest benefits, but in most jurisdictions were not allowed to vote. Further, as illustrated above, the poor do not register and vote in the same proportion as those with greater incomes, suggesting that any antipoverty political movement might focus most productively in its initial stage on voter registration and turnout. In the 1968 California primary, some precincts in Mexican American communities had a 100 percent turnout, a credit to the efforts of Chávez and his farm worker volunteers and illustrating the potential for galvanizing poor voters to register and vote. Compounding low turnout and registration is the impact on the right to vote in many jurisdictions of felony convictions, falling disproportionately on African Americans and Latinos through racial profiling.

Comprising poor voters of color and whites, the antipoverty coalition could fracture on familiar lines exploiting the selfishness that desperation breeds. Certain issues, such as affirmative action in education and jobs, and punitive anti-immigrant proposals, tend to pit one or more groups within such a coalition against each other, causing collapse. For example, the political campaign for California's Proposition 187 (denying education and social services to undocumented immigrants) aimed to convince African Americans that undocumented Latino and Asian immigrants were taking jobs and social services from them—not only did 47 percent of black voters back the initiative, but so did the same percentage of Asian American voters.[115]

Despite their mutual interests, poor whites and poor communities of color are hampered in coalition by the continued presence of derogatory stereotypes and of racism in U.S. society. Some white poor voters succumb to negative views of blacks, Latinos, and other subordinated groups and, to distance themselves from the consequent ill treatment of these groups in U.S. society, exert their whiteness as a tangible "asset" in an otherwise impoverished life. In this way, these voters, though their interests are more aligned with those of poor communities of color, join middle- and upper-class whites in supporting measures and politicians harmful to minorities and immigrants. Further, African American law professor Derrick Bell's theory of interest convergence, as summarized by Richard Delgado, suggests a related barrier to white/community of color cooperation:

> White elites arrange things so that Black gains come only when they will also advance White self-interest. A corollary explains why working-class Whites cast their lot with elite Whites, when one would think they could advance their interests more effectively by joining with Blacks and Latinos

to challenge their common exploiters. This happens because elite Whites convey to their working-class counterparts the idea that Blacks covet their paltry prerogatives and that Whites are better off by maintaining a sharp separation between themselves and those at the true bottom of society.[116]

Even the Latino middle class is prone to distance itself from the struggles and issues of poor Latinos, particularly immigrant Latinos—for example, as many as one in four Latino voters supported Proposition 187.[117]

Any chance that middle- and upper-class whites will join in an anti-poverty coalition out of compassion for the poor increasingly is undercut by the growing sentiment expressed by commentators such as Victor Davis Hanson, who view the immigrant poor, particularly Mexicans, as ingrates whose life is far better even mired in American poverty than the life they left behind in Mexico. As Hanson claims:

> Our young professors at California State University, Fresno, some with Ph.D.s from Berkeley and Stanford, will be lucky to take home $2,000 a month after deductions—appearing on the pay stub in some ten categories including state, federal, Social Security and Medicare taxes, health, dental and vision insurance fees, state retirement, parking and union dues. Some undocumented [Mexican] workers in construction can put in 200 hours of work per month, and at $10 cash per hour they match the English professor—without the tie, the decade's worth of degrees, the need to master the lingo of postmodernism, and the entire drain of life insurance, lawn care, and braces for the kids.[118]

Of equivalent insult to intelligence is Hanson's portrayal of the equal privilege of Mexican immigrants—"[t]he alien's water is, of course, as clean as a millionaire's. He drives on the same freeway. His windbreaker from Wal-Mart looks no different than the Wall Street tycoon's informal wear."[119] Hanson propagates the view that the Mexican poor are threats to middle-class neighborhoods and survive only through our largess: "The Mexican gang member may shoot and stab with abandon, but in the agony of his last hour he demands without appreciation or knowledge the technology of the twentieth-century American emergency room to rebuild his liver and stitch up his shredded kidneys."[120]

These images of the ungrateful and undeserving immigrant poor, and of poor populations generally, threaten to squelch the charity of the middle class in the voting booth and beyond. Middle- and upper-class white opinion has soured before, as when the Civil Rights Movement in the 1960s shifted from moral to economic equality:

> The civil rights movement generated powerful white support so long as it concentrated on issues perceived as moral questions (such as segregation, voting rights, antiblack violence); it lost that capability when the movement's focus shifted to the economic aspects of racial inequality. As the civil rights movement moved north after 1964 and pressed demands for open housing, busing, and affirmative action, the northern white civil rights constituency began melting away and undermining the political foundations of anti-poverty policy.[121]

In the minds of the American public, welfare once had an Anglo face, which darkened in recent years. Condescending references to "welfare mothers" abusing their privilege was code among politicians, both Democrat and Republican, and the public for African American single mothers. Along with urban violence and unrest, these derogatory perceptions prompted the shift in middle-class public opinion away from helping the poor:

> In hindsight, the "window of opportunity" for the [War on Poverty] was very brief; the historian Charles Noble estimates it at about twenty months, from early 1964 to late 1965. Identification with African Americans and with racial conflict and upheaval made the poverty war a target for growing white backlash. Accusations that liberal policies and programs fomented black rebellion, at worst, and were unappreciated by blacks, at best, eroded support for the poverty war among white Americans.[122]

By 2007, critics such as Pat Buchanan, Victor Davis Hanson, and Samuel Huntington had helped place an increasingly Latino face on discussions of welfare abuse. Although white Americans still make up a sizable por-tion of welfare recipients,[123] middle- and upper-class whites no doubt view poverty-based initiatives as primarily aiding black and brown Americans, and of declining relevance to whites.

In 2006, Barack Obama also attributed the palpable decline in compas-sion for our nation's poor to complacency fostered by media and popular culture:

There was a time ... when such deep intergenerational poverty could still shock a nation—when the publication of Michael Harrington's *The Other America* or Bobby Kennedy's visits to the Mississippi Delta could inspire outrage and a call to action. Not anymore. Today the images of the so-called underclass are ubiquitous, a permanent fixture in American popular culture—in film and TV.... Rather than evoke our sympathy, our familiarity with the lives of the ... poor ... [mostly has] bred indifference.... [W]e take these things for granted, as part of the natural order, a tragic situation, perhaps, but not one for which we are culpable, and certainly not something subject to change.[124]

CHAPTER ELEVEN

Immigration: Walls and Wages

The immigration service and the border patrol always worked on the assumption that it is not really illegal for these [undocumented] people to be here provided they are working, are being useful to the growers. The moment they stop being useful—either because they strike or because they don't work any more since the crops are finished—then of course it becomes very illegal and they are thrown out. It's a very corrupt system.

—César Chávez[1]

Taking hold in earnest in the 1980s but with deeper roots in history, anti-immigrant hatred directed at Mexicans continues unabated into the twenty-first century. Some hate radio commentators and best-selling authors contend that immigrants from Mexico and other Spanish-speaking countries are scourges to blame for street crime and the nation's drug problem, strains on the welfare and education system, and even the alleged breakdown of the country's historical, cultural, and moral identity. Publicity for Patrick Buchanan's latest book sounds this alarm in calling Mexican immigration "the greatest crisis facing America today."[2]

Now, unchecked Mexican immigration is far and away the defining social and political issue for Latinos in the United States. By contrast, in 1968, the farm worker movement and organizer César Chávez dominated discourse and the societal view of Latinos. Of course, there are parallels between the farm labor movement and immigration, explored below, which led Chávez to remark once during a strike seeking collective bargaining with growers that "if we could get the illegals out of the ... fields, the growers would have to come and meet with us in 24 hours."[3] But in the 1960s, U.S. society viewed Latinos as just poor farm workers concentrated in the California fields and rallying against Anglo growers but not displacing Anglo workers. By the 1990s, Latino immigrants surged in number throughout the United States, particularly in the South, East, and Midwest,[4] and were employed in substantial numbers in industrial, construction, and other sectors far from migrant field work. These developments helped fuel vicious anti–Mexican immigrant sentiment throughout the country.

The late 1960s and early 1970s saw César Chávez and the farm workers union oppose immigrants from Mexico used as strikebreakers, even to the point of allegedly patrolling the U.S./Mexico border during labor strikes in the borderlands. Still, the farm union immigration policy sought to ensure protection of striking workers from undercutting by immigrant strikebreakers lured by growers, while advocating at the same time for removal of barriers to immigrant citizenship. Thus, the union's beef was not with Mexican immigrants, but with strikebreakers. Misapplied by anti-immigrant voices today to support their xenophobic positions, the farm union's tactics targeted strikebreakers of any background—documented, undocumented, or citizen—and the union always was motivated by economic concerns to protect the most underprivileged workers in the United States, most of them of Mexican origin. By contrast, today's purveyors of anti–Mexican immigrant rhetoric often seem motivated by deep-seated hatred toward Mexicans and Latinos and aim to protect their view of U.S. "culture" with no regard for ensuring the economic survival of existing Mexican American workers.

Robert Kennedy and his brother John recognized the contribution of immigrants to the U.S. social fabric, and would have been unpersuaded by the alarm being sounded by today's crop of anti-immigrant hatemongers. Rather, they would value the contributions of Mexican immigrants and respect their courage and conviction in bettering the lives of their families under the American dream and flag.

Published in 2003 in the immigrant-bashing frenzy of California's gubernatorial recall election, Victor Davis Hanson's *Mexifornia: A State of Becoming* well articulates the anti-Mexican view that has taken hold in California and elsewhere. Brimming with contempt toward Mexican immigrants, Hanson's book accuses them of bringing to the United States values and tendencies that imperil the welfare of California and the country. In Hanson's xenophobic vision of "Mexifornia," Mexican immigrants are dirty people with no respect for the environment ("[F]or some reason—perhaps it is an atavism from the old country [Mexico] where trash is everywhere dumped outside city limits?—illegal aliens still go out to the country to dump their refuse, furniture, cars, and pets on farmland"),[5] the Anglo dead ("The graveyard where everyone from my great-great-grandmother to my parents ... are [sic] buried is no longer a staid ... European field of memory, but a more raucous picnic ground to commemorate the days of the dead with talking and snacks"),[6] or private property ("But increasingly, keeping illegal aliens and Mexican gang members off [my] property is a hopeless task; in the banter that follows my requests, some trespassers seem piqued that anyone in California should dare to insist on the archaic notion of property rights").[7] Hanson views Mexican immigrants as possessing criminal characters that pose a threat to his safety and that of all Californians ("The other *vatos* in his car, I noticed, seemed to be eying my car, truck, lawn mower—and me as well;"[8] "Hundreds of gang-bangers venture out into the rural counties to fornicate, shoot drugs, steal, rape, and murder").[9] Their supposed insistence on speaking and hearing the Spanish language allegedly threatens the culture and even the economy of the state ("No economist calculates the billions that are lost in time and efficiency in California daily when thousands of aliens must have translators and be instructed in the basics that millions of Californians take for granted").[10]

Although he is an academic, Hanson's warning unfolds as vicious rants and personal narratives against Mexican immigrants. Representative of those pointing blame at Mexican immigrants but grounding their attacks in scholarly suppositions and statistics is influential Harvard professor Samuel Huntington's *Who Are We? The Challenges to America's National Identity*. Of note, the single biggest "challenge" Huntington identifies is the influx of Mexicans into the United States. He criticizes Mexican Americans for maintaining their fluency in Spanish,[11] and worries over other supposed lapses in Mexican American assimilation, such as their lack of educational assimilation and a less than stellar work ethic (pointing out a Mexican philosopher who attributed to Mexican Americans such value statements as "Who cares? That is good enough," and "Tomorrow it will be ready").[12]

Overall, these writings represent the national momentum today against undocumented immigrants, particularly those from Mexico. Any program of immigration reform, such as the one I propose in chapter 15, must overcome this sentiment, which stymied immigration reform proposals during the first seven years of Bush's presidency.

The mid-1960s were a time of dramatic developments on the immigration front, particularly changes impacting Mexican immigration. At the start of the 1960s, immigration policy guaranteed farmers a near unlimited supply of Mexican laborers. Immigration law in effect at the time employed a discriminatory national origin quota system based on the 1890 census to favor immigration from northern and western Europe over southern and eastern Europe.[13] Still, Mexican immigrants were exempt from these national origin quota restrictions, as were immigrants from the Western Hemisphere generally.[14] At the same time, employers recruited agricultural workers from Mexico in droves through the so-called Bracero Program, initiated during World War II, under which Mexicans worked in the United States for temporary periods governed by agreed-upon wages and working conditions.[15] Agricultural growers favored bracero workers because their wages were set separate from principles of supply and demand or from union collective bargaining agreements.[16] As yet a third source of Mexican immigration in the 1960s, undocumented immigration from Mexico as an alternative to these legal but administratively burdensome means of entry was rampant given the lax border enforcement at the time.[17]

The coincidence of these immigration conditions in the early 1960s created a challenging environment for unionizing farm workers. The farm workers union opposed the grower-slanted Bracero Program, with Chávez describing the bracero agreements as fostering "slave labor conditions in California agriculture."[18] As one commentator summarized bracero abuses:

> They were routinely paid as little as twenty cents an hour, subjected to hazardous working conditions, and fired if they dared so much as to speak with labor organizers. They were promised pensions and benefits that they never received. They were confined by law to a contract system that conditioned their entry on working a single crop for a single employer, so they were not free to shop around for better wages and working conditions. And they were only a phone call away from being deported under Operation Wetback, the federal program established in 1954 to make certain that *braceros* did not wear out their welcomes after the harvest came in. All of which caused some commentators to compare *braceros* to convict labor.[19]

By the end of 1964, a coalition of the Chávez-led union, religious organizations, Mexican American groups, and national labor unions such as
the AFL-CIO succeeded in their campaign against the Bracero Program,
which Congress let lapse in December 1964.[20]

Enacted the next year to reform the immigration system, based previously
on discriminatory national origin quotas, the Immigration and Nationality
Act of 1965 for the first time imposed restrictions on Mexican and Western
Hemisphere immigration, limiting Western Hemisphere immigration to
120,000 immigrants a year.[21] As one commentator summarized the 1965
immigration reform: "In effect, Congress coupled more generous treatment
of those outside the Western Hemisphere with less generous treatment of
Latin Americans."[22] Robert Kennedy opposed the new Western Hemisphere limit, as did the Johnson administration. In testimony before the
Senate, Kennedy warned:

There is one provision of this bill [the Immigration and Nationality Act of
1965], however, that is in my judgment a serious mistake. The bill would put
a ceiling on immigration from the Western Hemisphere, roughly equivalent
to the present rate....

This provision would impose a statutory limit on immigration from
Latin America and Canada for the first time in our history. Even in 1920
and 1924, when the national origins system sharply limited immigration
from the rest of the world, the Congress recognized the special relationship
between the United States and our neighbors to the north and south, and
refused to place a flat numerical limitation on immigration from the Western
Hemisphere. This provision ignores that history, and that special relationship. In a world which is searching for increased cooperation and closeness
between nations, the relationships of the United States with Canada and
Latin America could serve as a goal and a model for others. We should not
go backward now....

[W]ith a population twice as great, and a gross national product more
than seven times as great, we are saying by this provision that we are fearful
of immigration from the Western Hemisphere.

Our relationship with Canada and Latin America is unique in the world.
In our relationship with Latin America, in particular, we are engaged in a
great experiment to see whether the societies which are rich and free can
help those who are less free and poor, and to live in a world society in peace
and harmony.

It is not in our interest to turn away from this experiment.[23]

Further, in September 1965, Robert Kennedy made a television statement about the undesirability of the Western Hemisphere quota and wrote to a State Department official commenting that it was "unfortunate" that the Department "acceded so rapidly to the [Western Hemisphere] quota."[24] Kennedy's opposition did not sway Congress, which enacted the Western Hemisphere limitation, which helped spur today's "illegal" immigration "crisis."

As historian David Gutiérrez observed, with the demise of the Bracero Program in late 1964, "Mexican immigration virtually disappeared as an issue in national politics. By the mid-1960s the intensifying Civil Rights Movement, urban unrest, and the escalation of the war in Vietnam all served to push the immigration issue out of the political spotlight."[25] The end of the Bracero Program and the new restrictions placed on immigration from Mexico in the 1965 act, combined with the accelerating and unquenchable demand of U.S. employers for cheap labor, however, eventually created the Mexican undocumented immigration "crisis" that still plagues commentators such as Hanson and Huntington.[26] In 1961, for example, the Immigration and Naturalization Service (INS) deported only 30,000 Mexicans. By 1967, the INS reported 108,000 such deportations.[27] Deportations reached near 500,000 by 1970 and near 1 million by 1977.[28] These undocumented immigrants from Mexico came primarily to work in the agriculture industry, effectively replacing Mexican bracero laborers with even more vulnerable undocumented Mexican workers. By 1969, Mexican undocumented immigrants were estimated to make up 20 percent of the U.S. farm laborers, and as many as six out of ten farm workers in California's Imperial Valley.[29]

Despite the end of the Bracero Program in late 1964 and the restrictions placed the next year on immigration from Mexico, both undocumented workers and green card (temporary work permit) holders created a surplus of farm workers in California at the time of the grape strike and the 1966 Senate hearings in California. Among the issues the Senate subcommittee examined in those hearings was the impact of the congressional termination of the Bracero Program on farm labor. In the last year of the Bracero Program, 1964, 264,500 farm workers were in California; in the month before the March 1966 hearings that brought Kennedy to California, the number had increased to 269,000, with the *Los Angeles Times* reporting a surplus in the fields in most areas of California.[30] These conditions spelled trouble for the grape worker strike that commenced in late 1965.

César Chávez and the farm workers union took the same position opposing grower use of green card holders and undocumented workers as they did for bracero workers—all were used by growers to replace striking workers and more generally to drive down labor costs. This union position on occasion generated confrontations with undocumented and green card labor. As early as 1966, the farm workers union intervened in a labor dispute in Texas where melon farmers replaced striking workers with Mexican immigrants. Union organizers and the striking farm workers allegedly prevented Mexican strikebreakers from crossing a bridge from Mexico into Texas, at one point lying down in the roadway to stop all traffic.[31]

A dramatization of the 1966 Senate hearings in Calfornia in the Fox television movie *RFK*[32] depicts a fictional conversation between Chávez and Kennedy after the hearings in which Kennedy asks "What do you need?" Chávez replies, "We need the INS off our backs," implying in the mind-set of today's viewer that federal immigration authorities were raiding the ranks of the organizing farm workers and deporting them. Rather, Chávez and Kennedy often discussed how to address the growers' use of undocumented and green card laborers as strikebreakers. For example, in their spring 1967 meeting at a Marin County fund-raiser event, Chávez recalled that Kennedy asked him what help he needed in Washington, and Chávez addressed in reply "the illegals and the 'green cards' who were breaking the strike and [I] ask[ed] him if [h]e could do something with the Department of Labor or the Immigration Service to help us with the problem."[33] Later, in August 1967, Chávez sent Kennedy a telegram requesting that Kennedy intervene with the INS:

> Request your assistance to compel US Immigration and Naturalization Service to conduct "in the fields" investigation to remove wetbacks (illegal entrance) and green carders who are currently being recruited and imported to break our strike against the Giumarra Vineyards Corp[.] Immigration and Naturalization Service steadfastly refuses to go into field to investigate our complaints and enforce US Department of Labor recent regulation on use of green carder to break strike.[34]

Under this federal regulation, green card holders who returned temporarily to Mexico (or other countries of origin) could not reenter the United

States with the intent of working at a strikebound farm. As a memo from Senate aide Peter Edelman to Kennedy explained, "In practical terms, this means that a grower cannot import strike breakers from Mexico once a labor dispute has been certified."[35] Pressure from Kennedy and others prompted the INS to conduct field interviews of Giumarra employees to determine their immigration status. As Dolores Huerta lamented to Edelman in a visit to Washington, of the 2,088 employees interviewed, the INS determined that 45 were undocumented immigrants, 1,249 were U.S. citizens, and the remaining 794 were green card workers who were in the country before the strike certification was made. Huerta disputed the legitimate status of these green card workers, contending that Giumarra was importing green card workers from Mexico as strikebreakers after the strike was certified in late July 1967.[36] Ultimately, the INS instituted deportation proceedings against several Giumarra workers that it claimed had violated this regulation. A letter from the farm workers union's attorney to Kennedy in March 1968[37] detailed the daunting issues of proof and lack of clarity in the labor regulation, and supported proposed legislation, introduced in the Senate in December 1967 by Edward Kennedy and cosponsored by Robert Kennedy, to more definitively restrict grower use of commuter (green card) laborers as strikebreakers. This bill would have prevented the reentry into the United States of commuter workers lawfully admitted for permanent residence in the United States but still living principally in Mexico, unless the secretary of labor certified that the commuter's employment would not adversely affect the wages of U.S. workers.[38] The union's hopes of curtailing green card strikebreakers eventually went sour, as the government dropped the Giumarra court proceedings when it embraced a narrow interpretation of the federal regulation on strikebreaking green card holders,[39] and the federal Ninth Circuit appeals court later struck down that regulation entirely as an abuse of discretion.[40]

The farm workers union's troubles with strikebreakers from Mexico continued after Kennedy's death. In the late 1960s and early 1970s, the union even at times picketed the federal INS, protesting its failure to enforce immigration laws—the union alleging that the INS was conspiring with growers and the INS responding that its inadequate funding prevented it from monitoring the status of strikebreakers.[41] Testifying before a Senate subcommittee on labor in the late 1960s, Chávez argued for laws to sanction employers who hire undocumented workers as strikebreakers: "What we ask is some way to keep the illegal and green carders from breaking our strikes; some civil remedy against growers who employ behind our picket lines those who have entered the United States illegally, and likewise those green carders who have not permanently moved their residence and domicile to the United States."[42]

At times while striking against growers, the union stood accused of reporting suspected undocumented immigrant strikebreakers to the INS, and in one controversial incident in September 1974, the union allegedly patrolled the border near Yuma by foot patrol, vehicles, and a plane to prevent strikebreaker immigrants from reaching citrus farmers in Arizona.[43] Dolores Huerta disputes reports that the farm union ever called immigration authorities to report undocumented border crossers. When the union went to the border, its purpose was to urge border crossers not to serve as strikebreakers. For example, Huerta and union officials stood at the border in Texas in the morning and again at night to talk to the undocumented day workers and urge them not to cross their picket line with the Di Giorgio company: "[The] UFW never called immigration. The whole thing is we just wanted people not to break the strike, period. . . . We're not against people who are undocumented. We just don't want them to break our strike."[44]

Growing consciousness among Latino organizations and supporters of the Chicano Movement in the late 1960s and early 1970s sought to protect undocumented workers from backlash, viewing them as scapegoats and as pawns for corporate farming labor greed. Chávez faced mounting criticism over the union's perceived immigration policy,[45] even from his own union officials. Responding to concerns expressed by a Florida UFW official, Chávez explained:

> We have gone to the [strikebreaker] illegals [in the fields] many times and told them they are breaking strikes and that they should leave, and that if they don't leave we are going to try to get the [INS] to get them out of the fields. . . . We are being against strike-breakers, and that's it.
>
> Our feeling is that if we really need them here these women and men should be given full immigration status so they can be free to move about wherever they want. We know the moment an illegal joins our picket line he is picked up by the Immigration Service, but as long as he remains in the fields breaking the strikes they leave him alone.[46]

Ultimately, the focus of Chávez and the union on strikebreaking undocumented and green card Mexicans changed to reflect the tension inherent in blaming workers who were near indistinguishable from the culture and history of the many Mexican immigrant workers organized by the union. Chávez shifted blame from the undocumented workers and placed it on the Nixon administration and on growers for their alleged conspiracy to limit enforcement of immigration laws in the fields.[47] Chávez issued a press statement July 1, 1974, that charged:

> [W]e believe there is a conspiracy between the Nixon Administration and agribusiness to make sure that this flood of desperately poor workers continues unchecked.
> The Border Patrol, which is part of the Justice Department, is not doing its job....
> We do not blame the illegals—who are our brothers and sisters—because they are tools used by others to try and destroy our Movement.
> But their presence hurts the aspirations of all workers for a decent life, a decent job, and a decent wage.[48]

The INS responded to the allegations against it, stating, "There is no lack of intent or incentive to enforce the immigration laws, only a lack of resources to do more." The INS letter then pointed a finger back at the union for having "illegal aliens" in its membership.[49]

Reflecting its evolving immigration position, the UFW stated in a letter to union membership in July 1974 that "all workers have the right to seek work in order to support themselves and their families."[50] In a policy statement that month, the UFW articulated its support for laws easing the citizenship process and protecting the rights of immigrants:

> [We] will support legislation, if introduced, which will make it easier for those already present in the United States or families wishing to come into the United States, in their application for permanent resident status or citizenship to be made in the language in which they are most literate. We must seek to stop the support of employer-oriented immigration schemes which only allow single people to enter the country. By so easing the requirements and the form in which lawful admission is sought, we can alleviate the threat of the employer calling the immigration authorities whenever the workers seek a redress of their grievances or seek to organize themselves into a union to represent their needs and interests.[51]

As early as 1968, shortly after Robert Kennedy's death, Chávez wrote to Senator Ted Kennedy proposing that the requirements for becoming a citizen be liberalized, for example by allowing immigrants to use their native language in the citizenship test.[52] Later in 1974, when criticized for supporting a Justice Department plan to deport one million undocumented immigrants, Chávez wrote to the editor of the *San Francisco Examiner* denying support for the planned deportation effort:

> [Attorney General] Saxbe advocates the mass deportation of working illegal aliens, mostly those from Mexico. We are against such drastic and unfair measures. We advocate amnesty for illegal aliens and support their efforts to obtain legal documents and equal rights, including the right to collective bargaining....
>
> We recognize the illegals as our brothers and sisters, and the union's position is that they should be allowed to enter the United States as legal residents. But they should not be used as strikebreakers.[53]

A UFW convention resolution formalized the UFW stance in stating that "if growers can bring illegal workers to this country for the purpose of exploiting them, then we can organize illegal workers to liberate them," and calling for laws to confer amnesty and legal status on undocumented workers.[54]

After that time, the UFW maintained its support for amnesty programs and other legal protections for undocumented workers. After tighter immigration restrictions were placed on Western Hemisphere countries in 1976, capping annual Mexico immigration at 20,000 immigrants,[55] the UFW urged higher immigration quotas for Mexico and the Western Hemisphere, and advocated "total amnesty" for existing undocumented workers.[56] Supported by the UFW,[57] the 1986 Immigration and Control Act signed by President Reagan gave legal status to undocumented immigrants who had lived in the United States since 1982 and to agricultural workers who had spent at least ninety days of a qualifying period engaged in agricultural labor in the United States.[58] The act gave legal "green card" status to 3.1 million immigrants, about 90 percent of them from Mexico[59] and about 750,000 of them farm workers.[60] Ironically, this legalization and the subsequent continued entry of undocumented immigrants crippled the UFW's ability to procure labor concessions, as replacement workers were in surplus.[61] In the 1990s and today, the UFW objected to temporary bracero-like guest worker program proposals in Congress,[62] but supported programs offering amnesty for existing undocumented field workers, such as under the AgJOBS (Agricultural Jobs, Opportunity, Benefits, and Security) bill considered by Congress in 2007 and prior years. Although slower to join the battle for immigrant rights, the national AFL-CIO union came to embrace legalization programs for immigrants, passing a resolution in 2000 supporting broadscale amnesty[63] and in 2006 rejecting guest worker proposals as a "greedy corporate model" that creates a "two-tiered society" that deprives workers of needed rights.[64]

Shortly before the September 11, 2001, terrorist attacks, George Bush and Mexican president Vicente Fox were engaged in promising negotiations to address the status of undocumented immigrants from Mexico in the United States, with Mexico pushing for amnesty and Bush preferring a temporary guest worker program. At the time, the Pew Hispanic Center estimated that undocumented workers made up 58 percent of the U.S. agricultural work force, as well as 23.8 percent in private household services (e.g., maids), 16.6 percent in business services, 9.1 percent in restaurants, and 6.4 percent in the construction industry.[65] After the attacks, negotiations between the two governments collapsed as U.S. priorities shifted toward heightened border security. By early January 2004, Bush unveiled a temporary worker plan, apparently hoping to draw Latino votes in the 2004 election. Under his proposal, immigrants with job offers in any industry could obtain a temporary three-year visa, renewable once, with the expectation that they would return home without citizenship outside the possibility of competing like any other worker for the limited number of legal immigration slots available each year. Bush stated his unstinting opposition to amnesty for undocumented workers already here—"Granting amnesty encourages the violation of our laws and perpetuates illegal immigration. America's a welcoming country. But citizenship must not be the automatic reward for violating the laws of America."[66] Latino organizations such as the National Council of La Raza and the League of United Latin American Citizens criticized Bush's plan as failing to contain a pathway to citizenship. Bush's anti-amnesty position, ultimately, would soften by 2006 to oppose only what he called "automatic amnesty," thus leaving the door open to legalizing some undocumented workers who pay a fine and any back taxes owed.

By contrast to Bush's anti-amnesty rhetoric in 2004, presidential candidate John Kerry's immigration proposal included a guest worker program with the potential for citizenship. Kerry also pledged to sign the Dream

(Development, Relief, and Education for Alien Minors) Act and the AgJOBS Act. Both with bipartisan sponsors, the Dream Act would enable children of undocumented immigrants to attend college with in-state tuition, and to eventually gain legal status, while the AgJOBS Act would give certain existing undocumented farm workers the opportunity to gain citizenship provided they worked at least 360 days in agriculture over six years. In the summer of 2004, the Bush administration allegedly instructed the senate majority leader to block this agriculture jobs bill.[67] Further, Bush's temporary worker proposal languished as anti-immigrant forces in the Republican Party opposed even the temporary presence of Latino immigrants. The AgJOBS bill was reintroduced in Congress in 2005 with a news conference joining the strange bedfellows of UFW president Arturo Rodriguez (César's successor), Idaho Republican senator Larry Craig, and Senator Edward Kennedy, all of whom helped draft the bill.[68] The list of sponsors for the AgJOBS Act of 2007 included Craig, Kennedy, Kerry, and 2008 presidential hopefuls Hillary Clinton, John McCain, and Barack Obama. Still, its prospects for adoption remained slim given the Republican Party's hostility toward amnesty proposals.

At the U.S./Mexico border in April 2005, hundreds of citizen militia volunteers gathered in Tombstone, Arizona, to patrol the border for undocumented immigrants. Dubbed the Minuteman Project, their effort was just the latest border vigilante campaign to round up undocumented immigrants, following citizen patrols for several years by armed Arizona ranchers. Regrettably, some of these vigilante efforts are in the sprit of the despicable mock set of Arizona State Game Commission guidelines for hunting and killing "wetbacks," distributed nationally as a "joke" in the 1980s and later. As the Minuteman Project website announced in recruiting these vigilante border agents: "The purpose of this political assembly in Arizona is to protest the refusal of the Congress and the President to protect our borders from illegal immigrants who have not had criminal background checks . . . thereby creating an imminent danger to all Americans, and creating the dilution of U.S. citizens' voting rights by foreign nationals."[69]

The website also invoked the Hanson/Huntington assimilation fears in contending:

> Future generations will inherit a tangle of rancorous, unassimilated, squabbling cultures with no common bond to hold them together, and a certain

guarantee of the death of this nation as a harmonious "melting pot." The result: political, economic and social mayhem.

Historians will write about how [a] lax America let its unique and coveted form of government and society sink into a quagmire of mutual acrimony among the various subnations that will comprise the new self-destructing America.[70]

Evidencing its compassionate immigration policy, the UFW condemned the Minutemen as "bigots on the border" and urged action on the AgJOBS bill to protect immigrants arriving to undertake crucial but demanding farm labor in the United States: "The spectacle of vigilantes intimidating human beings who perform such vital labor for our country should prompt Congress to enact the bipartisan AgJobs proposal jointly negotiated by the United Farm Workers and the nation's agricultural industry."[71]

Although the UFW went to the border in the 1970s to dissuade undocumented Mexicans from crossing as strikebreakers, its purpose was far removed from the bigotry of the Minuteman Project. The UFW sought to protect the wages and the right to organize of impoverished and underprivileged farm workers of all ethnicities. By contrast, the Minuteman Project seems primarily a vehicle to release frustration and animosity toward immigrants from Mexico and to safeguard the culture of the United States from Mexican influence. Another fundamental difference between efforts to stanch the border flow today and the short-lived UFW effort to dissuade border-crossing strikebreakers is that in the 1960s and 1970s the border was not a challenge to cross aside from a few official checkpoints. Union members could confront and discourage the strikebreakers as they crossed into the United States daily on roads in populated areas to replace striking union workers in nearby fields. Today, after President Clinton's obsession with border security, the remaining sites of undocumented entry are desolate and treacherous, and border crossings are a life-and-death struggle for survival. Vigilante efforts to secure these desolate entry points must be viewed against this backdrop of government having designed, implemented, and tolerated a deadly gauntlet of entry that has changed the landscape and morality of citizen border patrols.

Chávez's position on undocumented immigrants remains at times profoundly misunderstood by today's supporters of border bigotry. In the throes of congressional immigration debate in spring 2006, CNN's Lou

Dobbs attacked Latino student demonstrators supporting immigrants as running counter to Chávez's objection to "illegal immigration with all of his heart and all of his energy."[72] But Dobbs, who vehemently opposes amnesty proposals, ignored the long-standing efforts of Chávez and the UFW to secure citizenship for undocumented Mexican workers in order to empower them, and misrepresented the aim of the union, which opposed strikebreakers of all persuasions. As César's brother Richard put it recently: "César once said that he was opposed to anybody coming to break the strike.... It's very simple, whether you're a citizen, or an illegal, or an immigrant [with papers], don't come and break my strike. Then they [Dobbs and others] got it out of context.... I'm sure that if he were around today, he'd be right in the middle of it fighting for [the rights of] illegal immigrants."[73]

Initiated in 2005, the Minuteman Project swiftly altered the terrain of immigration reform. Previously, immigration debate under the Bush presidency had centered on whether undocumented workers should be given the right to continue working as guest workers, or whether they deserved a pathway to citizenship. The Minuteman Project lent credibility to border security proposals that give no recognition to the needs of U.S. employers or the human rights of immigrant workers. Rather, the well-publicized citizen vigilante project fueled the public perception that immigration reform was needed to seal the borders from the cultural, terrorist, and economic threat of immigrant workers. Congressional lawmakers in the House reacted to this surging public opinion by passing in December 2005 the profoundly anti–Latino immigrant Border Protection, Antiterrorism, and Illegal Immigration Control Act. One writer described the bill as the "most repressive immigration bill in decades."[74] Some thirty Democrats joined the rush of Republican representatives to approve this bill despite opposition from the business community, labor unions, and churches. Among other provisions, this act would add seven hundred miles of fencing to the existing seventy miles of barrier along the nearly two-thousand-mile U.S./Mexico border. By the time of his 2006 State of the Union address, Bush had embraced this prevailing "border security" rhetoric in calling for "stronger immigration enforcement and border protection" to ensure "orderly and secure borders." Although the House Border Protection bill ultimately was not enacted in 2006, the frenzied border security sentiment led to enactment that year of the similarly intentioned Secure Fence Act, which approved the seven hundred miles of additional border fencing in the interest of achieving "operational control" of the U.S./Mexico border.

The 2008 presidential hopefuls, both Democrat and Republican, tapped into the border security theme. On the Democratic side, Hillary Clinton's website accuses the Bush administration of failing to allocate sufficient resources to guard our borders.[75] Before it addresses support for a tortuous pathway to citizenship for undocumented immigrants, Barack Obama's website urges securing U.S. borders with "additional personnel, infrastructure and technology."[76] Implementing this border security philosophy, both Clinton and Obama voted in favor of the Secure Fence Act of 2006. Among Republican candidates, Tom Tancredo is the clear champion of the citizen militia and contends he will secure U.S. borders while remaining "100% opposed to amnesty."[77]

Inflamed anti-immigrant and anti-Mexican sentiments have seeped from the border to the ballot box and have begun to influence major elections, particularly in California, where voters often turn against Mexican immigrants in times of economic stress. For example, in 1994, California voters overwhelmingly approved Proposition 187, the initiative targeting undocumented Latino immigrants and imperiling their prospects for health care and education for their children. Sixty-four percent of Anglo voters approved the measure, while 73 percent of Latino voters rejected it.[78] Sensing his defeat in preelection polls putting him 23 percentage points behind front-runner Kathleen Brown, Republican governor Pete Wilson aligned his campaign for reelection with Proposition 187, and hate ushered in both Wilson and the anti-Mexican measure.[79] Wilson's campaign commercials included shadowy images crossing the U.S./Mexico border at San Ysidro with the warnings "they keep coming" and "enough is enough,"[80] thereby shifting blame for California's economic woes to Mexican immigrants. Dolores Huerta and the UFW campaigned against Proposition 187, as well as subsequent anti–bilingual education and anti–affirmative action initiatives in California, but all passed.[81] Although Proposition 187 was effectively gutted in subsequent court challenges,[82] the success in 2004 of Arizona's similar Proposition 200 (dubbed the Arizona Taxpayer and Citizen Protection Act, which denies "public benefits" to undocumented immigrants), netting 56 percent of the vote, spurred efforts to bring a new version of Proposition 187 to California voters and launched initiative petition drives and legislative proposals in other states, such as Georgia.

Pete Wilson was back at the helm in 2003 as manager for Arnold Schwarzenegger's successful campaign for California governor in the recall election that swept Democrat Gray Davis from office. Schwarzenegger voted for Proposition 187, and presumably for Wilson, in 1994.[83] A 2003 poll among California voters revealed that they ranked immigration as the fifth most critical problem in the state, ahead of crime, health care, and energy.[84] Spotlighting attention on the issue of undocumented immigration, Gray Davis signed a bill weeks before the recall election enabling undocumented immigrants to obtain driver's licenses. Although Latino candidate Cruz Bustamante voted as an assemblyman in the mid-1990s to require legal status as a condition to obtaining a license, he supported the new legislation, with explosive results in the racially charged recall election. Schwarzenegger made repeal of the driver's license bill a top priority. His campaign ads for television exploited the driver's license controversy with text reading "Driver's Licenses for Undocumented Immigrants" and a voiceover from a person on the street opining "Makes no sense at all. If they're here illegally, why should they be able to drive legally?" At the same time that his mainstream ads were tapping anti-Mexican sentiment, Schwarzenegger's Spanish-language ads touted his immigrant background.[85] An exit poll revealed that a staggering 70 percent of voters of all backgrounds favored denying driver's licenses to "illegal immigrants"; of those voters, 73 percent voted for Republicans Schwarzenegger or Tom McClintock.[86] Schwarzenegger rewarded the anti-immigrant vote by signing repeal legislation shortly after taking office and then in September 2004 vetoing a bill to restore driver's licenses to undocumented drivers.[87] Congress too caught the anti-immigrant fever in 2005, enacting the REAL ID Act to require that all states demand proof of lawful presence in the United States when issuing driver's licenses, or the license would be invalid for federal identification purposes such as airline travel.

At the same time that Schwarzenegger was playing to the anti–undocumented immigrant vote, Bustamante was inflaming voters who associated him with undocumented immigrants and nativism that favored Mexico and Mexican Americans over other state interests. In a crucial debate Bustamante responded that he could not think of any benefits he would deny undocumented immigrants—later he suggested to a columnist only voting and passports.[88] Bustamante supported amnesty for undocumented immigrants (an estimated two million of whom reside in California) and citizenship for every immigrant who works and pays taxes.[89] Bustamante also came under attack when Fox News and other media reported his past membership in the student group MEChA (Movimiento Estudiantil Chicano de Aztlán) while attending Fresno State University in the 1970s. Conservative commentators labeled MEChA a nativist group whose supposed motto is "for the [Mexican] race, everything. For those outside the race, nothing."[90] In a postelection comment, Victor Davis Hanson, author of *Mexifornia,* accused Bustamante of having played identity and racialist politics,[91] presumably conjoining Bustamante's Latino heritage and his support for causes of downtrodden undocumented immigrants as somehow advocating a racist agenda.

Bustamante's 2003 campaign illustrated the risks today of a politician's associating with the working class, immigrants, farm workers, and particularly Mexicans and Mexican Americans, who are inexorably tied with these backgrounds. A *Los Angeles Times* article accused Bustamante of "veering left" and leaving moderate Democrats behind with his appeals to immigrants and the working class.[92] In his campaign, Bustamante advocated raising taxes of the wealthy, and aligned with labor by criticizing employers such as Wal-Mart as being anti-worker and by vowing to force companies to provide employee health insurance. As he told union members at a campaign rally, "It's about time that we have a governor in the state of California who is going to remember his roots ... and work on behalf of the working class people of this state."[93] Responding to a reporter question of whether he saw a difference between legal and undocumented immigrants, Bustamante reminded voters of his connection to farm workers: "Have you been out to the fields? I have. I grew up out there."[94] During the recall campaign, a UFW website headline announced the union's endorsement of Bustamante in historical context: "Bustamante accepts UFW support at site where Robert Kennedy embraced Cesar Chavez in 1968," with the subtitle "Arnold on wrong side of farm worker battle." But in 2003, sadly, a political candidate who embraced the issues and concerns of farm workers, himself a child of migrant workers, alienated voters distressed by the scare tactics of "Mexifornia." In order to be successful today in California and elsewhere, presumably a Mexican American (or Anglo) politician must steer clear of a prominent immigrant-rights and labor agenda.

Robert Kennedy spoke up for Mexican and other immigrants in the 1960s, and no doubt would resist the tide of anti-immigrant and anti-Mexican sentiment sweeping California and the United States. In the introduction to his slain brother's posthumous revision of his position statement on the value of immigrants to our country, *A Nation of Immigrants,* Robert wrote that his and President Kennedy's attitudes toward the immigrant "gradually matured to a full appreciation of the contribution he can make and has made to American life."[95] In this fond tribute to our nation's immigration history, John Kennedy recounted the history of Irish immigrants, such as his great-grandfather, who faced discrimination because of their Catholic faith and their ethnicity (punctuated by signs such as "No Irish Need Apply"), noting parallels to the history of Latino and particularly Mexican immigration. John Kennedy observed that "[t]he same things are said today of Puerto Ricans and Mexicans that were once said of Irish, Italians, Germans and Jews: 'They'll never adjust, they can't learn the language, they won't be absorbed.'"[96] More generally, President Kennedy recognized the prospects for transformation of America's ethnic composition, suggesting that U.S. society "is a process, not a conclusion."[97] Those trying to freeze America's cultural heritage, such as advocates of the Minuteman Project, should consider Kennedy's words.

In a 1967 speech to the Irish Institute in New York, Robert Kennedy lamented about the loss of ethnic cultural traditions among later generations of Irish in the United States:

[A]s Americans, I think we can all sense that as the immigrant tradition dies, we lose one of our most precious possessions: the diversity and color, the rub of difference and discovery that have made this country more than the sum of all its particular heritages.... I want that [Irish] tradition—and those of all the other immigrant groups that built this country—to live. I for one would not be happy to see this nation bland and homogeneous, its speech and literature reduced to the common denominator of mass-circulation magazines, its life settled down into a uniform suburb stretching from coast to coast.[98]

In a 1965 statement in the Senate, Robert Kennedy invoked the U.S. history of immigration to declare that "we *need* immigration": "Our strength is in variety, not sameness.... Our greatness [as a country] we owe not to the bayonet, or to the atomic bomb, but to our capacity to attract and absorb the richness of diversity—because to all men we attempt to secure the same measure of freedom and opportunity."[99]

In the twenty-first century, the Spanish-language culture of Mexican Americans and other Latinos is under attack—from such distinct forces as employers adopting English-only rules in the workplace to state laws ending bilingual education programs. By contrast to this burgeoning anti-Spanish sentiment, Robert Kennedy complemented his fondness for the Irish tradition by bolstering Latino and Mexican American traditions, particularly the culture of the Spanish language. After breaking bread in Delano with Chávez in 1968, ending Chávez's hunger fast, Kennedy addressed the crowd in broken Spanish. As Chávez's brother Richard recalled, "Everybody just loved him for it. They just went wild."[100] Supporting the Spanish-language culture of his constituent Puerto Ricans in New York City, Senator Robert Kennedy cosponsored a provision of the 1965 Voting Rights Act that abolished state English-language literacy tests for voters in certain circumstances.[101] At the time, New York law adopted in the early 1920s (aimed primarily at Yiddish-speaking Jews)[102] required voters to pass a literacy test if they had not completed eighth grade in an English-language school. In a statement accompanying an early version of the Kennedy language provision, he explained that:

> There are now between 450,000 and 480,000 Puerto Rican citizens of voting age in New York City.... Depending on which estimate is correct, the number of these citizens who are not registered to vote is anywhere between 225,000 and 330,000.
>
> Many of those who are not registered have been refused because they cannot pass New York's State English-language literacy test, even though they are literate in Spanish, having been educated in that language under the American flag in Puerto Rico....
>
> The amendment ... does not single out New York ... [and] applies to any state in which an English-literacy test discriminates against persons educated in American-flag schools in which the main classroom language was other than English.[103]

As adopted by Congress in 1965 with some modifications, Kennedy's amendment, which is still part of the federal Voting Rights Act, provides:

> (e)(1) Congress hereby declares that to secure the rights under the fourteenth amendment of persons educated in American-flag schools in which

the predominant classroom language was other than English, it is necessary to prohibit the States from conditioning the right to vote of such persons on ability to read, write, understand, or interpret any matter in the English language.

(2) No person who demonstrates that he has successfully completed the sixth primary grade in a public school in, or a private school accredited by, any State or territory, the District of Columbia, or the Commonwealth of Puerto Rico in which the predominant classroom language was other than English, shall be denied the right to vote in any Federal, State, or local election because of his inability to read, write, understand, or interpret any matter in the English language, except that in States in which State law provides that a different level of education is presumptive of literacy, he shall demonstrate that he has successfully completed an equivalent level of education in a public school in, or a private school accredited by, any State or territory, the District of Columbia, or the Commonwealth of Puerto Rico in which the predominant classroom language was other than English.[104]

Although the Kennedy provision enfranchised many Puerto Rican voters in New York and other states with English-literacy laws, generally it did not aid Mexican American or Cuban American voters educated outside the United States.[105] In 1970, however, the California Supreme Court struck down the California English-language literacy test that disenfranchised some Mexican American voters—as applied to people literate in a language other than English (here Spanish), the California law violated the equal protection clause of the federal Constitution.[106]

Robert Kennedy also cosponsored legislation, signed by President Johnson in 1968, titled the Bilingual Education Act, to aid the education of English-illiterate and limited-English-proficient (LEP) immigrant students.[107] Although the act did not mandate bilingual education, it authorized grants to low-income school districts to develop bilingual education programs to transition LEP students to English. The act initially authorized the president to request $30 million in grant funds the first year of the federal program, and there was outcry in Congress when Johnson's war-pinched budget requested only $5 million.[108] Ultimately, in 2002, the Bush administration's No Child Left Behind Act eliminated the Bilingual Education Act and replaced it with a new federal program under which federal funds will continue to support education of LEP students, but "the rapid teaching of English will take precedence at every turn."[109] Consistent with this new emphasis, the program discourages native-language instruction. As language policy expert James Crawford summarized, whereas the 1968 Bilingual Education Act as amended "included among its goals 'developing the English skills ... and to the extent possible, the native-language skills' of LEP students, the [Bush education act] stresses skills in English only."[110] California voters in 1998 also dismantled bilingual education at the state level by passing an initiative mandating an English-only classroom absent a narrowly prescribed allowance of parental waiver.

Chávez too championed the language rights of Latinos. In 1975, Congress amended the 1965 Voting Rights Act to require bilingual voting materials in localities with sufficient numbers of voters lacking English proficiency. California voters in 1984 overwhelmingly approved a ballot initiative directing their governor to urge federal officials to repeal this federal multilingual ballot law. But Chávez campaigned actively against the initiative, contending that repeal of the federal protections, which still stood in 2007, would "disenfranchise American citizens."[111]

The legacy of immigration reform in the 1960s, particularly the Western Hemisphere limitation that Kennedy opposed, shapes all Latino issues in today's political arena. In this atmosphere of attack on undocumented immigrants, each Latino political issue is viewed by the public through the lens of its potential to encourage or facilitate undocumented immigration. Spanish-language recognition in the voting booth, for example, prompts concern that it aids the undocumented in their supposed efforts to hijack the voting franchise. Fear of mass undocumented voting in state elections led Arizona voters in 2004 to approve a proof of citizenship initiative as a condition to voting. Bilingual education has come under attack as a means of targeting the children of undocumented immigrants in schools. Although the Supreme Court has struck down as unconstitutional a state's refusal to educate these children, eliminating bilingual education and tossing these children into the deep end of the assimilation pool will likely survive constitutional scrutiny and is thus seen as a legitimate way of punishing these innocent children.

In the 1960s, Latino initiatives such as establishing language rights in the voting booth and the classroom had to overcome racial prejudice against Latinos, particularly Mexican Americans and Puerto Ricans. In those times of the civil rights reforms, opponents of these initiatives often were blatantly racist in articulating their opposition. Eventually, these opponents found cover for some anti-Latino initiatives in the interest of law and order. Today, the criminalization of undocumented immigration from Mexico and other Latin American countries gives license to pursue all varieties of anti-Latino policies in the name of preventing undocumented immigration. The security dimension to border patrol prompted by the September 11 attacks elevates Latino issues beyond law enforcement to the level of national security and defense.

Even farm worker reform must survive this gauntlet. In the 1960s, farm worker reform faced an uphill battle against long-standing prejudice that viewed Latino farm workers as a lesser class of people who were happy to work long hours in dangerous labor for minimal pay. Broader-minded reformists, such as Kennedy and Chávez, made progress toward constructing a more enlightened view of the Latino workforce. But today, farm worker reform is not seen as predominantly an issue of economic reform or, in the eyes of cynics, economic redistribution. Rather, the lens of undocumented immigration distorts farm worker reform. Through this lens, economic protection of farm workers, whether in the workplace or by community programs of health care and education, is seen as encouraging undocumented immigration, and even the entry of terrorists into the country, and most reform proposals are politically dead on arrival. The prospects, then, for meaningful economic reform for farm workers and other Latino laborers seem even more dim than they did in the 1960s.

Ironically, unchecked immigration in the 1960s—whether green card workers or bracero laborers brought into the country as strikebreakers, or undocumented immigrants arriving after the 1965 immigration act—hampered farm labor efforts to obtain vital economic reforms from employers. Since then, the replacement of legal bracero workers with "illegal" undocumented workers has doubly crippled the efforts of farm labor organizers. As in the 1960s, the oversupply of potential underpaid workers with no legal rights keeps employers from the bargaining table. This market imbalance requires political intervention. But any efforts to gain legislative or public support for the farm labor cause are stymied by the impression among the increasingly intolerant public that aiding workers encourages further immigration. To restore order to the labor markets, then, requires a multifaceted approach to immigration reform that recognizes this connectivity between immigration policy and worker rights. I propose such an agenda for labor and immigration reform in chapter 15.

César Chávez speaking at a rally for presidential candidate Robert Kennedy (United Farm Workers Collection, Walter P. Reuther Library, Wayne State University).

Robert Kennedy shaking hands with grape strike supporter, Delano, CA, c. 1966 (United Farm Workers Collection, Walter P. Reuther Library, Wayne State University).

Andy Imutan, Dolores Huerta, Larry Itliong, and Robert Kennedy standing amidst UFWOC flags before the breaking of César Chávez's 25-day fast, 1968 (United Farm Workers Collection, Walter P. Reuther Library, Wayne State University).

César Chávez holding the hand of Juana Chávez at the conclusion of his 25-day fast (Robert Kennedy at left) (United Farm Workers Collection, Walter P. Reuther Library, Wayne State University)

Robert Kennedy passing a communion wafer to César Chávez to break Chávez's 25-day fast (United Farm Workers Collection, Walter P. Reuther Library, Wayne State University).

Robert Kennedy standing at the microphone beside Dolores Huerta during the 1968 fast, March 10, 1968, Delano, CA (United Farm Workers Collection, Walter P. Reuther Library, Wayne State University)

Portrait (head and shoulders) of César Chávez before the breaking of his 25-day fast (United Farm Workers Collection, Walter P. Reuther Library, Wayne State University).

Robert Kennedy at the conclusion of César Chávez's 25-day fast (Robert Kennedy at left) (United Farm Workers Collection, Walter P. Reuther Library, Wayne State University).

PART III

Lessons from 1968:
Latino Politics Today

CHAPTER TWELVE

Latinos and National Politics

*[Robert Kennedy] taught me the importance of what one person can do in the
political realm.*

—Dolores Huerta[1]

During the 2004 presidential campaign, New Mexico governor Bill Richardson declared the Latino vote "up for grabs," suggesting that it was "a
sleeping giant about to explode."[2] Journalist Jorge Ramos captured this
development in his 2004 book subtitled "How Hispanics Will Elect the
Next American President." Ramos looked to Latinos as a potentially decisive
swing vote in immigrant-rich, contested states such as California, Texas,
Florida, Illinois, and New York.[3] There is no doubt that Latinos deserve
to be taken seriously by politicians on both sides of the political fence. For
better or worse, Latinos increasingly tend to swing their votes between the
political parties. Once Latinos begin to better wield this electoral clout,
politicians will ignore their prerogatives at their peril.

In contrast to their voting record in the 1960s, Latino voters, particularly
Mexican Americans, have since shifted dramatically from voting Democratic in bloc to sometimes supporting Republican candidates in considerable numbers. The shift is most evident in presidential elections, but is
reflected in state and local campaigns as well, such as the 2003 California
recall election, in which exit polls suggest that Latinos voted 31 percent for
Arnold Schwarzenegger and 9 percent for Tom McClintock—a total of 40
percent for Republican candidates in an election against Democrat Latino
candidate Cruz Bustamante, who drew only 52 to 55 percent of the Latino
vote according to various exit polls. In presidential elections, the decline

among Latinos in Democratic voting is compelling. In the 1960s, Mexican Americans[4] voted in bloc for Democratic presidential candidates:

1960: 85 percent for Democrat John Kennedy,[5] 15 percent for Nixon

1964: 90 percent for Democrat Johnson,[6] 10 percent for Republican Barry Goldwater

1968: 87 percent for Democrat Humphrey, 10 percent for Nixon.[7]

The strong preference for Democratic Party candidates continued in the 1970s, although one poll for the 1972 election gave Nixon 36 percent of the Mexican American vote but another poll gave him only 15 percent.[8] In the 1976 election of Democrat Jimmy Carter, exit polls gave Carter 92 percent of the Mexican American vote and 82 percent of the overall Latino vote.[9]

By the 1980s, however, the overwhelming Mexican American/Latino preference for Democrats began to erode dramatically, with Republican Reagan gaining 22 to 37 percent of the Latino vote in 1980[10] and, depending on the exit poll, 32 to 47 percent of the Latino vote[11] in his successful reelection campaign in 1984. In the 1988 election of Republican George H.W. Bush, exit polling showed between 30 and 38 percent of Latinos voting for Bush.[12] In the 1992 campaign, Latinos voted significantly (6 to 14 percent) for third-party challenger Ross Perot, with Democrat Clinton receiving between 51 and 62 percent of the Latino vote.[13] In 1996, however, although 10 percent of the Latino vote went to third-party challengers such as Perot, Clinton received 71 to 72 percent of the Latino vote.[14] As discussed below, George W. Bush's record of success among Latino voters in 2000 and 2004 signals some permanency in the Latino departure from their 1960s record of voting overwhelmingly Democratic, after their brief flirtation in 1996 with Clinton.

From the time that Robert Kennedy entered the political arena to the present, Latinos have enjoyed little influence in national politics, and have typically been disappointed by presidents, even ones they helped elect. Although the Latino community enjoyed a special relationship with John Kennedy, his administration frustrated many of the Latino leaders who campaigned for him and expected more Mexican American appointments to head new social programs, and more involvement in formulating Latin

American policy.[15] Although Johnson established the laudable War on Poverty agenda, represented by several federal programs of largess to the urban landscapes of poverty, the Vietnam War effort ultimately diverted the budget from aid to the underprivileged. For example, although Congress passed the Bilingual Education Act in 1967 with an authorization of $30 million for the first year toward programs to help limited-English-proficient minority students in low-income school districts, President Johnson's budget sought only $5 million for the first year of federal grants. César Chávez criticized Johnson on federal policies affecting rural opportunity. In a January 8, 1968, letter to Johnson, Chávez blasted the president for his administration's treatment of farm workers and their issues, including the failure to include farm workers in the National Labor Relations Act ("This is our greatest need, and we cannot support any administration that does not remedy this injustice") and Johnson's inability to regulate green card workers and undocumented border crossers, used unjustly by growers as strikebreakers against U.S. farm workers. Chávez ended the letter scolding Johnson, "[U]nfulfilled promises are a poor substitute for food, wages, and justice."[16]

A staunch opponent of the farm worker campaign, Nixon had a mixed record with Latinos. Although he attracted a relatively strong Latino vote in 1972 following his unprecedented record of Latino appointments in his first term (including a Latino U.S. treasurer), Nixon phased out these appointments after the 1972 election.[17] Under Nixon's direction, the federal government tried to quash the farm worker boycotts.[18] On the urban front, Nixon dismantled much of the Johnson War on Poverty effort and devolved control of spending at the federal level to the states through block grants to governments less responsive to prerogatives of the poor and communities of color.[19] One commentator contended that Nixon's economic and social policies were "largely responsible" for the early 1970s decline in Latino average income despite increases in income of the population generally.[20]

The only two-term elected Democratic president of recent times, Bill Clinton, had a surprisingly poor record on Latino issues. As governor of Arkansas, Clinton signed Official English legislation, although he disavowed it while campaigning for president[21] and while in the White House. As president, Clinton signed legislation that tightened welfare laws and also stripped undocumented and even documented immigrants of most federal poverty and health benefits.[22] The Clinton administration oversaw a border enhancement program, known as Operation Gatekeeper, that prompted the deaths of hundreds of undocumented immigrants in the Southwest by sealing traditional and safer border immigration routes.[23] Clinton also signed legislation that ensured that many states would not offer resident college tuition to undocumented immigrant state residents—this law demanded that states conferring resident status on undocumented students do so for any student living in the United States.[24]

In contrast to Clinton, as governor of Texas George Bush came out against state English-language laws; Bush also opposed the anti-immigrant Proposition 187 from California. But as president, Bush stood in the way of immigration reform that included amnesty for undocumented farm workers, and his No Child Left Behind education law helped move schools away from bilingual education programs. Still, in his second term, Bush made the most significant presidential appointment of a Latino—the conservative Alberto Gonzales as attorney general (who in 2007 succumbed to bipartisan calls for his resignation for his role in the firing of federal prosecutors), and Bush softened his position on amnesty for undocumented workers willing to pay a fine and learn English.

Republican Bush secured 31 to 35 percent of the Latino vote in the 2000 presidential election,[25] and his supporters targeted 40 percent of the Latino vote in 2004. Bush exceeded expectations, garnering 40 to 44 percent of the Latino vote in 2004.[26] Looking back to the 1960s, particularly 1968, in which Nixon won only 10 percent of the Mexican American vote, the Republican gains in 2004 are dramatic. Latinos voted for Bush in large numbers in an election whose overall voter turnout of just under 60 percent was the highest percentage turnout since 1968. Looking carefully at the Latino statistics reveals where Bush's Latino support made the strongest gains—among Mexican American men. Puerto Ricans voted in near bloc for Democrat John Kerry, with Bush receiving only 28 percent of the Puerto Rican vote, down from 35 percent in 2000.[27] Cuban Americans voted as they did in 2000, substantially for Bush. It was Mexican American voters, who compose a majority of the Latino vote, who surprised observers in their voting percentage for Bush. First-time Latino voters, who made up 21 percent of Latino voters, presumably many of them Mexican Americans and recent immigrants, provided a further surprise by voting 50 percent for Republican Bush.[28]

Exit polling and postelection interviews found that while 35 percent of Latinas voted for Bush, Bush received 46 percent of the Latino male vote;[29] a 2005 Pew Hispanic Center survey found a lesser gender disparity of 37 to 43 percent.[30] Among voters of all ethnicities, the male vote in 2004 was 55 percent for Bush and 44 percent for Kerry, while the female vote was 48 percent for Bush and 51 percent for Kerry.[31] The Latino gender gap was arguably greater than in the electorate generally, accentuated by the two-point gain by Bush in 2004 among males of all racial/ethnic backgrounds, and his substantial five-point surge among female voters of all backgrounds.[32] Conservative commentator Raoul Lowery Contreras proffered a chest-beating explanation that the "huge increase" in the 2004 Latino male vote for Bush, an almost 30 percent increase over 2000, was due to patriotism and the Bush-led War on Terror.[33] The director of the Hispanic Voter Project at John Hopkins University theorized that Bush's campaign message to Latino voters, focusing on moral values and security, seemed designed to garner male votes.[34] Related to the Latino gender gap, polling also revealed a gap between married and single Latino voters, with 47 percent of those "married or living as married" voting for Bush.[35]

Income played a role in the Latino Bush vote—only 28 percent of Latino voters with family incomes under $15,000 favored Bush, but 45 percent of those with family incomes of $50,000 to $74,999, and 47 percent of those with $75,000 or more, voted for Bush.[36] As is the case with Catholics generally, who as a group have trended toward voting Republican,[37] the burgeoning middle class among Latinos may account for some of the attrition from the Democratic Party.

A comprehensive survey of Latino voters conducted in 2004 by the Pew Hispanic Center reveals much about the trend among Latinos toward voting Republican. Nearly half (45 percent) of registered Latinos identified as Democrat, while only 20 percent claimed Republican affiliation and 21 percent claimed to be Independent. Of Cuban American voters (making up only 6 percent of the Latino electorate), the numbers were decidedly Republican as expected—52 percent claiming Republican affiliation and only 17 percent Democratic. Again as expected, Puerto Rican voters (accounting for only 15 percent of the Latino electorate) were substantially Democratic in party affiliation—50 percent Democrats, with only 17 percent choosing Republican affiliation. Among Mexican American registered voters (accounting for some 60 percent of the Latino electorate), 47 percent identified as Democrat, only 18 percent as Republican, and 22 percent as Independent. Given these numbers, presumably a very significant number of Independent-identified Latino voters, as well as some Democrat-identified Latinos, voted for Bush in the 2004 election. Especially interesting is a survey statistic that a third of all Latinos who identify as Republican once identified as Democrats; by contrast few Latino Republicans have switched party allegiance.[38]

A voter survey suggests that Latino voters rank education (with 54 percent) at the top of their issues of concern, ahead of the economy and jobs (51 percent), the War on Terror (45 percent), the war in Iraq (40 percent), and moral values (36 percent). On the issue of abortion, 49 percent of Latino registered voters believe abortion should be legal all or some of the time, with 44 percent who feel abortion should be illegal in all or most cases. These views are similar to those of the general population—a May 2004 survey determined that 54 percent of Americans thought abortion should be legal. A surprising statistic, which points to an increasing conservatism ahead among Latino voters, is the 2004 Pew Hispanic Center survey revealing that only one third (34 percent) of noncitizen Latinos thought abortion should be legal—far less support for abortion rights than among citizen, registered Latino voters.[39]

On the issue of gay marriage, 45 percent of registered Latinos favor a constitutional amendment to define marriage to exclude same-sex marriage, with 48 percent opposing this amendment (by contrast, in the general population, voters favored the restrictive amendment 51 percent to 45 percent).[40] But a 2003 New York Times/CBS News poll recorded Latino views as more conservative than voters generally on the question of whether homosexual relations between consenting adults should be legal (which the Supreme Court established in 2003).[41] Latinos were evenly divided on the question, but U.S. voters generally supported legality 54 to 39 percent.[42]

Of general-population voters in the 2004 election, exit polls found that of those who believed abortion should always be legal, 73 percent voted for Kerry, as did 61 percent of those who believed abortion should be mostly legal. Those who believed abortion should be mostly illegal or always illegal, by contrast, voted 73 percent and 77 percent for Bush.[43] Similarly, on the issue of same-sex marriage, 77 percent of those voters who believed in same-sex marriage voted for Kerry, while 70 percent of those who opposed legal recognition of same-sex couples voted for Bush.[44]

Perhaps the best explanation for the surge in Latino, particularly Mexican American, support for Bush in 2004 lies in these moral issues, especially gay marriage and abortion. An AP exit poll determined that 20 percent of Latino voters identified "moral issues" as the deciding factor in their vote for Bush or Kerry.[45] Bush's 2004 campaign website aimed at Latinos— "Viva Bush"—highlighted his contributions to the economy, health care, education, and the War on Terror, but it also showcased Bush's stands on abortion and same-sex marriage. The website stated that "President Bush supported the ban on partial birth abortion and believes in promoting a culture of life." The website contrasted the views of Kerry as "out of touch" with Latino values given Kerry's support for partial-birth abortions. The Viva Bush website also communicated that "President Bush supports an amendment to protect traditional marriage," implying that Bush opposes same-sex relationships as contrary to moral values.[46] As Professor Antoinette Sedillo Lopez opined, the reason that many Latinos, who traditionally had voted Democratic, voted for Bush in the 2004 election came down to the "wedge" issues of abortion and gay marriage: "The Republican Party used churches, targeted mailings and a whisper campaign to reach Hispanic voters on these two issues. Some Hispanics came to believe that voting for Bush was the 'moral' or 'Christian' thing to do."[47]

The president of the Hispanic Clergy Association of New Jersey, Rev. Arturo Soto, opined during the campaign that Kerry's voting record in the Senate was inconsistent with Latino values—"He has consistently voted against requiring that parents be notified before their teenage daughters have an abortion. He was one of the only 14 Senators who voted against the [antigay] Defense of Marriage Act."[48] As examined in the next chapter, the Catholic Church, the religious affiliation of most Latinos, took a particularly aggressive stance on the issues of gay marriage and abortion in the 2004 election, politicizing the church. Several Catholic bishops made headlines by suggesting that Kerry should be denied communion because he supported abortion rights, and one bishop even suggested that voters supporting such politicians should be denied communion.[49] Republicans in Los Angeles also helped organize Spanish-language evangelical churches to prompt conservative, religious Latinos to vote.[50]

Other potential explanations for the surge toward Bush among Latino voters in the 2004 election include the economy and the War on Terror. The 2004 National Hispanic Survey from the Latino Coalition revealed that Latino voters had the economy foremost on their minds, and a majority believed that the most effective approach to stimulate the economy was to cut taxes on families and business. A nationwide poll of Latino voters in October 2004 concluded that while 25 percent of Latino voters supporting Bush attributed their allegiance to his religious beliefs and values, 39 percent supported Bush because of his national security stance.[51]

Aside from Dolores Huerta, there were no nationally powerful and persuasive Latino voices favoring Democrats in the 2004 election, as there had been for years in César Chávez among Mexican American voters. Indeed, a 2003 national poll revealed the paucity of Latino leadership in its response to the survey question of which three people were the most important Hispanic leaders in the United States right now. Although 22 percent named at least one person, an astounding 78 percent of Latinos polled could not name any leader![52] Even Bill Richardson, the Latino governor of New Mexico, who carried that state in 2002 by a landslide, saw Latino votes for Bush in his state increase from 32 percent in the 2000 election to 44 percent in 2004, helping to change New Mexico from a Blue to a Red state.[53] Prominent Latinos in California lost high-profile elections in the 2000s—Antonio Villaraigosa, who volunteered as a teenager for Chávez during the grape boycott, lost the 2001 mayoral race in Los Angeles (but emerged victorious in 2005 after the incumbent victor faltered), and Cruz Bustamante lost the 2003 governor recall election to Arnold Schwarzenegger. In the 2004 presidential election the next year, Latinos in California voted 34 percent for Bush, an increase of 6 points from the 2000 election.[54]

At the time of the 1968 presidential election campaign, race was a salient issue in national politics. Martin Luther King, Jr. was assassinated by a white man in April 1968, further incinerating unrest in the urban ghettos. The signing of the 1964 Civil Rights Act a few years earlier ushered in the short-lived civil rights era, still relevant in 1968. Resistance to desegregation in the South launched the 1968 campaign of racist third-party presidential candidate George Wallace. César Chávez and the farm workers union's struggle for fair wages and working conditions in California represented the prominent role of Latino issues on the national stage. Robert Kennedy's 1967 book *To Seek a Newer World*, a blueprint for new directions in U.S. domestic and foreign policy and eventually for his presidential campaign, devoted one of its two chapters on domestic issues entirely to the confluence of race and poverty in a chapter titled "Race and the City: The Slums and Community."

The 2004 presidential campaign illustrated the pronounced shift in priority and impetus of racial issues since 1968. Instead of being confronted directly, racial issues were replaced by coded dialogue about crime and the need for sacrificing civil liberties in fighting the War on Terror.[55] Whereas in 1968, minority groups were voicing issues proactively whether from burning cities, through militant dialogue, or by labor strikes, today's advocates of racial equity are on the defensive. For example, in the anti-immigrant climate of hate in California and elsewhere, proponents of driver's licenses for undocumented immigrants are vilified as promoting terrorist entry, and proponents of bilingual education are seen as threatening the core of American identity in the post-9/11 campaign to protect this identity against attack. Right-wing journalist Michelle Malkin tapped this post-9/11 mindset in contending that licensing undocumented immigrant drivers "undermines safety by giving terrorists a ticket to the American mainstream," and that facilitating their access to higher education under Dream Acts is bad policy at a time when terrorist immigrants supposedly are using U.S. universities to enhance their ability to produce weapons of mass destruction.[56]

In 1968, unrest in Latino urban and rural communities led many Latinos to challenge existing institutions and conditions through labor strikes in the field and school walkouts in the barrio, ushering in the antiwar and antipolice rallies in the urban barrios that punctuated the Chicano Movement. In the 1980s, particularly, Latinos seemed far less prone to such uprisings, although the turnout of nearly one million pro-immigrant marchers in Los Angeles in March 2006, followed by school walkouts on César Chávez's birthday in support of immigration reform, may signal a return to the activism of the 1960s. Perhaps the War on Terror has diverted attention to the Middle East and Afghanistan, and away from such domestic woes as tragic school drop-out rates, woeful educational funding, anti-immigrant backlash, underpaid jobs, and inadequate health insurance. And, as examined in chapter 13, emphasis in the churches on the moral issues of curbing homosexual rights and outlawing abortion deflects attention from the economic and community ills of Latinos.

The legacy of the friendship between Robert Kennedy and César Chávez suggests the need for changes in the political philosophy of the Democratic Party and the Latino voter.

Several characteristics of the Latino population signal that Latinos should support the Democratic Party. Mexican Americans, and Latinos generally, are substantially an immigrant population. Despite the significant number of later-generation Latinos (in my case, both my mother's parents came from Mexico in the early 1900s), 57 percent of Latinos are immigrants,[57] and a large number are only one step removed from immigrants to the United States. Latinos embody their connection to immigrants in their support of immigrant rights—85 percent of registered voter Latinos favored a proposal granting undocumented workers the opportunity to legalize their status, and 62 percent concurred that undocumented immigrants help the U.S. economy.[58] By contrast, the same study found that 67 percent of Anglos (and African Americans too) believed that the undocumented harm our economy.[59]

As a group, Latinos are under attack in the United States on several fronts, particularly through immigration, language, and affirmative action policies. Armed vigilantes patrol the U.S./Mexico border, while hate radio commentators and authors such as Victor Davis Hanson blame society's ills on Latino immigrants, particularly those from Mexico. California voters, for example, enacted initiatives that dismissed any role of the Spanish language in government, rejected bilingual education of limited-English students in California classrooms, and denied undocumented immigrants essential public services and education. These immigrant and cultural attacks run counter to the overwhelming favorable bipartisan sentiment among Latinos for cultural preservation and immigrant rights. For example, the 2004 Pew Hispanic Center National Survey found that 88 percent of Latinos responded that it was very or somewhat important for Latinos living in the United States to speak Spanish, with only 4 percent who believed it was not at all important.[60]

The economic indicators for Latinos are staggeringly low. Latinos dominate the agricultural industry, but agricultural workers earn paltry wages, with the median annual income of individual workers determined in the 1990s to be less than $10,000.[61] In the wake of September 11, doubts about the patriotism of Latinos and other immigrants further imperiled Latino prosperity with increased emphasis on citizenship for jobs often held by immigrants. The most compelling example was the 2001 enactment by Congress of the Aviation and Transportation Security Act, imposing a citizenship requirement on airport screeners, and leading to the discharge of 80 percent of the security screeners at the San Francisco International Airport, many of them Latino immigrants.[62]

Education, which best offers the pathway to improve the economic standing of Latinos, continues for them to lag way behind the attainment of Anglos. A 2004 study determined that 27 percent of registered Latino voters, 38 percent of non-registered but citizen Latinos, and 58 percent of noncitizen Latinos had not completed high school. Moving along the educational spectrum, only 16 percent of registered Latino voters, 5 percent of nonregistered citizens, and 4 percent of noncitizen Latinos had completed "college or more."[63]

Health care is unattainable for many Latinos, with more than one of three Latinos without health care insurance (18 million total), and millions more struggling to pay their premiums. A 2004 survey of Latino voters found that 81 percent favored federally provided health insurance, with only 13 percent opposing such government coverage.[64] Housing is deficient for significant numbers of Latinos, with agricultural workers often living in abysmal, crowded conditions.

Latinos are racially profiled by local, state, and federal law enforcement and make up a disproportionate percentage of those searched, arrested, and imprisoned, particularly for offenses in the War on Drugs. Latinos consistently need to fight for rights in the criminal justice system—from recognition of the right to Spanish-language interpreters[65] to attacking racial profiling. Finally, Latinos are lured to the military by their lack of educational and employment opportunities. In their entry-level roles in the military, they are disproportionate victims of the War on Terror in Iraq and elsewhere.

Principles of the Democratic Party are surely more consistent with these needs and demands of Latino life in the United States than are the policies and practices of the Republican Party. Although the ideological gap between the two parties is narrowing, with some Democrats (notably Bill Clinton) mimicking Republicans, nevertheless there are differences that should cause the Latino voter to favor Democrats. Democrats have tended to advocate economic and taxation policies that favor the disadvantaged. By contrast, Republicans disfavor minimum wage increases, protection of organized labor, funding of social service programs, and universal health care. Republicans proffer law and order policies that reject a shift in the War on Drugs from enforcement to treatment. Republicans are particularly aggressive in fighting terrorism through military intervention without exhausting options for peaceful resolution of conflict. Republicans have supported anti-immigrant positions; most notably Republican governor Pete Wilson's campaign for reelection in 1994 built on his embrace of the anti-immigrant Proposition 187, and Arnold Schwarzenegger's campaign for California governor in 2003 spotlighting his opposition to driver's licenses for undocumented immigrants. A survey of Californian voters in 2003 at the time of Arnold's election revealed the partisan nature of anti-immigrant sentiment—only 9 percent of Republicans felt that undocumented immigration had a positive benefit; by contrast, 40 percent of California Democrats felt that undocumented immigration made a positive impact. Further, although 72 percent of Republican voters opposed government benefits for undocumented immigrants, only 36 percent of Democrats opposed benefits.[66] Republicans have supported restrictive anti-Spanish laws, and have targeted affirmative action, most notably through the Bush administration's opposition to the affirmative action policies at the University of Michigan. Democrats traditionally favor greater levels of spending for education, and exhibit more support for bilingual education programs than Republicans do. The Bush administration has blocked progress of the Dream Act, which would level the playing field in college tuition for undocumented immigrants.[67] Bush's plans for immigration reform, announced in his 2004 campaign, failed to include amnesty for existing employed undocumented workers, by contrast to Kerry's 2004 proposal, which included the possibility of citizenship for these workers. Kerry's Latino campaign website, Un Futuro Mejor (A Better Future), well captured the party differences in promoting an increased minimum wage, better funding for the bipartisan No Child Left Behind Act, and health care for all Americans. Latino voters surveyed in 2005 demonstrably favored the Democratic Party over Republicans on issues of which party did the better job in creating jobs, improving education, providing affordable health care, representing Latino views on immigration, and being in touch with the Latino community.[68]

But despite the overwhelming factors that should prompt Democratic votes among Latinos, as mentioned above moral issues swayed many to vote Republican in 2004. A 2004 survey revealed that 44 percent of registered

Latino voters thought abortion should be illegal, and 45 percent favored a constitutional amendment denying legal marriage to same-sex couples.[69] Not merely by coincidence, exit polling showed up to 44 percent of Latinos voting Republican in the 2004 presidential election. In the absence of prominent Latino leadership such as that of César Chávez and of Democratic candidates who connect with the Latino community as Robert Kennedy did, the challenge to overcome the role of the churches and conservative voices on moral issues will be daunting. Much of the job of reconnecting Latino voters with their roots in the Democratic Party will depend on the ability of Democratic Party leaders to reformulate a strategy that rekindles the Kennedy compassion for the least privileged, and builds coalitions of those hurt most by the Republican divestment of education, social services, inner cities, and job creation[70] in the United States. If the Democratic Party fails to reconnect with Latinos, Republican control of government will be near assured: "To remain viable as a party, Democrats need to win Latinos back. At stake is nothing less than control of the presidency and Congress. If the GOP maintains its current share of the Latino vote, says Simon Rosenberg of the New Democrat Network, 'then the Democrats will never be the majority party again in our lifetimes.'"[71]

Latino leadership too has a key role to play in the resurgence of Democrat allegiance among Latino voters by sparking voter participation. Voter apathy among Latinos often runs higher than for other groups, and Latinos are significantly excluded from political participation as a group because of the youth and lack of citizenship of many Latinos. For example, in the 2004 presidential election, about half of Anglo residents voted, a ratio of one voter to two Anglos in the United States. But due primarily to lack of participation, lack of citizenship, and youth, only one in five Latinos voted in 2004—meaning it took five Latinos to produce a single Latino voter.[72] Of eligible voters, only 58 percent of Latinos registered in 2004; by contrast 75 percent of Anglos and 69 percent of African American eligible voters registered.[73] Of these registered voters, the Latino turnout (82 percent in the 2004 election) lagged behind rates for Anglo (89 percent) and black (87 percent) voters.[74] Despite the tremendous gain in the Latino population from 2000 to 2004—5.7 million Latinos—the increase yielded only 2.1 million eligible voters and 1.4 million actual voters in the 2004 election, boosting the Latino share of the national vote only half a percent from 5.5 in 2000 to 6 percent of the votes cast in the 2004 election.[75]

César Chávez's record suggests that Latino leadership must be the catalyst for enhancing Latino voter participation. Although to a lesser extent than in 1968, Latino voters remain concentrated in barrios now found throughout the United States. Chávez demonstrated in 1968 that a grassroots voter registration and turnout drive in Latino barrios can translate to even 100 percent voter participation. In proposing a strategy of political mobilization of the poor to Ted Kennedy shortly after Robert Kennedy's death, Chávez recognized the potential for grassroots political organizing among the Latino poor. He proposed nonpartisan voter registration centers in areas where the poor reside, as well as citizenship classes to aid resident aliens in becoming citizens and then registering to vote. Aside from the youth of the Latino population, Chávez's strategy addressed effectively the two other fundamental shortcomings of Latino political participation—noncitizenship and low participation rates. Reshaping this strategy for current times, and implementing it, will require the commitment of national and local Latino leaders, who will need to recapture the cachet of Chávez, whose farm worker volunteers were able to go door to door in East Los Angeles in the 1968 Democratic primary and urge "This is the day César says to vote for Robert Kennedy."[76]

Given the surge in Latino votes lately for Republican candidates, Democratic leaders might question the wisdom of efforts to spur Latino political participation. Still, several factors suggest the value to Democrats of increasing the Latino voting ranks and participation. Among them are the disproportionate poverty of Latinos and the correlation, documented earlier, between class and voter participation, as well as class and party affiliation. Efforts that target the Latino poor are likely to pay political dividends to the Democratic Party. Latino voters remain substantially unaffiliated, with great potential for a Democratic platform that taps Latino values to resonate with this unaffiliated electorate. As an overgeneralization, Latinos tend to be social conservatives and economic liberals.[77] The youth of the Latino population are a resource for the Democratic Party if these voters upon reaching eligibility share the same liberal economic values as Latinos but bring more progressive positions on social issues such as abortion and gay marriage. Apart from the benefits to Democratic candidates, mobilizing the Latino electorate is important to counterbalance the increasing anti-immigrant voices in the Republican Party, as Latinos widely favor immigrant rights and will help protect against anti-immigrant initiatives and laws.

By contrast to their status as a bloc vote in the 1960s for Democrats, Latino voters today are nearly as likely to vote for Republican candidates as Democrats. Latinos must seize this shift as an opportunity for influence. As detailed previously, disaffection with the Democratic Party at the time of Democratic allegiance among Latinos led some Mexican Americans to form their own race-based political party in the late 1960s and 1970s, the short-lived La Raza Unida Party. That party flirted with the idea of channeling Latino voters toward the Democratic or Republican candidate who best reflected prevailing Latino prerogatives, but organizers ultimately rejected both mainstream parties and ran their own candidates, with few successes. Perhaps what is needed today is a political organization that does not constitute an independent political party, but instead serves the channeling function of auditioning mainstream party candidates and embracing those who best reflect Latino prerogatives. By contrast to the 1960s, when Latino activism helped influence the mainstream issues that defined and separated the political candidates, Latinos today have not capitalized on their potential political clout to help boost the issues that matter to the Latino community into mainstream campaign agendas. For example, Latinos need to proudly embrace their contributions to the country and insist that politicians confront their desires for cultural recognition (such as by resisting anti-Spanish measures), appreciation of immigrant contributions (such as by creating a pathway to citizenship for undocumented workers), protection of workers and jobs (through both economic and workplace safety measures), and quality publicly funded education for their children. Bringing these issues to the foreground of political debate should expose the deep schisms between most Democrat and Republican candidates on these issues, and perhaps lead to a softening of hard-line positions. The impact of Latinos as a swing vote was already felt in the 2004 presidential election, when Bush was able to capitalize with some Latino voters on his willingness to accept a guest worker program as the touchstone of his immigration reform package. But the impact was not realized in the 2003 California recall election, where Republican candidates drew 40 percent of the Latino vote but failed to exchange any ideas that resonated beyond mainstream appeal. It also was unrealized in the 2006 elections, in which several Republican candidates embraced hard-line anti-immigrant positions. Still, the swing of many Latino voters toward Democratic candidates in 2006, with the resulting shift in control of Congress, should signal to

Republicans the folly of running so strongly against the grain of Latino prerogatives. As Democratic and Republican platforms converge on issues of Latino resonance, Latinos might then more comfortably make their political choices on the issues of broader impact that have dominated recent elections—such as the economy, protecting against terrorism, and enforcing a shared sense of morality.

Latino leadership is needed both to develop the Latino platform and to convey the platform to mainstream party political candidates. César Chávez had the cachet to influence Democratic leaders on labor issues and, when Democrats such as Jerry Brown were in office, to reap political gains in labor reform. Under Republican leadership, farm laborers suffered. But even under Democratic leadership the gains were not dramatic—the separatist Latino political party emerged in the late 1960s from disaffection at a time when Latino political allegiance was overwhelmingly Democratic. Even Chávez lamented about the failings of the Democratic Party among Mexican Americans and other marginalized groups fighting to eradicate poverty: "A Democrat comes in [to political office], it's a little better, but it doesn't change things. A Republican comes in, it becomes oppressive.... [T]he Democratic administrations never really helped us that much. They never really like making a special case out of it."[78]

Fortunately, today's Latino leadership can rely on the emerging Latino swing vote to influence both Democrat and Republican politicians on labor and other crucial Latino issues. Born in the time of widespread allegiance among Latinos for the Democratic Party, La Raza Unida Party never had a realistic chance to broker Latino votes between mainstream political parties. Ironically, then, the increasing embrace of the Republican Party by Latinos carries the potential for Latino influence as both parties scramble for the Latino swing vote. Because Cuban American voters tend to vote Republican, and Puerto Rican voters Democrat, Mexican American voters are likely to wield the most clout as swing voters given the recent advances for the Republican Party among Mexican Americans. As the dominant group in the public eye on the issues of immigration and farm labor, Mexican American voters are poised to play a tremendous role in reshaping U.S. politics, if only their community leaders can harness and communicate a Latino platform. César Chávez was once that leader, and Robert Kennedy was a receptive listener, but replacement leaders and listeners are missing today.

Latinos with backgrounds other than Mexican, Cuban, and Puerto Rican also will gain political prominence given their independent streak as voters—a survey in 2004 found that these Latinos more often identified as politically independent than did Latinos of Mexican, Cuban, or Puerto Rican background.[79] A particular challenge in identifying and developing leaders who resonate with Latinos today is that immigrants now come in substantial numbers from countries in Central and South America aside from Mexico. Moreover, even Mexican immigrants increasingly are Mexican Indians from the central and southern states of Mexico, for whom Spanish may not be a first language.[80] Organizing these increasingly diverse workers, both economically in the workplace by union organizers, and in the political spaces of the United States, is a daunting task, perhaps even more than it was in the 1960s.

CHAPTER THIRTEEN

Mexican Americans and the Catholic Church

There was a kind of mystical aura about [Robert Kennedy], something that was electrifying and almost religious in its intensity.

—César Chávez[1]

In the course of [the farm worker] movement, César became ... a spiritual leader for all Chicanos.

—Mexican American poet Gary Soto[2]

Latinos in 1968 and still today are overwhelmingly of the Catholic faith, with one recent source identifying 77.4 percent of Latinos as Catholic[3] and another claiming 70 percent as Catholic.[4] As mentioned previously, the best explanation for the surge in Latino, particularly Mexican American, support for Bush in 2004 and the trend toward Republican voting among Latinos is found in religious-based values voting, particularly driven by the issues of gay marriage and abortion. In the mid-1960s, these issues held little significance in the voting booth for Latinos and for voters generally. Instead, at the time of the 1968 election, political issues that dominated the campaign seemed aligned with principles of the Catholic Church that did not emphasize individual lifestyle and privacy. Easing the economic and racial tensions in the inner cities and resolving the military involvement of the United States in the Vietnam War paralleled teachings on the poor and peace in the church. Further, the Catholic Church had begun to move from opposition or neutrality toward support of the reforms sought by the Mexican American farm labor movement. Overall, Democratic candidates best channeled these positions.

César Chávez invoked spiritual and Catholic influences in organizing farm labor. The key symbol of the labor movement was the Virgin of Guadalupe, whose image graced the head of union processions and parades. While locked in the grape struggle with the Di Giorgio company in the late 1960s, the farm workers erected a shrine to the Virgin outside the Di Giorgio ranch and kept a constant vigil there.[5] As one commentator noted:

> By bringing the [Catholic] church into the farmworker movement ... Chávez identified himself as belonging in the mainstream of the Mexican and Mexican American communities. The symbol of the Virgen [Spanish for virgin] had played an important role in Mexico's independence, in the Cristero revolt (a Catholic uprising), and the Mexican Revolution of 1910. Few things were as ingrained in the Mexican mind as Catholicism and the Virgen de Guadalupe. Staying close to the church placed the farmworker's movement within a conservative and legitimate boundary ... acceptable to many moderate and conservative Mexican Americans.[6]

Chávez also used religious services and prayer to anchor his movement, ending his fast in 1968 with Robert Kennedy at his side in a religious ceremony. The vast majority of farm workers whom Chávez sought to organize were Catholic;[7] Chávez himself was born into a Catholic family and attended Catholic mass regularly.[8]

Although Chávez relied on religion and Catholic Church influences in his organizing from the outset, the Catholic Church initially was not supportive of his labor movement. Apparently, growers controlled the Catholic parishes in Delano; the church there even denied Chávez use of its auditorium for union meetings.[9] As Chávez summarized in an essay titled "The Mexican American and the Church," which he wrote during his 1968 fast:

> In fact, we could not get any help at all from the [Catholic] priests of Delano. When the strike began [in 1965], they told us we could not even use the Church's auditorium for the meetings. The farm workers' money helped build that auditorium! ...
>
> Then the workers began to raise the question: ... "What does the Bishop say?" But the Bishop said nothing. But slowly the pressure of the people grew and grew, until finally ... our own [local] Catholic Church has decided to recognize that we have our own peculiar needs, just as the growers have theirs.[10]

Eventually, at the 1966 California hearings of the Senate subcommittee on migratory labor that forged the friendship between Kennedy and Chávez, the Catholic Church broke its official neutrality and embraced some of the farm labor goals. As the *Los Angeles Times* reported following the Delano session on the third and final day of the Senate hearings: "The hierarchy of the Catholic Church in California united Wednesday for the first time in an urgent appeal for collective bargaining rights and a minimum wage for farm workers."[11] Bishop Hugh Donohoe of Stockton, California, presented the church's statement on behalf of Cardinal McIntyre of Los Angeles and other Catholic officials. The church's statement recognized the right of workers to organize, declaring further that it was "unjust for farmers or grower organizations to strive to prevent by reprisal the legitimate efforts of farm laborers to form worker associations or unions."[12] As the bishop explained, "It is becoming evident that unless farm workers are given a chance to organize, they are going to become wards of the State."[13] The church's statement supported the reform package of federal legislation by calling for extending the National Labor Relations Act (NLRA) unionizing protections to farm workers, as well as the federal minimum wage.[14] Further, the church challenged the Delano growers' assertion that organizers of farm labor were troublemakers bucking the desire of local workers to preserve the status quo, stating bluntly "those who seek to organize farm laborers are not to be looked upon as outside agitators."[15]

When the farm workers union implemented the nationwide grape boycott, Chávez asked the Catholic bishops in 1968 to endorse it. Political leaders such as Robert Kennedy and eventually the 1968 Democratic candidate Hubert Humphrey backed the boycott, but church leaders initially did not directly support it. In their 1968 statement, the U.S. Catholic bishops, short of endorsing the grape boycott, recognized the legitimacy of the farm workers' rights to organize and strike, and appealed to Congress to include farm laborers under the NLRA. Arguably, their statement implicitly approved the boycott by not condemning it.[16] Finally, in 1973, the U.S. bishops for the first time endorsed a UFW boycott, this time the 1970s boycott of non-UFW iceberg lettuce and table grapes prompted by the UFW struggle with the Teamsters union to represent farm labor. At their annual meeting in November 1973, the National Conference of Catholic Bishops considered a presentation by Bishop Donnelly, chair of the Bishop's Committee on Farm Labor. Donnelly outlined the history of the UFW's battle with the Teamsters, and sided with the UFW:

We must be clear about the fact that the very existence of the UFW is at stake in this struggle [with the Teamsters union].

The Bishop's Committee on Farm Labor has met to reconsider its own role in the light of this urgent crisis. The committee is convinced that the cause represented by Cesar Chavez and the UFW is a just cause. We are persuaded that the UFW represents the best interests of the nation's agricultural workers and that it deserves our whole-hearted support in its struggle to protect the legitimate economic rights of one of the most disadvantaged groups of workers in the American economy.[17]

The bishops resolved to support secret-ballot elections to determine which union, the UFW or the Teamsters, would represent farm workers, and also approved the UFW boycott until secret elections were held. Some California priests, however, opposed the UFW. One Catholic pastor in Coachella, California, distributed a "position paper" detailing why churchgoers should oppose the boycott and not take sides in the UFW battle with the Teamsters.[18]

In 1974, Pope Paul VI demonstrated the changing position of the church toward the farm labor movement in a statement honoring César Chávez and the Mexican American community. The Pope cited Chávez's "sustained effort to apply the principles of Christian social teaching," and observed that "in striving to do so you [Chávez] have faithfully worked together with the Bishops of your country and with the support of their authoritative representatives, the members of the United States Catholic Bishops' Ad Hoc Committee on Farm Labor."[19]

The marriage of Chávez, the Catholic Church, and the Democratic Party in the late 1960s and early 1970s was a mostly happy one based on mutual interests. Protecting the basic rights and needs of laborers and building a better life for the most underprivileged of Americans were consistent with the focus of the church on the downtrodden in the community. The candidacies in 1968 and 1972 of Richard Nixon, an avowed supporter of the grape growers and opponent of the farm labor movement, further crystallized the opportunity for Catholic Latinos to implement Catholic social theology in their votes for Democratic candidates who supported farm labor organizing and reform to bring dignity to farm workers and their families. But, eventually, the farm workers' pursuit of the family values of dignity and opportunity were eclipsed by other "family values" that lent themselves to Republican votes. This shift among Latinos, particularly

Mexican American voters, was part of a similar shift toward the Republican Party among Catholic voters generally.

For generations, Catholic voters faithfully supported the Democratic Party. But by the 2004 election, Catholics of all ethnicities (representing 27 percent of the electorate) supported Bush over Kerry 52 percent to 47 percent, a substantial gain for Bush over the Catholic vote in 2000, when he received only 47 percent of the Catholic vote.[20] Catholic allegiance to the Democratic Party had begun to shift toward the Republican Party earlier, however, prompted by circumstances such as the Supreme Court's recognition in 1973 of constitutional limits on abortion laws, the class-climbing of Catholics leaving blue collar roles in factories and unions behind for the suburbs, and the concomitant departure of Catholics from ethnic urban enclaves, after which they shed their minority, persecuted status.[21] A brief review of the role of Catholic voters in modern presidential elections confirms the shift.

John Kennedy's candidacy in 1960 presented the opportunity for an electoral coalition among Catholic voters. Ultimately, over seven of ten Catholics supported Kennedy, a showing eclipsed only by the Democratic Party leanings of African American voters, Jewish Americans (four out of five of whom supported the Catholic Kennedy), and Latinos (most of whom were Catholics).[22]

Also a Catholic, Robert Kennedy in 1968 offered another opportunity for Catholic voters to implement Catholic social teaching. For example, a liberal Catholic publication, *Commonweal,* supported Kennedy's Vietnam policy, as well as that of the other Catholic candidate in the 1968 election—Senator McCarthy.[23] Still, Robert Kennedy took stands on reproduction issues inconsistent with the church's official positions. He challenged the church's condemnation of birth control, especially as it applied to Latin America.[24] By contrast, after Kennedy's assassination, Pope Paul VI in July 1968 condemned the birth control pill. Shortly before his death, Robert Kennedy also was embroiled in the effort to relax New York State abortion laws. New York law enacted in the 1800s allowed abortions only when necessary to save a mother's life. Efforts in the late 1960s to liberalize state law drew fire from Catholic leadership, who issued a letter urging all Catholics to fight abortion reform efforts with "all their power."[25] Based on the influential American Law Institute Model Penal Code, the New York reform proposal sought to legalize abortions in additional circumstances, such as when there was risk to the mother's physical or mental health, the child would be born with a grave physical or mental defect, or the pregnancy resulted from incest or rape. Although Kennedy did not specifically endorse the reform bill, he expressed general support for liberalizing abortion laws, stating, "There are obvious changes [in abortion law] that have to be made."[26] In a letter to a constituent in January 1968, Kennedy argued, in support of reform of New York law, that abortions were being performed illegally under current law, and cited the Model Penal Code liberalization of abortion law, as adopted in Colorado and North Carolina, as providing "some understanding of the form our abortion laws should take in the future."[27] After Kennedy's death, New York relaxed its abortion law in 1970 dramatically to become the most liberal in the country at the time, going well beyond the Model Penal Code approach to allow abortion on demand for any reason up to the twenty-fourth week of pregnancy.[28]

Following Kennedy's assassination, Catholics supported Democratic nominee Humphrey in the 1968 election despite his Catholic running mate's (Edmund Muskie's) evasive stance on birth control and Humphrey's repudiation by the liberal Catholic publication *Commonweal* for his defense of Johnson's Vietnam policy.[29]

By the 1972 election, incumbent Republican Nixon embraced an anti-abortion strategy that garnered the first Catholic majority for a Republican presidential candidate. Nixon's Catholic vote was at least 52 percent, up from 33 percent in 1968.[30] In the late 1960s and early 1970s, the abortion issue attracted major national attention, reflected in the states by reform legislation to liberalize abortion laws, and in the courts with the Supreme Court hearing oral argument in the *Roe v. Wade* litigation in 1971 and 1972. Against the advice of most of his campaign officials, Nixon relied on counsel from his aides Charles Colson and Catholic Patrick Buchanan (himself a presidential candidate in later years) to issue a public statement, in the form of a letter to New York's Catholic archbishop, who published it, opposing abortion and repudiating New York's legalization of abortion in 1970. Nixon charged that unrestricted abortion rights were "impossible to reconcile with either our religious traditions or our Western heritage."[31] In spring 1972, Nixon also repudiated the findings of a population growth commission he had appointed, calling the commission's advocacy of public-funded abortions "an unacceptable means of population control."[32] By contrast, 1972 Democratic candidate George McGovern, and his Catholic running mate, Kennedy's brother-in-law Sargent Shriver, advocated for abortion rights and apparently led many Catholic voters to abandon the Democratic Party in national elections. Nixon received over half the Catholic vote in 1972, at a time when 60 percent of Catholics were registered Democrats. In 1973, the Supreme Court issued its decision in *Roe v. Wade* recognizing a constitutional right to abortion, unrestricted in the first trimester of pregnancy.[33] The Catholic Church decried the *Roe* decision, condemning the ruling as "an unspeakable tragedy for the nation," and contending that the Court acted "as a superlegislature" that "defied the will of the people."[34] The National Conference of Catholic Bishops even issued a warning that any Catholic involved in an abortion would be excommunicated.

Democrat Jimmy Carter proclaimed his personal opposition to abortion in the 1976 election, as did Republican Gerald Ford, but Catholic officials blasted the 1976 Democratic platform that supported abortion rights. Still, with the specter of Watergate and his pardon of Nixon hanging over Ford, Catholics helped Carter win the election, with 57 percent supporting him. By the 1980s, the battle lines between Democrat and Republican candidates had been drawn along the lines of abortion—the Republican platform touted a constitutional amendment outlawing abortion while Democrats sought federal funding for abortions for poor women. At the same time, the Catholic Church took to active campaigning in support of antiabortion candidates; the *Roe* decision previously had ignited Catholic political advocacy, with Catholic cardinals appearing before Congress to support a right-to-life amendment to the Constitution.[35] In the 1980 election of Ronald Reagan, for example, a Boston cardinal distributed a letter encouraging Catholics to support antiabortion candidates.[36] Galvanizing these Catholic voters, Reagan and his morality agenda cemented the emerging trend of Catholic voters to favor Republican candidates by attracting 51 percent of Catholic voters, luring several voters away from incumbent Democrat Carter. The Catholic antiabortion vote was evident particularly in 1984, as Reagan beat Democrat Walter Mondale and his running mate Geraldine Ferraro, a Catholic congresswoman, with 55 percent[37] of the Catholic vote, even eclipsing Nixon's high-water mark among Catholics in 1972. Ferraro's outspoken views on abortion angered Catholic Church officials, leading some to rebuke her publicly.

In the 2004 election, several U.S. Catholic bishops asserted that John Kerry (the first Catholic candidate nominated by a major party since John

Kennedy in 1960) should be denied communion because he supported abortion rights, with at least one bishop even contending that Catholics who voted for politicians who favored abortion and gay marriage should be denied communion unless they confessed their voting as a sin.[38]

At a time of increasing economic disparity between the rich and poor, and in the throes of global war pursued by the United States, the Catholic Church chose to prioritize the moral issues of abortion and gay marriage, taking positions overwhelmingly correlating with votes for Republican Bush. There is little reason to anticipate that Catholic Church leadership will depoliticize issues of abortion and gay marriage and make them the province of individual choice for church members. In a book published shortly before his death, Pope John Paul II reiterated the church's opposition to abortion, even comparing abortion to the Holocaust, and further suggesting that gay marriages imperiled society with "evil."[39] Former cardinal Joseph Ratzinger, elevated to Pope in 2005, expressed similar hard-line positions on abortion and gay marriage; in 1986 he co-issued with Pope John Paul II the church's strident condemnation of same-sex relationships. Their statement contended that "[i]t is only in the [heterosexual] marital relationship that the use of the sexual faculty can be morally good."[40]

These voices of Catholic leadership, in my opinion, have misplaced the social justice imperatives of the Catholic Church and must reconsider the social teaching that once dominated the church and drew Catholics to the Democratic Party. Particularly given its influence in the Latino community, the Catholic Church needs to carefully consider its political positions when the candidates it favors have such detrimental impact on the lives of Latinos.

Compassion for the impoverished and imperatives for peaceful resolution of conflict still play major roles in Catholic social teaching. A 1998 publication of reflections of U.S. Catholic bishops articulated major themes of Catholic social teaching to include putting "the needs of the poor and vulnerable first," and respecting the basic rights of workers—"the right to productive work, to decent and fair wages, [and] to organize and join unions."[41] Another tenet of Catholic social teaching is that "Christians must be peacemakers."[42] Reflecting this tenet, the Pope in 2003 condemned U.S. involvement in Iraq as an unjust war.[43] Other tenets aligned with principles of the Democratic Party include attention to environmental justice, curbing the easy availability of weapons in the interest of preventing violence, eliminating racism, and providing universal health care coverage as a basic human right. As one Latina commentator summarized, "the Catholic church's teachings on social justice look more like the Democratic platform than the Republican platform."[44]

Protection of immigrant rights is also consistent with church teachings.[45] In the 2005 effort by Congress to prohibit states from issuing driver's licenses to undocumented immigrants, Catholic bishops and other religious leaders criticized the REAL ID Act, which Bush ultimately signed into law in spring 2005.[46] In a May 2005 press conference, Catholic cardinal Theodore McCarrick announced the responsive Justice for Immigrants campaign within the Catholic Church that seeks to counter the increasingly prevalent anti-immigrant rhetoric and vigilante attacks against immigrants. The goals of the long-term campaign are to educate Catholics and the public generally about the benefits of immigration, to advocate for immigration reform that offers legal status to migrant workers and their families, and to assist immigrants in accessing the benefits of immigration reform. This church immigration initiative prompted political activism by the church in 2006, when U.S. Catholic bishops opposed the border-arming sentiments of the proposed Border Protection, Anti-Terrorism, and Illegal Immigration Protection Act, which passed the House in late 2005. Cardinal Mahony of Los Angeles wrote President Bush criticizing this proposal, which might have criminalized Catholic social services provided to undocumented immigrants, even contending in a news conference that the church would defy the law.[47] The church's increasingly aggressive stance on immigration mirrors the demographics of the Catholic Church, whose lifeblood has become Latino immigration—Latinos not only account for some four of ten Catholics in the United States, they also represent 71 percent of new U.S. Catholics since 1960.[48]

By contrast to the church's emphasis on certain morality issues, however, there is little chance that the church will politicize issues of poverty policy and immigrant rights at election time. If it did, few, if any, candidates would survive a gauntlet of voting advocacy from the church that approved only abortion and gay marriage opponents who also advocated for the poor and immigrant populations. Today's "religious right" candidate is likely to embrace anti-immigrant sentiment, along with contesting abortion and gay marriage, all in the name of "family values"—a recent study confirmed that 63 percent of white evangelicals viewed immigrants as "a threat to U.S.

customs and values."[49] As one Catholic official put it, the church dichotomy between conservative family values and pro-immigrant social justice attitudes leaves Catholics "politically homeless."[50] Change, then, must come not from church officials but from church membership, or from political candidates who better embrace the social justice teaching of the church instead of a more narrow conception of family values.

Latino Catholics, in particular, must realize that the Catholic Church sometimes has failed their interests historically and recently. Among these inadequacies, the Catholic Church has continued to advocate against birth control in poor countries where reproduction practices consistent with church teachings ensure a life of poverty. Church schools have strictly imposed assimilationist ideals on young Latinos—as a youngster in Catholic school in East Los Angeles I witnessed scoldings for speaking Spanish, and was never exposed to Latino culture by the Anglo faculty despite the overwhelming Latino composition of the student body. Despite its eventual recognition of the farm labor struggle in California, the church was slow to join the movement and rarely stands at the forefront of movements for social change in the Latino community. Rather than seizing the opportunity to acknowledge the Latino and other dominant membership of color in the church, in selecting Cardinal Ratzinger Catholic officials chose to promote an Anglo with conservative positions out of step with the needs of the Latino community. This reflects the relative absence of Latino priests in the church—although Latinos make up about 40 percent of church membership in the United States, less than 8 percent of U.S. Catholic priests are Latino.[51] Collecting money from Latino parishioners in poor neighborhoods, the church historically invested these monies in opulent structures of worship rather than in meaningful social programs for the community. If the Catholic Church was bound by the same community reinvestment standards as banks, it would fail miserably in the Latino communities. In the late 1960s, the Mexican American activist group Católicos por la Raza confronted the Catholic Church on its irresponsiveness to the needs of the Chicano poor, even storming a 1969 Christmas Eve mass at St. Basil's, a Los Angeles Catholic church, until the protesters were beaten back by police.[52] The opulent new St. Basil's church undercut claims of the church hierarchy that it lacked funds for projects to aid the striking farm workers.[53] César Chávez too was critical of church priorities in an essay he wrote during his 1968 fast: "In a nutshell, what do we want the Church to do? We don't ask for more cathedrals. We don't ask for bigger churches or fine gifts. We ask for its presence with us, beside us, as Christ among us. We ask the Church to *sacrifice with the people* for social change, for justice, and for love of brother. We don't ask for words. We ask for deeds. We don't ask for paternalism. We ask for servanthood."[54]

In an interview, Chávez expressed additional criticism of the absence of activism in the church: "You know there are many changes in the Church today. But many of these changes, like the new ritual of the Mass, are merely external. What I like to see is a priest get up and speak about things like racism and poverty. But even when you hear about these things from the pulpit, you get the feeling that they aren't doing anything significant to alleviate these evils. They are just talking about them."[55] The human rights perspective that the church brings to the current immigration debate is a refreshing change in direction from the church's history of failing to embrace issues of concern to Latinos. Still, the church campaign for immigrant rights launched in 2005 came too late to build the momentum needed for the congressional debate in late 2005 and early 2006—where was this initiative when California voters using Proposition 187 and Congress through Operation Gatekeeper targeted immigrants in the mid-1990s? As with the Chávez campaign in the fields in the 1960s, the church eventually joined the struggle, but it rarely takes the lead on human rights issues that intersect with Latinos and other marginalized groups.

The political activism of the Catholic Church on moral fronts is not responsible entirely for the shift in Mexican American political allegiance from the Democrat to the Republican Party over the years. A significant and growing role is played by the Protestant faith, which is fervently Republican in orientation. In the 2004 presidential election, Bush captured 52 percent of the overall Catholic vote of all ethnicities (a gain of 5 percentage points over the 2000 election), but gained an even more substantial 59 percent of the overall Protestant vote, including a whopping 70 percent of those Protestant voters who attended church weekly.[56] The number of Latino Protestant voters is growing (a recent publication counted 23 percent of Latinos as Protestant),[57] a reflection of a survey finding that Latinos turn to the Protestant faith in later generations. Indeed, were it not for the constant influx of immigrants from Mexico, who are predominantly Catholic, the percentage of Latino Catholics would have declined even more rapidly in recent years.[58] The consequence of the shift to the Protestant faith among later-generation Latinos is that the Protestant faith is likely to be represented increasingly in the voting booth among citizen Latinos. Elections statistics from 2004 bear out this trend. The share of Protestant (and other Christian) voters jumped to 32 percent of Latinos voting in the 2004 election, up from 25 percent in 2000.[59] Catholic Latino voters were 55 percent of those Latinos voting in the 2004 race. The affinity of Protestant (and other Christian)[60] Latino voters for Bush was dramatically evident in the 2004 campaign, with 56 percent supporting Bush (up from 44 percent in 2000). By contrast, Latino Catholics voted for Bush in lesser numbers—33 percent in 2004.[61] Another source reported an even greater differential—finding that the Latino Protestant vote for Bush in 2004 was 63 percent and the Latino Catholic vote only 31 percent.[62] This differential between Catholic and Protestant voters probably stems from the abortion issue—among registered voters, Catholic Latinos are more likely to support legal abortion (51 percent) than are Protestant (37 percent) or evangelical Christian Catholics (39 percent).[63] Further, Latino registered voters who are evangelical Christians or Protestants are more likely (56 and 52 percent) to support a constitutional amendment to prohibit gay marriage than are Catholic Latino voters (44 percent).[64] The differential could also be linked to findings that Latino Protestants were more likely than Latino Catholics to respond that their churches engaged in political action, such as encouraging votes for certain political candidates.[65]

Despite the Protestant vote for Bush, there are roots for Protestant support of a progressive antipoverty and labor-oriented Latino agenda. Although Chávez was a devout Catholic, he counted on support for the farm workers union among ministers and parishioners from Protestant churches.[66] Further, regard for the underprivileged is the foundation of the scripture binding most devout Americans: "[In the Old and New Testament] [t]aken as a whole, the message is strong and clear. Whether one interprets the Judeo-Christian ethic from a religious perspective or from an ethical perspective, there is a direct imperative to help the poor. In fact, this message lies at the heart of the Judeo-Christian ethic."[67]

CHAPTER FOURTEEN

Mexican Americans and the Civil Rights Movement

Although they never met as a group, César Chávez, Robert Kennedy, and Martin Luther King, Jr. shared kindred visions and were the civil rights icons of the 1960s. Among their linkages, all were reviled in some quarters for their efforts toward equality—Kennedy among many Southerners for his enforcement of racial integration imperatives as attorney general, Chávez by growers in California who regarded him similarly as a meddling outsider in local labor issues, and King by those who resented his dream of racial and economic quality. But their connections ran deeper.

All three men shared firm religious convictions that shaped their approach to resolving the prevailing inequalities. The black Civil Rights Movement of the 1960s helped to guide the techniques of the farm worker struggle led by César Chávez. Like Martin Luther King, Jr., Chávez drew inspiration from the nonviolent techniques of Gandhi—Chávez kept a picture of Martin Luther King, Jr. and a poster of Gandhi in his office, along with a crucifix and a picture of the Virgin of Guadalupe. King sent Chávez a telegram during Chávez's 1968 hunger fast praising his commitment to nonviolence:

> I am deeply moved by your courage in fasting as your personal sacrifice for justice through nonviolence. Your past and present commitment is eloquent testimony to the constructive power of nonviolent action and the destructive impotence of violent reprisal. You stand today as a living example of the Ghandian[sic] tradition with its great force for social progress and its healing

spiritual powers. My colleagues and I commend you for your bravery, salute you for your indefatigable work against poverty and injustice, and pray for your health and your continuing service as one of the outstanding men in America. The plight of your people and ours is so grave that we all desperately need the inspiring example and effective leadership you have given.[1]

When King was assassinated a month later, Chávez sent his widow Coretta Scott King a touching telegram of remembrance and hope for the future of the cause of bringing dignity to the underprivileged through nonviolent struggles for justice:

> We are deeply saddened to learn of the death of your husband. Our prayers are for you and your children in your sorrow. It is my belief that much of the courage which we have found in our struggle for justice in the fields has had its roots in the example set by your husband and by those multitudes who followed his nonviolent leadership. We owe so much to Dr. Martin Luther King that words alone cannot express our gratefulness. Despite the tragic violence which took your husband, there is much that is good about our nation. It was to that goodness that your husband appealed. It was that compassion in all of us that he reached out to touch. His nonviolence was that of action—not that of contemplating action. Because of that, he will always be to us more than a philosopher of nonviolence. Rather, he will be remembered by us as a man of peace.[2]

In 1974, Coretta King would award Chávez the Martin Luther King Nonviolent Peace Award. After King's death, Chávez published an essay in his memory further extolling the strength of their shared commitment to nonviolence in the following excerpt:

> In honoring Martin Luther King, Jr.'s memory we also acknowledge nonviolence as a truly powerful weapon to achieve equality and liberation—in fact, the only weapon that Christians who struggle for social change can claim as their own....
> Our conviction is that human life is a very special possession given by God to man and that no one has the right to take it for any reason or for any cause, however just it may be.[3]

Kennedy joined their condemnation of violence as a means of social change. Speaking in Cleveland the day after Martin Luther King, Jr.'s assassination, Kennedy asked "What has violence ever accomplished? What has it ever created? ... No wrongs have ever been righted by riots and civil disorders."[4]

Chávez and King shared a vision of the importance of the rural struggle for justice in the larger national Civil Rights Movement, which encompassed urban ghettos and the rural fields, and even stretched beyond the bounds of color. By telegram to Chávez in 1966, King endorsed the farm worker struggle and situated the rural effort in this broader campaign for dignity:

> As brothers in the fight for equality, I extend the hand of fellowship and good will and wish continuing success to you and your members. The fight for equality must be fought on many fronts—in the urban slums, in the sweat shops of the factories and fields. Our separate struggles are really one—a struggle for freedom, for dignity, and for humanity. You and your valiant fellow workers have demonstrated your commitment to righting grievous wrongs forced upon exploited people. We are together with you in spirit and in determination that our dreams for a better tomorrow will be realized.[5]

As discussed previously, in chapter 10, King eventually steered the Civil Rights Movement toward more of a class-based struggle. Indeed, on his death he was planning the Poor People's Campaign, which was to focus more on economic equality than racial equity, but the new direction of the movement fractured on his death, and on that of Robert Kennedy weeks later.

Chávez and King also shared an appreciation for the role of politics in the pursuit of social change. Among their strategies in the struggle for political rights was registering new voters. Chávez spent much of his young career orchestrating voter registration, primarily of poor Mexican Americans in rural and urban landscapes throughout California. King's efforts to register black voters in Selma, Alabama, in 1965 helped prompt the federal Voting Rights Act to overcome racist state policies that had curtailed the black vote.[6]

Kennedy's relationship with King was somewhat more strained than the collaborative bond between Chávez and King. Although Kennedy was credited with aiding King's release from jail on trumped-up charges in 1960, and as attorney general in 1961 with helping to protect King and the Freedom

Riders (protesters riding by bus through the South to enforce federally man-
dated integration in interstate transportation),[7] Kennedy also briefly allowed
FBI director Hoover to wiretap King in Hoover's crazed pursuit of Communist involvement in the Civil Rights Movement. Still, at the time of his death
weeks before Kennedy's own assassination in spring 1968, King was said
to be planning to declare his support for Kennedy in the presidential race.[8]
Surely their alliances on issues were multifold. Kennedy was emerging as one
of the strongest opponents of the Vietnam War, a position that King had
taken much earlier. Kennedy and King also shared the goal to spark a class-
based coalition, with Kennedy said to have spurred King's decision to lead
a poor people's march on Washington, D.C., by suggesting to an NAACP
lawyer that Congress needed the prompting of "a whole lot of poor people"
to come to Washington and embarrass Congress into action.[9] Kennedy had
an honorable record on civil rights during his time as attorney general, and
was held in high esteem by the black and Mexican American communities.
Indeed, one observer remarked that during the five-mile march through an
all-black crowd following King's funeral, Kennedy and entertainer Sammy
Davis, Jr. drew the loudest cheers.[10] When Kennedy's motorcade drove
through black neighborhoods during his 1968 campaign, black children
ran alongside; in Mexican American barrios, Kennedy received a hero's
welcome. After Kennedy's assassination, California politician Jesse Unruh
remarked about the overwhelming black voter turnout for Kennedy, "We
can't get them out again. They'll never come back like that."[11]

The 1960s witnessed the potential for coalition among the poor, as well
as between blacks and Mexican Americans (and other Latinos). Demonstrating this potential, Chávez and the farm workers extended their political campaign for Kennedy in spring 1968 into the black neighborhoods of
South Central Los Angeles. But the later 1960s in particular also witnessed
discontent within these groups. As the black movement began to splinter between those following King's credo of nonviolence and the violence-tinged
principles of the Black Power movement, so too in the Mexican American
community tensions emerged between Chávez's nonviolent campaign
in the fields and the more urban Chicano Movement, which sometimes
drew inspiration from Black Power principles.[12] For example, in 1965, the
Latino organization League of United Latin American Citizens sent a
resolution to President Johnson distancing Latinos from the supposed black
militancy that sparked the 1965 Watts riots.[13] Within the black Civil Rights

Movement, King was jeered by some Black Power members,[14] and within the Mexican American community in the late 1960s and beyond, Chávez too encountered hostility, here directed toward his traditionalist Democratic Party leanings and his focus on rural issues.

In the 1980s, particularly, a new dynamic emerged in black-brown relations that has come to define their relationship and threatens their prospects for coalition—undocumented immigration that has brought Mexican Americans and other Latinos increasingly into the jobs and geographies occupied previously by African Americans. Before the immigration influx, black-brown solidarity was threatened primarily by the perception among some blacks that Latinos are situated on the color line as a racially mobile group with better access to the privilege of whiteness given the lighter color of their skin.[15] Politically, though, in the 1960s, Mexican American and black voters were situated very similarly on the political spectrum in voting overwhelmingly for Democrats. But today, the immigrant influx and the trend of Latino voters toward Republicans create new wedges in black-brown relations. During the 2006 mass nationwide pro-immigrant rallies, many Latino immigrants invoked the black Civil Rights Movement and King's struggles as their own, pointing out the parallels in these struggles. Black representatives such as Jesse Jackson, long a proponent of an antipoverty coalition, hailed these pro-immigrant rallies. But some blacks objected to any comparison to the black experience and the Civil Rights Movement; as well, some blacks feared competition from immigrant laborers, whom they saw as undermining wages for low-income workers generally.[16]

In 1968, Latino representatives from the United Farm Workers Organizing Committee went to Watts to secure African American votes for Robert Kennedy. Ultimately, as Mexican Americans voted Democrat in the 1968 election in substantial numbers (87 percent), African Americans voted in virtually identical strong numbers for Democrat Humphrey, casting only a smattering of votes for Nixon (about 12 percent).[17] By 2004, the potential for political coalition between Latinos and African Americans was evaporating. African Americans voted 88 percent for Kerry and 11 percent for Bush, while Latinos voted 53 percent for Kerry and as much as 44 percent for Bush. Only Puerto Rican voters, representing about 15 percent of the Latino electorate, approached the Democratic bloc vote of African Americans. Although Bush improved his share of the black vote by three percentage points over the 2000 election, his sour harvest of 11 percent of their vote essentially matched the average draw of Republican presidential candidates from black voters since 1964—11.7 percent.[18]

At the same time that Latinos are drifting toward the Republican Party and away from African American voters in their potential for coalition, Asian American voters are becoming more Democratic in their voting. Fifty-five percent of Asian American voters supported George Bush Sr. in 1992, and in 1996 they handed Clinton only 43 percent of their vote, but by 2000 a majority of Asian American voters (54 percent) supported Democrat candidate Al Gore in his campaign against the junior Bush.[19] In 2004, the Asian shift to the Democratic Party continued, with 56 percent of Asian American voters favoring Kerry to Bush's 44 percent.[20]

As Latino voters, particularly Mexican American voters, trend toward Republican voting at the same time that African Americans continue to vote for Democrats en masse and Asian American voters drift toward Democratic candidates, the potential for interracial/ethnic coalition evaporates. Even when Latino candidates run, coalition is not assured. The 2004 Pew Hispanic Center study revealed that over half (55 percent) of Latino voters disagreed strongly or somewhat that they would be more likely to vote if there was a Latino on the ballot. The 2003 California recall election reflected this ambivalence, in which African American voters supported Latino Cruz Bustamante in far higher numbers (65 percent) than did Latino voters, whose support as gauged in exit polls ranged from 52 to 55 percent,[21] the weakest Latino support given in modern elections to a Democratic gubernatorial candidate in California. Earlier, in the 2001 Los Angeles mayoral campaign, African American voters overwhelmingly favored an Anglo Democratic candidate, James Hahn, at 80 percent, while 80 percent of Latino voters went for Latino Democrat Antonio Villaraigosa.[22]

The affinities and alliances that Chávez, King, and Kennedy saw in the 1960s among blacks and Latinos in the mutual struggle for dignity are present today despite the dynamic of immigration that increasingly has come to define U.S. perceptions of Latinos. Stalwart issues of a class-based coalition, such as employee wage reform and public school financing, situate blacks and Latinos on the same side of the political spectrum. But the increasing values voting of many Latinos, prompting support of Republican candidates, threatens this potential for political coalition. Latino leadership must navigate the turbulent waters of the immigration tide and forge new alliances with the black community in order for any antipoverty coalition to emerge. In crafting an alliance, Latino leaders have significant leverage to draw on—recently, the black vote has been written off, at least in national elections, given the overwhelming Democratic leanings of black voters. But the Latino swing vote, as discussed previously, can wield considerable power in shaping issues of concern to both black and Latino voters, particularly economic issues of the poor such as the minimum wage and funding of public education, as well as such social issues as police-community relations. Representatives of the black community should realize the potential power of association in aligning with Latinos to forge change across party lines on these issues of concern to both communities of color. The weight of these issues overcomes the immigration issue that has stymied black-brown cooperation. Once leadership gets past this temporary roadblock, the potential for interracial cooperation can resume the path laid by Chávez, King, and Kennedy, with the added clout of the increase in numbers of these groups since the 1960s and the power of the Latino swing vote that has emerged.

Although Chávez was loyal to the Democratic Party, King's experience provides an example of the potential power of the ethnic swing vote. King voted Republican in 1956, and lobbied Vice President Nixon in 1957 on federal civil rights legislation by stressing the burgeoning black voter rolls and the potential for blacks to vote Republican.[23] Ironically, Nixon was a near champion at the time for civil rights reform favoring integration and equality; Nixon had even endured hostility from some Southern Democrats for his membership in the NAACP. Unfortunately for Nixon, though, the promise of King's delivering the black vote evaporated when Robert Kennedy intervened to gain King's release from jail shortly before the 1960 presidential election, which helped sway black voters to his brother. By 1968, Nixon recovered and resurrected his political fortunes with a racialized "Southern strategy" that preached states' rights and aligned itself with segregationists rather than black interests. Since that 1960 election, the black vote has generally followed the Democrats, and Republicans have largely abandoned the black vote and black issues. But King's wielding of the black vote in the late 1950s as a racial power broker demonstrates the utility of the racial swing vote, particularly in the hands of an icon who can deliver that vote. The challenge today is not merely identifying leadership within racial and ethnic communities to broker and deliver the vote but, in the context of interracial or antipoverty coalitions, to find individuals or groups capable of representing and speaking for the diverse interests of groups such as blacks and Latinos. No such comprehensive leader exists today, and as mentioned previously, other than Dolores Huerta no such leader arguably exists even for the subgroup of Mexican Americans that Chávez once represented, or for blacks, whom King once spoke for.

The experience of Nixon and Republicans in 1968 and beyond also suggests that to be effective, the swing vote must outweigh the potential for white backlash that helped sway Nixon toward Southern segregationists in 1968. Even a black-brown alliance that overcame disagreements on immigration policy might stumble in attracting Republican attention given the specter of backlash on racial and class grounds. Although tapping an interracial antipoverty coalition might ease the racial tension, class warfare would still pose problems in garnering Republican alliance. The coalition will have the most success on issues that present a confluence of classwide interest, such as immigration policies that fuel social security reserves or boost the housing industry.

The 1970 Census counted 9.6 million Latinos and 22.6 million African Americans. But by the 2000 Census, Latinos (35.3 million) and African Americans (36.4 million) stood virtually even in population, and the Census Bureau announced officially in January 2003 that Latinos had become the most numerous minority group in the United States. In the coming years, the Latino population is expected to dramatically outpace the growth of the African American population, leaving Latinos and blacks at a crossroads of alliance or departure. Shouldering the responsibility for charting the destiny of our most populous minority group, hundreds of Latino leaders gathered in Los Angeles in summer 2006 for a historic National Latino Congreso (congress) to consider the pressing political, social, and economic issues facing Latinos. Delegates passed a resolution acknowledging the need for Latino and African American cooperation on issues of the day, its preamble explicitly recognizing the 1960s vision of Chávez and King, who embraced the common goals of these groups. With an eye toward a mutual future of struggle against discrimination, the resolution stated: "Now, therefore be it resolved, that Congreso participants undertake new efforts to meet with African American community leaders at the local level to listen, learn, communicate and teach about our communities and develop ways to work in common concert on issues of equality and freedom."[24]

CHAPTER FIFTEEN

Looking Ahead: The Future of the Democratic Party and Immigration Reform

Education ... can be a means to the solution of some of our most pressing social problems—of race, of poverty, or crime.
—Robert Kennedy[1]

We would do better to build the economies of countries like Mexico, so people can live their own dream in their own nation. If we don't help build the economy of the nations who surround us, we will continue to have people fleeing for both economic reasons and because they're being persecuted.
—U.S. Representative Sheila Jackson Lee (D-TX), who introduced the Save America Comprehensive Immigration Act of 2005 with cosponsors from the Congressional Black Caucus, proposing to legalize undocumented immigrants who have lived in the United States for five years with no criminal record[2]

In 2004, *Time* magazine reported that only 45.2 percent of the U.S. public identified with the Democratic Party, down from 49 percent a decade before in 1994; at the same time, the Republican Party gained membership from 40 percent a decade ago to 45.5 percent.[3] Since Robert Kennedy entered the presidential race in 1968, Anglo voters have defected to the Republican Party in large numbers, along with many Latino voters, while African American voters have remained loyal to the Democratic Party. Reacting to the loss of Anglo votes particularly, Democratic candidates have embraced a so-called New Liberalism. Abandoning a platform that builds upon the social programs and civil rights–oriented reforms of the 1960s, this political approach tries to out-Republican the Republicans. One commentator described this Democratic strategy as follows: "[T]he advocates of New Liberalism believed that the only way for the Democrats to win at the presidential level and govern effectively was to shed their traditional support for and identification with the poor, the working class, and minorities and to reach out to disaffected whites and economic elites by moving to the right on issues such as crime, affirmative action, welfare, and economic justice."[4] Bill Clinton best embodied this philosophy, evident particularly in his support for repressive welfare and immigrant benefit reform in the 1996 Personal Responsibility and Work Opportunity Reconciliation Act.

In this current climate of immigrant bashing, with Minutemen patrolling the U.S./Mexico border and xenophobes warning of "Mexifornia," Democrats who embrace a New Liberalism should remember the potential for backlash by Latino voters against anti-immigrant candidates and proposals. Pete Wilson, the California governor who embraced the anti-immigrant Proposition 187 in his 1994 reelection campaign, received almost 45 percent of the Latino vote in his 1990 election. But in 1994, surging Latino turnout handed him only 25 percent of their vote,[5] and by 1998, his conservative Republican successor candidate, Dan Lungren, obtained less than a quarter of the Latino vote while Latinos helped Democrat Gray Davis win office.[6] In his 1996 campaign for the presidency, Republican Bob Dole jumped onto the anti-immigrant bandwagon, attacking Clinton for "failing to control the nation's borders."[7] Clinton upped his percentage of the Latino vote dramatically, going from estimates of 51 to 62 percent of the Latino vote in 1992 to 71 or 72 percent of the Latino vote in 1996.

President George W. Bush avoided any immigrant policy backlash among Latinos in the 2000 presidential election given his Latino-friendly record as governor of Texas, where he came out against state English-language laws and Proposition 187; in 2004 Bush bettered his already-impressive showing among Latinos from 2000. Arnold Schwarzenegger managed to walk an immigration tightrope in securing the California governorship in 2003—blasting driver's licenses for undocumented immigrants, but positioning himself favorably among many Latinos given his own immigrant past, which he touted in ads run in Spanish-language media.[8] Eventually, Schwarzenegger revealed the range of his anti-immigrant sentiment, or a desperate move to restore his plummeting public approval, by praising the armed Minuteman citizen patrol at the Arizona border as doing a "terrific job."[9] Although Schwarzenegger warmly likened the armed group to a "neighborhood patrol,"[10] President Bush rightly called them vigilantes. Welcomed to California by the governor, the Minuteman Project expanded its vigilante border patrol in 2005 to California and the other southern border states. But Schwarzenegger eventually sensed the ill political winds of an anti-immigrant stance, and during his successful campaign in 2006 for reelection he disavowed his earlier support for both the Minutemen and Proposition 187, which no doubt helped him earn 39 percent of the Latino vote.

The 2006 elections should signal to Democrats (and Republicans) the risk of anti-immigrant positions—fervent anti-immigrant rhetoric prompted many Latino voters to swing to Democratic candidates, helping the Democrats gain control of Congress. CNN's exit polling in 2006 determined that Democrat House candidates secured 69 percent of the Latino vote, compared with only 55 percent in 2004.

After the Bush victory in 2004, several pundits proffered strategies to resurrect the Democratic Party from its wayward course of mirroring the Republican Party on issues of economic and social justice. Fresh from her loss to Schwarzenegger in the 2003 California recall election as an independent candidate, Arianna Huffington called for a return to the soul-based politics of Robert Kennedy by tying economic issues and moral values together under the slogan she coined "economic issues are moral values."[11] In a similar vein, evangelist Jim Wallis criticized the unrealistic separation by Democrats of religious values from political leadership, and called for championing the poor as a moral value.[12] Although Democrats gained ground in the 2006 elections, arguably that success was more of a backlash against President Bush than a recognition of fundamental change in the Democratic Party and its candidates. Moreover, in the climate of immigrant bashing, many Democrats jumped on the border security bandwagon, such as Arizona's Governor Napolitano and New Mexico's Latino Governor Richardson, who both declared a state of emergency at the U.S./Mexico border in their states.

In my vision, the Democratic Party must articulate a moral and family values agenda that emphasizes antipoverty initiatives and educational opportunity. Further, Democrats must embrace a bold plan for immigration reform that intersects with these antipoverty and educational initiatives. Although addressing these areas is a daunting task, I concur with Arianna Huffington that Democrats need to recapture the drive and devotion of Robert Kennedy, who as attorney general in 1963 once locked the entire presidential Cabinet into a room for four hours and made them discuss how best to solve the crisis of poverty in the United States.[13]

Needed immigration reform is closely aligned with the antipoverty coalition agenda articulated in chapter 10. Although some Democratic politicians have embraced aspects of this reform, they sometimes fail to perceive the connection between immigration reform and combating poverty, as well as fail to develop solutions that extend beyond our borders. César Chávez and Robert Kennedy both well understood the interplay of immigration and labor economics in which employers manipulate undocumented and temporary guest workers to ensure inadequate wages and substandard working conditions for other employees. Thus, the foundation of any immigration reform plan must begin with a workers' rights agenda that guarantees a decent, inflation-indexed federal minimum wage, extends to farm workers federal protections in union organizing, and ensures safe working conditions. In addition to addressing poverty among working families in the United States, labor-oriented reforms will help stabilize immigration by decreasing the incentive to hire an undocumented immigrant willing to work for less than fair U.S. wages.

For undocumented immigrants already here, and for documented but noncitizen immigrants, reform along the lines of the AgJOBS bill, but more expansive to encompass additional sectors of employment, is needed to lay a pathway to citizenship for those immigrants with skills sufficient to find work for a specified period of time. Supported by the UFW, the 1986 Immigration and Control Act was criticized by some for its amnesty program that gave legal "green card" status to 3.1 million immigrants. Critics contend that U.S. immigration policy tolerates the undocumented, and when the pressure for amnesty builds and the political winds blow right, another amnesty program comes along. The key to breaking this cycle of building pressure and release though amnesty programs is to couple amnesty not merely with employer sanctions for hiring future undocumented immigrants, as the 1986 act did, but to embrace a more comprehensive economic and even international reform package to address the roots of the impetus for future immigration.

Immigrants already here must be treated better, and not denied such basic rights as the ability to obtain a driver's license and therefore car insurance, and the entitlement to core services that other taxpayers receive such as immunizations and education for immigrant children.[14] Denying these services does nothing to discourage undocumented immigration—immigrants desperate enough for jobs to risk a deadly desert crossing will be undaunted by denial of these government services once they arrive. Although some of these immigrant rights reforms are best executed at the state level, the federal government has a significant role to play in setting the tone for reform and by reversing such abusive laws as the 2005 REAL ID Act that governs driver's licenses and the 1996 Personal Responsibility and Work Opportunity Reconciliation Act restricting entitlement of both documented and undocumented immigrants to certain fundamental benefits.

With regard to future immigration, party leaders must accept the proposition that our immigration policy, while properly guarding against terrorists, cannot humanely jeopardize the lives of workers trying to better the lives of themselves and their families. As one commentator captured it pointedly: "Our national [immigration] policy seems to be: 'Amigo, if you can brave the deserts in the middle of summer and outrun our Border Patrol agents, then we will reward you by allowing you to live in the shadows while you work as our gardeners, nannies and waiters.'"[15]

Since Bill Clinton's border-arming plan in 1994, which concentrated on fortifying the border in urban areas, hundreds of Mexican immigrants have perished annually trying to cross the border in the unforgiving desert. This Democrat-approved immigration philosophy has failed miserably. Rather, immigration reform needs to reverse this strategy and secure the remote border areas away from urban checkpoints, in order to protect against the possibility of terrorist entry or drug smuggling on the one hand, and on the other to prevent perilous desert crossings by Latinos and their children. With the border flow directed back to the urban checkpoints as it was before the 1994 policy, immigration law must return to a practice closer to the pre-1965 law that exempted the Western Hemisphere from quota ceilings. Today, Mexican and other Central and South American undocumented immigrants pay exorbitant fees to "coyotes" to guide them through the cruel desert gauntlet into the United States. In place of this system, immigration reform must stabilize the border by allowing immigration of residents from these countries freely on payment of a fee sufficient to finance vigorous but rapid security background checks.[16] By contrast to President Bush's proposed guest worker program, which requires a U.S. job as a prerequisite to temporary entry, these immigrants should be allowed a specified period of time to find suitable work, and also a pathway to citizenship for those (and their immediate families) who contribute to the U.S. economy through their sustained work.

The missing piece of most current plans for immigration reform is supplied by the teachings and example of Robert Kennedy, who looked internationally in addressing our domestic strife. In a 1965 speech, Kennedy advocated policies of increased economic aid to disadvantaged countries:

> We are not now meeting our responsibilities. Our economic aid to the rest of the world amounts to ... perhaps one-third of one percent of our national income....
>
> In order to solve the pressing problems of world poverty, developed countries must make a greater contribution—of money and mind, of time and toil.... The United States can and must make the greatest share of these contributions.[17]

Kennedy embraced the Alliance for Progress, championed by his brother President John F. Kennedy in 1961 and accepted by all Latin American countries except Cuba. The alliance pledge established the responsibility of the United States toward the political, economic, and social development of Latin America, including at least a billion dollars a year in assistance to counter the imbalance of global aid that saw the United States provide $30 billion to Europe and only $2.5 billion to the Americas in the fifteen years after World War II.[18] As a senator in 1965, Robert Kennedy traveled to several South American countries to help cement the alliance. During the Cuban Missile Crisis in 1962, in perhaps the most critical moment of human fate in modern times, these Latin American countries (except for Cuba) unanimously supported the U.S. military blockade that led to disarmament.[19] Under the Bush administration, by contrast, relations with South America have deteriorated, particularly in countries such as Bolivia and oil-rich Venezuela. Leftist leaders in these and other countries campaigned on antipoverty platforms to address widespread poverty in the region—Chilean voters elected a socialist doctor in 2006 who defeated a conservative multimillionaire to become the country's first female president. These leaders increasingly disdain help or influence from the United

States. At a time when hemispheric and even international debate is needed to address our immigration issues, sentiment in the United States increasingly wants to wall off the rest of the world from immigration debate and immigrant entry.

Seizing on Robert Kennedy's initiative in addressing poverty, particularly in Central and South America, immigration reform today must extend internationally and work to stabilize the rural economies devastated by NAFTA and past U.S. intervention in foreign politics, particularly rampant under the Reagan administration, which rattled entire economies and led to mass emigration.[20] The investment of money now will pay off when economic advances in countries such as Mexico decrease the incentives, which are overwhelmingly economic, to immigrate to the United States, leaving familial and cultural roots behind. Mexico's President Vicente Fox recognized this crucial need to boost Mexico's economy: "How can we narrow the gap on income on both sides of the border? How can we in the long term equal the levels of development between our countries so that we become real friends, real partners and real neighbors? How can we build up the opportunities in Mexico so that our kids, 12- [and] 14-year-olds, don't have to leave home, don't have to move to the United States looking for opportunities?"[21] Fox's successor, Felipe Calderón, similarly has called for comprehensive immigration reform while recognizing the need for Mexico to create jobs to slow immigration north.[22]

There are at least five starting points from which to construct or view any immigration reform proposal. One could seek primarily to protect an Anglocentric vision of U.S. culture and heritage from "dilution" by Latino immigration, as Victor Davis Hanson and Samuel Huntington might; one could endeavor to fortify the border to protect against entry by terrorists or the criminal element, as the Minuteman Project has undertaken; the primary emphasis of immigration reform could be to protect worker rights; reform could honor the human rights of immigrants; or the starting point of immigration reform could be protecting the interests of U.S. employers. In the 1960s, Robert Kennedy's immigration stance balanced concern for workers' rights with a strong recognition of and fondness for the role of immigrants in U.S. society. Kennedy appreciated the devastating effect of documented green card and undocumented immigrants from Mexico and elsewhere on labor organizing in the United States for fair wages and worker protections. Therefore, he supported enforcement of immigration laws and reform to protect against employer use of noncitizen labor in strike zones. At the same time, Kennedy opposed the imposition of ceilings on the number of Western Hemisphere immigrants seeking citizenship. Kennedy's balance also marked the UFW (and predecessor) union position on immigration. The UFW opposed the use of immigrants (and anybody else) as strikebreakers, and opposed the bracero guest worker program because they saw it as ensuring employers a steady stream of insufficiently protected workers who would undermine the cause for workers in the United States. But the UFW supports empowering programs of legalization for undocumented workers currently employed in the United States, such as under the AgJOBS bill.

Today, Senator Ted Kennedy best reflects the immigration reform mindset of the UFW to respect the human rights of immigrants while protecting worker rights. Kennedy issued a statement in 2006 to frame the Senate's consideration of immigrant reform proposals:

> I look forward to working with [Senate Judiciary Committee] Chairman [Arlen] Specter on comprehensive immigration reform so that temporary workers can come here safely, and the 11 million illegal workers already here will have a way to earn permanent residence and citizenship. I have concerns about his proposal that would establish for the first time in our nation's history a class of millions of people who are forever in a temporary worker status, thereby creating a second-class status for immigrant workers. And I am concerned that his enforcement provisions contain punitive measures that would horribly affect many immigrants and their families and do nothing to fix the broken immigration system.... It would unfairly punish and criminalize countless hardworking immigrants and divide American families. This proposal will only drive immigrants further into the shadows. We need to enact responsible reforms consistent with our country's ideals and our heritage as a nation of immigrants and a nation of laws.[23]

Particularly evident in the presidencies of Nixon from 1968 and Bush from 2000 is the Republican Party support of agribusiness and of employers generally that led César Chávez to charge Nixon with refusing to enforce immigration laws when growers needed strikebreakers, and Bush in 2004 to tout an expansive guest worker program for U.S. employers that carried no possibility of citizenship beyond the narrow channels available under existing law. Bush refused to support the AgJOBS bill that year, despite its bipartisan sponsorship, because it represented a compromise between employer interests (a free supply of workers) and labor interests (the possibility down the road of empowering citizenship). But even the employer-friendly posture of the Republican Party has been challenged lately by the shrill alarm of anti-immigrant forces in the Republican Party who disdain any worker rights immigration platform, or even the traditional employer-friendly immigration platform of the Republican Party. Instead these voices, like those of academics such as Victor Davis Hanson and Samuel Huntington and those of the Minutemen, would have us shut the U.S./Mexico border in order to protect our culture, our economy, and our lives from the supposed threat of welfare-minded, criminally inclined, and even terrorist-bent Mexicans. This anti-immigrant lobby has come to dominate immigration policy in the 2000s, seizing on the terrorist attacks of September 11 to drape its anti-immigrant proposals with the U.S. flag in the name of patriotism and national security. Anti-immigrant forces have shown their clout nationally in preventing serious consideration of the labor and employer compromise AgJOBS bill, and in fast-tracking adoption of the REAL ID Act, signed by Bush in 2005, to prompt the denial of state driver's licenses to undocumented immigrants in the name of national security. As well, the passage by the House in late 2005 of the border-security-at-any-cost Border Protection, Anti-Terrorism, and Illegal Immigration Control Act and by Congress in 2006 of the Secure Fence Act well represents the prevailing poisonous anti-immigrant/security dynamic that has emerged on Capitol Hill and throughout the states.

With its increasing co-option by anti-immigrant forces, the Republican Party will not move us forward in addressing an issue of critical importance to Latinos and all other Americans—immigration. It is up to Democrats to forge an internationally minded immigration plan that captures and balances both the Kennedy tradition of valuing immigration and the diversity it brings, and the César Chávez and UFW legacy of according opportunity and dignity to workers on the lowest rungs of U.S. society.

As this book went to press in 2007, Congress was in the throes of debating a compromise immigration reform bill that failed these aims on several grounds. Its tortuous pathway to citizenship for undocumented immigrants already in the United States demands payment of a whopping fine for these struggling workers, totaling $5,000, as well as insisting they "touchback" in their countries of origin. Many Republican voices decried the compromise—2008 presidential candidate Rudy Giuliani opposed it while fellow candidate Mitt Romney denounced it as offering amnesty to the undocumented, but Senator John McCain, an architect of the plan, defended it. Another key architect, Ted Kennedy, admitted that the bill wasn't exactly as he had hoped, but was "the best chance we will have to finally fix this broken system."[24] Still, the bill reflected the shift in comprehensive immigration proposals toward Republican prerogatives of border security and employer needs that led some Democrats, notably presidential candidate Bill Richardson, to oppose the plan. For most future immigrants, the bill resurrects the bracero program with guest worker provisions that allow entry for three two-year work terms provided the worker returns to his or her own country for a year in between terms. Needed worker protections and a pathway to citizenship are absent, as is any design for restoring the economies of surrounding countries. Our special neighbor relationship with the Western Hemisphere that prevailed in our immigration policy until the 1960s is again forsaken for a plan that puts U.S. employers ahead of U.S. workers, and immigrant workers and their families. By the summer of 2007, opposition primarily from Republicans had scuttled the bill, but it may be revived in future proposals. Should this reform bill ever be enacted, which is doubtful in the supercharged anti-immigrant climate, much work toward restoring dignity in these sectors will be left behind for the Democratic Party.

Aside from reshaping immigration policy, the Democratic Party and U.S. voters must attend to the woeful state of our underfunded educational system. New Mexico's Latino governor Bill Richardson suggested in 2004 what was needed to stanch the flow of Latino voters to the Republican Party: "It is going to take a political platform that recognizes that Hispanic children need good schools, our parents need to retire in dignity, that our families must have quality health care, and that we all need good jobs at good wages."[25]

No doubt education tops the Latino voting agenda. A recent study by the Pew Hispanic Center confirmed that Latinos are more concerned about education than any other group of voters—54 percent of Latinos said that education would be "extremely important" in determining their vote in the 2004 election (by contrast, 51 percent said the economy, jobs, health care, and Medicare would be extremely important).[26] A later 2005 study by the Pew Hispanic Center established that 96 percent of Latinos identified education as an "extremely" or "very" important issue for the Latino community.[27] Elected in 2005, the Mexican American mayor of Los Angeles, Antonio Villaraigosa, labeled the high school dropout crisis as "the new civil rights issue of our time."[28] One recent study found that only 44 percent of Latinos graduate from high school in four years.[29]

In the 2004 election, Democratic candidate Kerry began to articulate the mainstream party differences on the crucial issue of education. For example, he highlighted the critical underfunding of the No Child Left Behind Act. Kerry suggested the shortfall in funding ($27 billion!) should be overcome by rolling back tax cuts for the wealthy.[30] But President Bush appealed to Latino voters with the sloganeering and empty bilingual statement he made in his acceptance speech at the Republican National Convention—"No dejaremos a ningún niño atrás—we will leave no child behind." Bush also ducked federal responsibility by stating that "the commitment for educational excellence must start at the local level."[31]

As the Democratic Party formulates its education policy for Latinos and voters nationally, party leaders must avoid the temptation to scapegoat immigrants for the educational funding crisis. That anti-immigrant sentiment yielded Proposition 187's prohibition of educating the children of undocumented immigrants, and the witch hunt it authorized through the California schools to weed out such unentitled children. One of Bob Dole's 1996 television clips tapped this sentiment by featuring gang members loitering in the street while the ad decried the costs of immigrants to California education, closing with a shot of a classroom of Anglo students.[32] In 2005, California's Pacific Research Institute blasted the California Teachers Association for not embracing Governor Schwarzenegger's attacks on undocumented immigrants. As the institute writer saw it, the Teachers Association could not fairly lay any blame on the governor for the $9.8-billion cut in K–12 education funding in California the last four years without acknowledging the need to control borders to relieve pressure on the educational system.[33] Democrats need to adopt and maintain a plan of compassion toward immigrants and their children, particularly for purposes of educational policy. This entails supporting the Dream Act, as Kerry did in the 2004 election, to enable Latino undocumented immigrant children to attend college at the same cost as resident children. It also means recognizing the value of bilingual education in teaching native Spanish-speaking children the English language, and the role of affirmative action programs in ensuring diverse classrooms in higher education.

A USC professor described concern for education as the one issue that unites the otherwise diverse national group of Latinos.[34] Education should further unite all Americans in a vision for betterment of our country and an expression of our compassion for the underprivileged. Barack Obama struck this chord of the U.S. community at the 2004 Democratic convention when he said:

Alongside our famous individualism, there's another ingredient in the American saga: a belief that we are connected as one people. If there's a child on the South Side of Chicago who can't read, that matters to me, even if it's not my child.... It's that fundamental belief—I am my brother's keeper, I am my sister's keeper—that makes this country work. It's what allows us to pursue our individual dreams, yet still come together as a single American family. "E pluribus unum." Out of many, one.

In addition to compassionate and patriotic reasons, all Americans have an economic stake in repairing the educational system for Latino children—elderly Americans will come to depend on the disproportionately youthful Latino population to finance our social security system, and ensuring their proper education will enhance these revenues.

Among the parallels in their souls, César Chávez and Robert Kennedy both cared passionately about the prospects for future generations, regardless of class.[35] Kennedy spoke often about the value of education in any vision for improving the lives of Americans. For example, in *To Seek a Newer World*, Kennedy argued:

Education is ... the foundation of [economic] progress in the modern world....

Education is also ... a passport to citizenship. As Horace Mann put it, "A human being is not, in any proper sense, a human being until he is educated." Men without education are condemned to live as outsiders—outside political life, outside the twentieth century, foreigners in their own land.[36]

Viva Kennedy campaign materials in 1968 quoted Kennedy's lament over the deficiencies in educating Latinos in U.S. schools: "Look at the world through the eyes of the young ... Mexican American. He goes to a school which teaches little that can help him in an alien world. His chances of graduating from high school are three out of ten. And if he does graduate there is only a fifty-fifty chance that he will have even the equivalent of an eighth grade education. The schools, bluntly, do not teach."[37] Kennedy's concern for youth led him to East Los Angeles in March 1968 to support the organizers of the high school walkouts there on the same trip that took Kennedy to Delano to celebrate the end of Chávez's fast for nonviolence in the grape struggle.

Later, Chávez lashed out against budget cuts in California's public education, calling public schools "the greatest opportunity for upward mobility to Hispanics and to all ethnic minorities in this state." He charged in a 1991 speech that:

In the 1960s and early '70s, another Republican governor—Ronald Reagan—was leading the fight for more support for public education. But there was a big difference. Back then, the majority of public school children were white, and they were from middle- or upper-middle-income families.... But [now] it is *our* children—the children of farm workers and Hispanics and other minorities—who are seeking a better life. It is for them, for their future—and for the future of California—that we must say "no" ... to making *our* children and *their* teachers scapegoats for the budget crisis.[38]

Democrats and their party must embrace a community standard that elevates youth of all backgrounds. Addressing a Mexican American group in 1972, Senator Edward Kennedy reminisced about his brother Robert's unifying vision of bettering the lives of the single American family, which Barack Obama saw too in 2004. As Ted Kennedy recounted:

[Robert Kennedy] walked the streets of the barrio in East Los Angeles, he broke the fast with César Chávez in Delano, and he committed himself to alter the conditions of poverty and discrimination in this country. For he believed, as I do, that this nation can never be completely free nor completely whole until we know that no child cries from hunger in the Rio Grande Valley, until we know that no mother in East Los Angeles fears illness because she cannot afford a doctor, until we know that no man suffers because the law refuses to recognize his humanity. It is not for the [Mexican American] alone that we must seek these goals. It is not for the disadvantaged alone that we seek these goals. It is for America's future.[39]

Conclusion

In the 1960s, the prospects for equality for farm workers, and for Mexican Americans generally, seemed within reach. Many Americans cared about the welfare of farm workers, and Robert Kennedy helped elevate the struggles of César Chávez for equality to the mainstream of U.S. consciousness in the 1960s, when anything seemed possible.

Today, regrettably, the prospects for fair treatment and equal opportunity for farm workers and Mexican Americans are bleak. Justifications for reform have been obscured by the passion and frenzy of the immigration debate, which views farm workers and Mexican Americans as unwelcome guests who are unentitled to economic equality and are straining social service budgets and ripping the cultural fabric. Organizers of farm workers, particularly the UFW, which Chávez helped to establish, are vilified in the mainstream media such as the *Los Angeles Times* as corrupt and undeserving of support. Politicians who work to ensure basic human rights and opportunity for farm workers and Mexican Americans, such as Robert Kennedy's brother, the indefatigable Ted Kennedy, are seen as radical idealists out of touch with national security and cultural preservation imperatives.

But there are signs of hope. The anti-immigrant assault in the mid-1990s, and again after September 11, distanced the U.S. public from farm workers, Mexicans, and Mexican Americans, but drew these targeted groups together. The 2003 Immigrant Workers Freedom Ride across the United States by bus and the protest in the streets of Los Angeles in March 2006 that brought out between 500,000 and 1 million protesters, most of them of Mexican heritage and many of them with roots in the fields, signal a new awakening of a people whose struggle for equality goes forward with renewed purpose. Survivors from different ethnic backgrounds of the struggle captured in this book, such as Dolores Huerta and Ted Kennedy, connect us to the time when we expected more from this great country than a walled fortress and a haven for the wealthy.

Interviewed by David Frost in the heyday of his lifelong activism, César Chávez responded to the question of whether he was an optimist or a pessimist: "I'm an optimist. I have lots of confidence in people."[1] Robert Kennedy's political vision was fueled by the same optimism and faith in the U.S. public and the American dream. There is still time to prove Chávez and Kennedy right.

¡Viva la Causa!

Notes

Notes to the Introduction

1. Sara Rosenbaum and Peter Shin, "Migrant and Seasonal Farmworkers: Health Insurance Coverage and Access to Care," Apr. 2005, Kaiser Commission on Medicaid and the Uninsured, 9 [hereinafter Kaiser Commission Report].
2. Ibid., 10 (statistics from 2000 National Agricultural Workers Survey).

Notes to Chapter 1

1. "The Fight in the Fields: Cesar Chavez and the Farmworkers' Struggle" (Paradigm Productions, 1997) [hereinafter "Fight in the Fields" video].
2. Although Chávez recalls his initial meeting with Robert Kennedy as taking place in 1959 (*Oral History Interview with Cesar Chavez* [Jan. 28, 1970] 3, in Wayne State University, College of Urban, Labor and Metropolitan Affairs, Walter P. Reuther Library [hereinafter Wayne State Library]), one publication (Arthur M. Schlesinger, Jr., *Robert Kennedy and His Times* [New York: Houghton Mifflin Company, 2002], 792) claims they met in 1960.
3. F. Arturo Rosales, *Chicano! The History of the Mexican American Civil Rights Movement* (Houston: Arte Público Press, 1997, 2d ed.), 106.
4. Fred Ross, *Conquering Goliath: Cesar Chavez at the Beginning* (Keene, CA: El Taller Grafico 1989), 4.
5. Richard Santillan, *Chicano Politics: La Raza Unida* (Los Angeles: Tlaquilo Publications, 1973), 9.
6. Rodolfo Acuña, *Occupied America: A History of Chicanos* (New York: HarperCollins, 1988, 3d ed.), 286 (noting 12,000 new voters were registered); Susan Ferriss and Ricardo Sandoval, *The Fight in the Fields: Cesar Chavez and the Farmworkers Movement* (New York: Harcourt Brace, 1997), 42 (15,000 were registered by 1949).
7. Armando B. Rendón, *Chicano Manifesto* (New York: Macmillan Com-pany, 1971), 242.
8. Ferriss and Sandoval, *Fight in the Fields*, 48; charges that undocumented immigrants were voting surfaced again in the anti-immigrant climate of the mid-1990s

and post-9/11, prompting Arizona's Proposition 200, adopted in 2004, that requires proof of citizenship when voting.

9. Acuña, *Occupied America*, 299.

10. Ibid., 319 (noting that during the 1960s the Latino population of San Francisco/Oakland also mushroomed, but comprised mostly Central and South Americans and Puerto Ricans).

11. Ibid., 318 (noting a study that suggested Mexican American voter registration actually declined in Los Angeles in the early 1960s, and attributing the decline to the CSO's loss of its Industrial Area Foundation funding in 1958, and the decline in emphasis in voter registration after the successful 1960 Viva Kennedy campaign).

12. Santillan, *Chicano Politics*, 33.

13. Kim Geron, *Latino Political Power* (Boulder, CO: Lynne Rienner Publishers, 2005), 150.

14. *Oral History*, 2.

15. Ibid., 3.

16. Ignacio M. García, *Viva Kennedy: Mexican Americans in Search of Camelot* (College Station: Texas A&M University Press, 2000), 44.

17. I use the term *Latino* throughout the book even though in the 1960s there was no inclusive mainstream term for Spanish-origin people in the United States, perhaps besides "Spanish" or "Latin people." In the 1970s, the government desire to coin a reference for Census Bureau purposes to encompass Mexican Americans, Cuban Americans, Puerto Ricans, and other Spanish-origin groups led to the adoption of the *Hispanic* label, which has gradually, but in some locations and contexts grudgingly, given way to the term *Latino*.

18. García, *Viva Kennedy*, 48. The Nixon campaign later jumped into the ethnic appeal race by adopting the "Arriba Nixon" slogan. Juan Gómez Quiñones, *Chicano Politics: Reality and Promise 1940–1990* (Albuquerque: University of New Mexico Press, 1990), 90.

19. Ernesto Chávez, *"¡Mi Raza Primero!": Nationalism, Identity, and Insurgency in the Chicano Movement in Los Angeles, 1966–1978* (Berkeley: University of California Press, 2002), 35.

20. Steven W. Bender, *Greasers and Gringos: Latinos, Law, and the American Imagination* (New York: New York University Press, 2003), 120–121.

21. John F. Kennedy, *A Nation of Immigrants* (New York: Harper and Row, 1964, rev. ed.), 18.

22. García, *Viva Kennedy*, 59.

23. Julie Leininger Pycior, *LBJ and Mexican Americans: The Paradox of Power* (Austin: University of Texas Press, 1997), 117.

24. "Little Brother Is Watching," *Time*, Oct. 10, 1960, 23 (crediting the Viva Kennedy clubs for registering these "new Spanish-speaking Democrats," although as discussed below it was the CSO that deserved credit; moreover, the registrations

were nonpartisan, although at the time Mexican Americans overwhelmingly voted for Democrats).

25. *Oral History*, 3.

26. Schlesinger, *Robert Kennedy*, 792; interview with Dolores Huerta, Apr. 9, 2007.

27. Letter from Robert F. Kennedy, *Time*, Nov. 7, 1960, 4. *Time* also published a letter from Herman Gallegos, president of the CSO, who corrected the story with dramatic flair: "As the group that actually did the job which you so generously attribute to [Viva Kennedy clubs], we feel forever justified in … squawking like young robbed eagles. The group which set this alltime registration record is the Community Service Organization. CSO is neither a Viva Kennedy, a Viva Nixon, nor a Viva any other politician outfit. CSO is strictly nonpartisan, and it saves its *vivas* strictly for human dignity, for the rights of oppressed minorities, for their speedy incorporation into all phases of the lifestream of the overall community."

28. Jack Smith, "200,000 Welcome Kennedy in Downtown L.A. Motorcades," *Los Angeles Times*, Nov. 2, 1960, § I, 1, 2.

29. Lou Fleming, "U.S. Must Move Ahead, Kennedy Tells Overflow Crowd of 35,000," *Los Angeles Times*, Nov. 2, 1960, § I, 1, 6.

30. García, *Viva Kennedy*, 106.

31. Ibid., 105.

32. Quiñones, *Chicano Politics*, 91.

33. Ignacio M. García, *Chicanismo: The Forging of a Militant Ethos* (Tucson, AZ: University of Arizona, 1997), 23.

34. Chávez, *Raza Primero*, 35.

35. Ibid., 35–36.

36. García, *Viva Kennedy*, 110.

Notes to Chapter 2

1. *Huelga* is Spanish for "strike."

2. Schlesinger, *Robert Kennedy*, 791.

3. Ferriss and Sandoval, *Fight in the Fields*, 62.

4. Ibid.

5. Peter Matthiessen, *Sal Si Puedes (Escape If You Can): Cesar Chavez and the New American Revolution* (Berkeley: University of California Press, 2000), 53.

6. Ferriss and Sandoval, *Fight in the Fields*, 97.

7. Ibid., 97–98.

8. Acuña, *Occupied America*, 325.

9. Susan Samuels Drake, "Dolores Huerta," *The Progressive*, Sept. 2000, 34–38.

10. Ferriss and Sandoval, *Fight in the Fields*, 65.

11. Richard Griswold del Castillo and Richard A. Garcia, *Cesar Chavez: A Triumph of Spirit* (Norman: University of Oklahoma Press, 1995).

12. Ferriss and Sandoval, *Fight in the Fields*, 67; see also Rosales, *Chicano!*, 134 (noting the NFWA collected some 80,000 registration cards from potential union members).

13. Acuña, *Occupied America*, 325.

14. Ferriss and Sandoval, *Fight in the Fields*, 98.

15. Rosales, *Chicano!*, 137.

16. Ferriss and Sandoval, *Fight in the Fields*, 92.

17. Quiñones, *Chicano Politics*, 97.

18. Pycior, *LBJ and Mexican Americans*, 150 (noting that 15,000 people attended an East Los Angeles rally with Mexican comedian Cantínflas and Viva Johnson speakers).

19. Ibid., 151.

20. Ibid., 150.

21. Rendón, *Chicano Manifesto*, 119.

22. Pycior, *LBJ and Mexican Americans*, 151.

23. See infra chapter 7 (also discussing the NLRA protections for employers against secondary boycotts, and how Chávez, once his union began using secondary boycott tactics, altered his lobbying effort to seek inclusion of agricultural workers in the union organizing protections for other workers, but without the employer protection against secondary boycotts).

24. See chapter 7 infra.

25. Ferriss and Sandoval, *Fight in the Fields*, 28–29.

26. Ronald B. Taylor, *Chavez and the Farm Workers* (Boston: Beacon Press, 1975), 11–12.

27. Ann McGregor, Cindy Wathen, and George Elfie Ballis, eds., *Remembering Cesar: The Legacy of Cesar Chavez* (Sanger, CA: Quill Driver Books, 2000), 88 (essay by Paul Schrade).

28. Jean Stein, *American Journey: The Times of Robert Kennedy* (New York: Harcourt Brace Jovanovich, 1970), 280.

29. Amending Migratory Labor Laws, Hearings before the Subcommittee on Migratory Labor of the Committee on Labor and Public Welfare (Washington, DC: U.S. Government Printing Office, 1966), 279.

30. Ibid.

31. Ray Christiansen, "Senators in the Field, A Look at Cal. Migrants," *San Francisco Examiner,* Mar. 13, 1966, § I, 22.

32. See Dick Meister, "Senate Probe of State Farm Labor," *San Francisco Chronicle,* Mar. 14, 1966, 52. Later, during Nixon's presidency, George Murphy introduced union-busting legislation that, although never enacted, "would have outlawed the boycott,

made it illegal to strike at any time a grower could be hurt and put farm labor relations under a presidential board." Dick Meister and Anne Loftis, *A Long Time Coming: The Struggle to Unionize America's Farm Workers* (New York: Macmillan, 1977), 156.

33. Amending Migratory Labor Laws, 361–362.

34. Amending Migratory Labor Laws, 362; Dick Meister, "Brown, Unionists Back U.S. Farm Labor Bills," *San Francisco Chronicle*, Mar. 15, 1966, 2.

35. Taylor, *Chavez*, 159.

36. Meister, "Brown, Unionists Back."

37. Ibid.

38. Ibid.

39. Taylor, *Chavez*, 159–160.

40. Amending Migratory Labor Laws, 336 (statement of Jack Miller, Citrus Industries of California and Arizona).

41. Harry Bernstein, "2 Senators Term Farm Housing in Tulare 'Shameful,'" *Los Angeles Times*, Mar. 16, 1966, § I, 3.

42. Ibid.

43. Peter Edelman, *Searching for America's Heart: RFK and the Renewal of Hope* (New York: Houghton Mifflin, 2001), 45.

44. Pycior, *LBJ and Mexican Americans*, 219.

45. Schlesinger, *Robert Kennedy*, 792.

46. Amending Migratory Labor Laws, 597.

47. Ibid., 363.

48. Although Peter Edelman recalls this confrontation as taking place in Visalia (Edelman, *Searching for America's Heart*, 44–46), the published transcript of the Senate hearings and a considerable number of other sources confirm it took place the following day in Delano, where the sheriff worked. Edelman's account of the initial parking lot conversation between Kennedy and Chávez (ibid., 45) while on break from the hearings likely did take place in Visalia as he specifies, rather than in Delano, as the two men toured and spoke together the next morning in Delano before the hearing began.

49. Ferriss and Sandoval, *Fight in the Fields*, 106; Bender, *Greasers and Gringos*, 200–201 (explaining that the Supreme Court in 1974 held that this essay was not actionable defamation against strikebreakers; see *Old Dominion Branch No. 496, National Association of Letter Carriers, AFL-CIO v. Austin*, 418 U.S. 264 [1974]).

50. Ferriss and Sandoval, *Fight in the Fields*, 105.

51. See generally W.J. Rorabaugh, *Berkeley at War: The 1960s* (New York: Oxford University Press, 1989).

52. Ferriss and Sandoval, *Fight in the Fields*, 107.

53. Ibid., 106.

54. Amending Migratory Labor Laws, 369.

55. Ibid.

56. Edwin O. Guthman and C. Richard Allen, *RFK: Collected Speeches* (New York: Viking, 1993), 198.

57. Amending Migratory Labor Laws, 629.

58. Later, in January 1968, Dolores Huerta and other farm union members went to New York to further the grape boycott. While picketing a produce market there, several union members were arrested for disorderly conduct. Interviewed after Kennedy's death, Dolores Huerta recalled that they went to see Kennedy on that trip at the Puerto Rican Commonwealth building in New York City. Dolores reported on the arrests, and Kennedy replied "Every time I see you, you have people in jail! They're either in jail in California, they're in San Francisco, or Texas." Dolores replied, "Well, now they're in jail in New York" (Stein, *American Journey*, 284). Dolores remembers that Kennedy dispatched his lawyers and the workers were released. Interview with Dolores Huerta, Apr. 9, 2007.

59. Amending Migratory Labor Laws, 629–630.

60. Ibid., 630.

61. Ibid.; see also Dick Meister, "Catholic Bishops Back Farm Unions," *San Francisco Chronicle*, Mar. 17, 1966, 1; C. David Heymann, *RFK: A Candid Biography of Robert F. Kennedy* (New York: Dutton, 1998), 411 (recollection of Senator Murphy that he said this to the sheriff facetiously).

62. "Fight in the Fields" video.

63. *Oral History*, 5.

64. Ibid.; Edleman, *Searching for America's Heart*, 46.

65. Rosales, *Chicano!*, 139.

66. Ferriss and Sandoval, *Fight in the Fields*, 117.

67. Sam Kushner, *Long Road to Delano* (New York: International Publishers Co., 1975), 164.

68. Matthiessen, *Sal Si Puedes*, 193–194.

69. Ferriss and Sandoval, *Fight in the Fields*, 117.

70. Letter from M.E. Headrick to Robert F. Kennedy, undated, JFK Library, RFK Collection, Labor-Migrant file.

71. Letter from R.B. Stiger to Senator Edward [sic] Kennedy, Mar. 21, 1966, JFK Library, RFK Collection, Labor-Migrant file (letter mistakenly addressed to Edward rather than to Robert).

72. Letter from César Estrada Chávez to Robert Kennedy, Mar. 25, 1966, JFK Library, RFK Collection, Labor-Migrant file.

73. Rosales, *Chicano!*, 144 ("Millions of people watched news reports of the hearings on national television, which both Kennedy and the union used as a forum to denounce the deplorable conditions of farm work").

74. Evan Thomas, *Robert Kennedy: His Life* (New York: Touchstone, 2000), 320; McGregor, Wathen, and Ballis, *Remembering Cesar*, 88.

75. Ellis E. Conklin and Cesar Chavez, "You Can't Struggle if You're Filled with Bitterness; You Got to Love the Fight," United Press International, Dec. 3, 1985.

76. Brian Dooley, *Robert Kennedy: The Final Years* (New York: St. Martin's Press, 1996), 16.

77. Alan C. Miller, "FBI Spied on Cesar Chavez for Years, Files Reveal," *Los Angeles Times*, May 30, 1995.

78. Carlos Larralde, *Mexican American Movements and Leaders* (Los Alamitos, CA: Hwong Publishing, 1976), 214, 216.

79. Thomas A. Hopkins, ed., *Rights for Americans: The Speeches of Robert F. Kennedy* (Indianapolis: Bobbs-Merrill, 1964), 19 (speech delivered May 6, 1961, at University of Georgia Law School).

80. Ibid., 47–48 (speech delivered Dec. 3, 1961, to National Conference of Christians and Jews Dinner, Cleveland).

81. Matthiessen, *Sal Si Puedes*, 194.

82. *Oral History*, 7.

83. Letter from Michael J. Miranda to Robert F. Kennedy, undated, JFK Library, RFK Collection, Labor-Migrant file.

84. Letter from Robert F. Kennedy to Michael J. Miranda, June 22, 1966, JFK Library, RFK Collection, Labor-Migrant file.

85. Harry Bernstein, "Big Changes Loom in Farm Labor Economy," *Los Angeles Times*, Mar. 21, 1966, § II, 1.

86. Fair Labor Standards Amendments of 1966, Pub. L. No. 89-601 (the law also included prohibitions against oppressive child labor on farms). California had established a minimum wage for farm workers in 1963.

87. Note, "Commuters, Illegals and American Farmworkers: The Need for a Broader Approach to Domestic Farm Labor Problems," 48 *New York University Law Review* (1973): 439.

88. Bernstein, "Big Changes."

89. Ibid.

90. Douglas Ross, *Robert F. Kennedy: Apostle of Change* (New York: Trident Press, 1968), 290 (Speech, U.S. Senate, June 28, 1966).

91. Letter from César E. Chávez to Senator Robert F. Kennedy, Jan. 12, 1968, Wayne State Library, UFW Office of the President, Box 39, Folder 6.

92. Letter from Robert F. Kennedy to César E. Chávez, Feb. 27, 1968, JFK Library, RFK Collection, Unions file.

93. Telegram from César Chávez to Senator Robert Kennedy, Apr. 21, 1966, JFK Library, RFK Collection, LAB-migrant file.

94. Letter from Robert F. Kennedy to César Chávez, May 6, 1966, Wayne State Library, NFWOC Collection, Box 1, Folder 12.

95. Ferriss and Sandoval, *Fight in the Fields*, 126.

96. Letter from Robert F. Kennedy to César Chávez, Aug. 16, 1966, Wayne State Library, NFWOC, Box 1, Folder 18.

97. JFK Library, RFK Collection.

98. Ferriss and Sandoval, *Fight in the Fields*, 129–133.

99. Frederick John Dalton, *The Moral Vision of César Chávez* (Maryknoll, NY: Orbis, 2003), 16–17.

100. Arlene Schulman, *Robert F. Kennedy: Promise for the Future* (New York: Facts on File, 1997), 32.

101. Robert F. Kennedy, *The Enemy Within* (New York: Harper and Row, 1960), 212.

102. Thomas, *Robert Kennedy*, between pages 160 and 161, illustration captions.

103. Kennedy, *The Enemy Within*, 162.

104. Ibid., 104, 118.

105. Ronald Goldfarb, *Perfect Villains, Imperfect Heroes: Robert F. Kennedy's War against Organized Crime* (Sterling, VA: Capital Books, 1995), 188.

106. Interview with Richard Chávez, Apr. 9, 2007.

107. Acuña, *Occupied America*, 326.

108. Heymann, *RFK*, 225.

109. Robert F. Kennedy, *Just Friends and Brave Enemies* (New York: Harper and Row, 1962), 84.

110. Letter from Jerome Cohen [attorney for UFWOC] to Senator Robert Kennedy, Oct. 21, 1967, JFK Library, RFK Collection.

111. Letter from Paul A. Pumpian, director of legislative and governmental services, FDA, to Robert F. Kennedy, Nov. 6, 1967, JFK Library, RFK Collection.

112. Letter from César E. Chávez to Senator Robert Kennedy, May 17, 1967, Wayne State Library, UFW Office of the President, Box 5, Folder 2. In his oral history transcript recorded in 1970 (see *Oral History*, 8), Chávez initially recalled the date of the fundraiser correctly as 1967, but in discussions with his brother Richard he corrected his oral recollection to situate the fundraiser as occurring in fall 1966, which seems inconsistent with the date of this letter. Chávez also wrote Kennedy in July of 1967 extolling the virtues of the California Rural Legal Assistance organization, a federal government–funded OEO program. Letter from César E. Chávez to Senator Robert Kennedy, July 22, 1967, Wayne State Library, UFW Office of the President, Box 39, Folder 6.

113. Edelman, *Searching for America's Heart*, 46.

114. John Gregory Dunne, *Delano* (New York: Farrar, Straus, and Giroux, 1971), 182.

Notes to Chapter 3

1. Dalton, *Moral Vision*, 130.

2. John C. Hammerback and Richard J. Jensen, *The Rhetorical Career of César Chávez* (College Station: Texas A&M University Press, 1998), 74.

3. Ferriss and Sandoval, *Fight in the Fields*, 131.

5. Ibid., 144.

6. Jacques E. Levy, *Cesar Chavez: Autobiography of La Causa* (New York: W.W. Norton, 1975), 286. Although not as well known, a later fast by Chávez in the summer of 1988 protesting pesticides in grapes lasted thirty-six days.

7. Dalton, *Moral Vision*, 131.

8. Luís D. León, "César Chávez and Mexican American Civil Religion," in Gastón Espinosa, Virgilio Elizondo, and Jesse Miranda, eds., *Latino Religions and Civic Activism in the United States* (New York: Oxford University Press, 2005), 58.

9. Ferriss and Sandoval, *Fight in the Fields*, 143 (remarks of Leroy Chatfield).

10. Ralph de Toledano, *Little Cesar* (Washington, DC: Anthem Books, 1971), 71 (suggesting that his wife, brother or guards were picking up strawberry milk shakes and grilled sandwiches at local restaurants for him during the fast).

11. "Chavez Ends Symbolic 25-Day Fast," *San Francisco Chronicle*, Mar. 11, 1968, 1.

12. Dalton, *Moral Vision*, 133.

13. Joseph A. Palermo, *In His Own Right: The Political Odyssey of Senator Robert F. Kennedy* (New York: Columbia University Press, 2001), 225.

14. Levy, *Cesar Chavez*, 284.

15. Letter from Robert F. Kennedy to César E. Chávez, Feb. 27, 1968, JFK Library, RFK Collection, Union file.

16. "Chavez to End 25-Day Fast at Meeting Today," *Los Angeles Times*, Mar. 10, 1968, A3; see also Jean Maddern Pitrone, *Chavez: Man of the Migrants* (Staten Island, NY: Alba House, 1971), 121.

17. Stein, *American Journey*, 281.

18. Edwin Guthman, *We Band of Brothers* (New York: Harper and Row, 1971), 325.

19. David Larsen, "Chavez Breaks Fast at Mass Attended by Kennedy, 6000," *Los Angeles Times*, Mar. 11, 1968, 1.

20. Guthman and Allen, *RFK*, 204.

21. Stein, *American Journey*, 282.

22. A Day at Delano: A Moving Tribute to the Character of Cesar Chavez, recording of events of Mar. 10, 1967 (1974) [hereinafter Day at Delano].

23. Matthiessen, *Sal Si Puedes*, 195.

24. Larsen, "Chavez Breaks Fast."

25. Stein, *American Journey*, 283.

26. Dolores Huerta had helped write the statement with Chávez the night before. Interview with Dolores Huerta, Apr. 9, 2007.

27. Day at Delano.

28. Richard J. Jensen and John C. Hammerback, eds., *The Words of César Chávez* (College Station: Texas A&M University Press, 2002), 166.

29. Day at Delano.

30. Wayne State Library, UFW Information and Research, Box 5, Folder 29 (slight alterations from this written text in the main text above reflect the audio version of the events from Day at Delano, in three instances: the added word "many" before allies, the omission of "to" in "God help us to be men," and the phrasing in the oral version of "our lives are all that we really have" by contrast to the written version of "our lives are all that really belong to us").

31. The written version of Kennedy's remarks, on file with the JFK Library, Statement of Senator Robert F. Kennedy, Mar. 10, 1968, Delano, CA, follows; the remarks in the main text above duplicate the audiotape of the event recorded in Day at Delano.

> This is a historic occasion. We have come here out of respect for one of the heroic figures of our time—Cesar Chavez. But I also come here to congratulate all of you, you who are locked with Cesar in the struggle for justice for the farm worker, and the struggle for justice for the Spanish-speaking American....
>
> The world must know, from this time forward, that the migrant farm worker, the Mexican American, is coming into his own rights. You are winning a special kind of citizenship: no one is doing it for you—you are winning it yourselves—and therefore no one can ever take it away.
>
> And when your children and grandchildren take their place in America—going to high school, and college, and taking good jobs at good pay—when you look at them, you will say, "I did this. I was there, at the point of difficulty and danger." And though you may be old and bent from many years of labor, no man will stand taller than you when you say, "I marched with Cesar."
>
> But the struggle is far from over. And now, as you are at midpoint in your most difficult organizing effort, there are suddenly those who question the principle that underlies everything you have done so far: the principle of nonviolence. There are those who think violence is some shortcut to victory.
>
> Let me say that violence is no answer.... It takes far greater commitment, far more courage to say "we will do what must be done through an organization of the people, through patient, careful building of a democratic organization." That road is far more difficult than lighting a match or firing a weapon.... So we come here, you and I, in a great pilgrimage to demonstrate our commitment to nonviolence, to democracy itself.
>
> [I]f you come here today from such great distance and at such great sacrifice to demonstrate your commitment to nonviolence, we in Government must match your commitment. That is our responsibility.
>
> We must have a Federal law which gives farm workers the right to engage in collective bargaining—and have it this year.
>
> We must have more adequate regulation of green-card workers, to prevent their use as strikebreakers—and we must have that this year.

We must have equal protection of the laws. Those are the words of the Four-teenth Amendment to the Constitution of the United States. The California Labor Code, the Federal Immigration Laws, the Federal Labor Department Regulations—these are laws which are supposed to protect you. They must be enforced. From now on.

So I come here today to honor a great man, Cesar Chavez. I come here today to honor you for the long and patient commitment you have made to this great struggle for justice. And I come here to say that we will fight together to achieve for you the aspirations of every American: decent wages, decent housing, decent schooling, a chance for yourselves and your children. You stand for justice and I am proud to stand with you.

Viva la Causa.

See also "Chavez Ends Symbolic 25-Day Fast," *San Francisco Chronicle*, Mar. 11, 1968, 1; Jan Young, *The Migrant Workers and Cesar Chavez* (New York: Julian Messner, 1972), 152. Dolores Huerta, who translated Kennedy's remarks into Spanish for the crowd that day, remembers that Kennedy "totally went off script. What he had written was not what he said." Interview with Dolores Huerta, Apr. 9, 2007.

32. Day at Delano; see also Lester David and Irene David, *Bobby Kennedy: The Making of a Folk Hero* (New York: Dodd, Mead and Company, 1986), 294. Kennedy's Senate aide, Peter Edelman, who accompanied Kennedy on the trip, prepared some Spanish-language words and phrases in phonetics for Kennedy on the back of an en-velope, such as the rallying phrase *Si Se Puede*. Interview with Peter Edelman, Jan. 8, 2006. Kennedy relied on these words in his speech on the platform truck, peppering his speech with poorly pronounced but sincere Spanish.

33. *Oral History*, 20.

34. Stein, *American Journey*, 283.

35. Guthman and Allen, *RFK*, 206.

36. Letter from Vera [unintelligible] to Senator Robert Kennedy, Mar. 1968, JFK Library, RFK Collection, LAB-Migrant file.

37. Letter from S.S. Anderson to Senator Robert Kennedy, Mar. 13, 1968, JFK Library, RFK Collection, LAB-Migrant file.

38. Letter from H.T. Lebrenz to Mr. Kennedy, Mar. 12, 1968, JFK Library, RFK Collection, LAB-Migrant file.

39. Letter from Senator Robert Kennedy to H.T. Lebrenz, Mar. 22, 1968, JFK Library, RFK Collection, LAB-Unions file.

Notes to Chapter 4

1. *Oral History*, 16.

2. Interview with Richard Chávez, Apr. 9, 2007.

3. Ferriss and Sandoval, *Fight in the Fields*, 145.

4. Cesar Chavez, "Cesar Chavez," in *That Shining Hour*, Patricia Kennedy Lawford, ed. (New York: Halliday Lithograph Corp., 1969), 121–122.

5. Levy, *Cesar Chavez*, 287.

6. Thomas, *Robert Kennedy*, 359. Kennedy's Senate aide, Peter Edelman, recalls that Kennedy declared his intention to run for president as early as the flight into Delano. Interview with Peter Edelman, Jan. 8, 2006.

7. Guthman and Allen, *RFK*, 320. Another transcript of the speech omits the line quoted above of "The Report of the Riot Commission has been largely ignored."

8. McGregor, Wathen, and Ballis, *Remembering Cesar*, 89.

9. *Oral History*, 30–31.

10. "Kennedy Chooses Chavez," *El Malcriado*, v. 2, no. 3, Apr. 1, 1968.

11. Levy, *Cesar Chavez*, 289.

12. "Kennedy Chooses Chavez."

13. Levy, *Cesar Chavez*, 288.

14. *Oral History*, 23.

15. As Chávez recalled, "we're dealing with a subject that I had been working on for many years. So I knew the state and what to do. So we had a beautiful campaign." *Oral History*, 23.

16. "Fight in the Fields" video.

17. Levy, *Cesar Chavez*, 289.

18. *Oral History*, 22.

19. Schlesinger, *Robert Kennedy*, 908.

20. *Oral History*, 22.

21. Ibid.

22. Wayne State Library, UFW Office of the President, Box 49, Folder 8.

23. *Oral History*, 34.

24. Wayne State Library, UFW Office of the President, Box 49, Folder 8.

25. *Oral History*, 17.

26. Ibid., 25.

27. Ibid., 44.

28. Ibid., 31 (also noting that the union got some campaign money from Kennedy).

29. Wayne State, *El Malcriado* file, vol. 2, Feb. 1968 to Feb. 1969. Radio spots featured such bilingual commentary from Chávez as "The election of Robert Kennedy would be a great help on our long way in the fight by the poor. Robert Kennedy is our friend. He helps in our fight for better wages, better lives, and for the dignity of all." JFK Library, Robert F. Kennedy 1968 Presidential Campaign, Media Division file, TV and Radio Ads Transcripts, Mexican Americans.

30. Wayne State Library, UFW Office of the President, Box 48, Folder 14, Viva Kennedy brochure.

31. Ibid.

32. Pycior, *LBJ and Mexican Americans*, 219.

33. Ibid., 220.

34. Ibid., 220.

35. Ibid., 219.

36. Ibid., 220.

37. Norman MacAfee, ed., *The Gospel According to RFK: Why It Matters Now* (Boulder, CO: Westview Press, 2004), 91, 96.

38. Jules Witcover, *The Year the Dream Died: Revisiting 1968 in America* (New York: Warner Books, 1997), 233–234.

39. JFK Library, Remarks of Senator Robert F. Kennedy, Olvera Street, Los Angeles, California, Mar. 24, 1968.

40. MacAfee, *Gospel According to RFK*, 65–66.

41. Jack Newfield, *Robert F. Kennedy: A Memoir* (New York: Berkley Publishing Corp., 1969), 262 [1978 edition].

42. Daryl E. Lembke, "Kennedy Campaigns on Caboose through San Joaquin Valley," *Los Angeles Times*, May 31, 1968, 3.

43. Jules Witcover, *85 Days: The Last Campaign of Robert Kennedy* (New York: G.P. Putnam's Sons, 1969), 206; Pycior, *LBJ and Mexican Americans*, 224.

44. Jack Smith, "L.A. Youth Gets Kennedy's 'Running Shoes,'" *Los Angeles Times*, May 22, 1968.

45. Ronald Steel, *In Love with Night: The American Romance with Robert Kennedy* (New York: Simon and Schuster, 2000), 173; Palermo, *In His Own Right*, 232.

46. Levy, *Cesar Chavez*, 289.

47. "The Triumph and the Tragedy," *El Malcriado*, June 15, 1968, 4.

48. Newfield, *Robert F. Kennedy*, 320.

49. Levy, *Cesar Chavez*, 289.

Notes to Chapter 5

1. Del Castillo and Garcia, *Triumph of Spirit*, 88.

2. Newfield, *Robert F. Kennedy*, 320.

3. Del Castillo and Garcia, *Triumph of Spirit*, 88.

4. "Triumph and the Tragedy."

5. Newfield, *Robert F. Kennedy*, 301.

6. Witcover, *85 Days*, 229.

7. Ibid., 255.

8. Stein, *American Journey*, 333–334.

9. *Oral History*, 32.

10. Newfield, *Robert F. Kennedy*, 320.

11. Ibid., 329.

12. Levy, *Cesar Chavez*, 290.
13. *Oral History*, 26.
14. Stein, *American Journey*, 334.
15. Guthman and Allen, *RFK*, 401–402.
16. Michael Knox Beran, *The Last Patrician: Bobby Kennedy and the End of American Aristocracy* (New York: St. Martin's Griffin, 1998), 206.
17. "Triumph and the Tragedy."
18. Warren Rogers, *When I Think of Bobby: A Personal Memoir of the Kennedy Years* (New York: HarperCollins, 1993), 158; Ray Rogers and Jack Jones, "Disbelief, Sorrow Sweep Negro, Latin Areas at News of Tragedy," *Los Angeles Times*, June 6, 1968, § II, 1 (quoting a Mexican American resident as saying "I think there were a lot of prayers heard in East Los Angeles last night. Everyone was praying to God that it was not a Mexican who shot him").
19. Witcover, *85 Days*, 270–271.
20. William Vanden Heuvel and Milton Gwirtzman, *On His Own: Robert F. Kennedy, 1964–1968* (Garden City, NY: Doubleday, 1970), 379–380.
21. Pycior, *LBJ and Mexican Americans*, 225.
22. Levy, *Cesar Chavez*, 289.
23. *Oral History*, 37 ("[They] explained to me and diagrammed where the bullet was and what they knew about it. They knew that it was difficult to pull [the bullet] out. So we sort of were prepared for it").
24. "Triumph and the Tragedy."
25. Rogers and Jones, "Disbelief."
26. Levy, *Cesar Chavez*, 290.
27. Chávez and other guests were summoned by telegram inviting the guests "to attend a requiem mass in memory of Robert Francis Kennedy," and stating that a funeral train would travel to Washington for the interment at Arlington Cemetery. Wayne State Library, UFW Office of the President, Box 30, Folder 13.
28. Witcover, *85 Days*, 304. Kennedy's body was transported to the mass by a hearse with Ethel and Ted Kennedy in the front seat. As the hearse passed Spanish Harlem, hundreds of Puerto Rican onlookers shouted "Viva!" Charles Kaiser, *1968 in America: Music, Politics, Chaos, Counterculture, and the Shaping of a Generation* (New York: Weidenfeld and Nicolson, 1988), 185. Dolores Huerta rode the funeral train but recalls that Chávez was not on the train (interview with Dolores Huerta, Apr. 9, 2007).
29. Stein, *American Journey*, 29.

Notes to Chapter 6

1. Mike Dorman, "Friends, Relatives Celebrate RFK," *Newsday*, May 23, 1993.

2. Oscar Zeta Acosta, *The Revolt of the Cockroach People* (New York: Vintage Books, 1973), 64 (my regrets for removing the expletive from Acosta's observation). Acosta, a criminal defense lawyer, fashioned constitutional arguments in the late 1960s challenging the grand juror selection process in Los Angeles County as discriminatory to Mexican Americans. Ironically the defense team for Sirhan Sirhan, Robert Kennedy's assassin, took Acosta's lead in raising similar challenges. Rendón, *Chicano Manifesto*, 227.

3. Antonio Orendain, "Our Friend, May He Rest in Peace," *El Malcriado,* June 15, 1968.

4. Pycior, *LBJ and Mexican Americans*, 232.

5. *Oral History*, 38.

6. McGregor, Wathen, and Ballis, *Remembering Cesar,* 88 (recollections of Paul Schrade).

7. Pycior, *LBJ and Mexican Americans*, 231.

8. Letter from Hubert H. Humphrey to César Chávez, Aug. 1, 1968, Wayne State Library, UFW Office of the President, Box 30, Folder 13.

9. Pycior, *LBJ and Mexican Americans*, 232.

10. Mark Kurlansky, *1968: The Year That Rocked the World* (New York: Ballantine Books, 2004), 361; Jeremy D. Mayer, *Running on Race: Racial Politics in Presidential Campaigns, 1960–2000* (New York, Random House, 2002), 83–89.

11. Mark Day, *Forty Acres: Cesar Chavez and the Farm Workers* (New York: Praeger Publishers, 1971), 89.

12. Pycior, *LBJ and Mexican Americans*, 232.

13. Wayne State Library, UFW Office of the President, Box 48, Folder 12.

14. Letter from James L. Drake, National Boycott Coordinator, UFWOC, to Richard Nixon, Sept. 7, 1968, Wayne State Library, UFW Office of the President, Box 46, Folder 14.

15. Taylor, *Chavez*, 236.

16. Pycior, *LBJ and Mexican Americans*, 232.

17. John P. Schmal, "Electing the President: The Latino Electorate (1960–2000)," Apr. 17, 2004, www.hispanicvista.com (cited May 10, 2005).

18. Mayer, *Running on Race,* 94 (observing that after this election Republicans would never reach out to the black vote in national elections, but never lose the white vote to Democrats).

19. Schmal, "Electing the President."

20. Quiñones, *Chicano Politics,* 157 (a rate more than one-sixth less than in 1960); Mark R. Levy and Michael S. Kramer, "Patterns of Chicano Voting Behavior," in F. Chris Garcia, ed., *La Causa Politica: A Chicano Politics Reader* (Notre Dame, IN: University of Notre Dame Press, 1974), 242 (observing that in Chicano precincts in Arizona, there were one-third fewer votes than were cast in 1960, with a similar drop-off in parts of Colorado).

21. Levy, *Cesar Chavez*, 290.

22. Ibid.

23. *Oral History*, 38.

24. Hammerback and Jensen, *Rhetorical Career*, 74.

25. Maurilio Vigil, *Chicano Politics* (Washington, DC: University Press of America, 1977), iv.

26. Letter from César E. Chávez to Senator Edward Kennedy, June 24, 1968, Wayne State Library, UFW Office of the President, Box 5, Folder 2.

27. Letter from Edward M. Kennedy to César Chávez, Sept. 16, 1968, Wayne State Library, UFW Office of the President, Box 39, Folder 7.

28. Nan Robertson, "New Fund Honors Robert F. Kennedy," *New York Times*, Oct. 30, 1968.

29. Del Castillo and Garcia, *Triumph of Spirit*, 89.

30. Letter from Pat Kennedy Lawford to César Chávez, Nov. 18, 1968, in Wayne State Library, UFW Office of the President, Box 39, Folder 11.

31. Letter from César E. Chávez to Pat Kennedy Lawford, Mar. 30, 1969, in Wayne State Library, UFW Office of the President, Box 39, Folder 11.

Notes to Chapter 7

1. Cindy Wathen, ed., *Remembering Cesar: The Legacy of Cesar Chavez* (Clovis, CA: Quill Driver Books, 2000), 1.

2. "Fight in the Fields" video.

3. Interview with Richard Chávez, Apr. 9, 2007.

4. Jensen and Hammerback, *Words of César Chávez*, 123.

5. Note, "Commuters, Illegals and American Farmworkers: The Need for a Broader Approach to Domestic Farm Labor Problems," 48 *New York University Law Review* (1973): 439, 455. Farm workers had also been excluded from the Social Security Act of 1935.

6. The farm workers union had undertaken secondary boycotting earlier in less comprehensive campaigns—for example, the boycott of stores selling Perelli-Minetti-label wine in 1966 and 1967. See Ferriss and Sandoval, *Fight in the Fields*, 133, 136.

7. Ibid., 456 (quoting *New York Times*, Mar. 26, 1972, 25).

8. Patrick H. Mooney and Theo J. Majka, *Farmers' and Farmworkers' Movements: Social Protest in American Agriculture* (New York: Twayne Publishers, 1995), 162.

9. Meister and Loftis, *Long Time Coming*, 159; in testimony before a Senate subcommittee in April 1969, Chávez concluded with: "The relief we seek from Congress today, however, is neither new nor very revolutionary. It has proved beneficial to the nation in the past when unions were weak and industry strong. We need and favor NLRA amendments along the lines of the original Wagner Act, but we oppose for this period in history the [secondary boycott and other]

restrictions of Taft-Hartley and Landrum-Griffin" (Jensen and Hammerback, *Words of César Chávez*, 45).

10. Ferriss and Sandoval, *Fight in the Fields*, 138.

11. Day, *Forty Acres*, 89.

12. Mooney and Majka, *Farmers' and Farmworkers'*, 162–163.

13. Ibid., 163.

14. Mooney and Majka, *Farmers' and Farmworkers'*, 163.

15. Ferriss and Sandoval, *Fight in the Fields*, 181.

16. Meister and Loftis, *Long Time Coming*, 178.

17. Ferriss and Sandoval, *Fight in the Fields*, 197. The U.S. Supreme Court spoke to the Arizona law in reversing a federal district court decision that had invalidated the act as unconstitutional. See *Babbitt v. United Farm Workers National Union*, 442 U.S. 289 (1979) (concluding that the district court should have abstained from deciding constitutional questions until material unresolved questions of state law were determined by the Arizona state courts).

18. Mooney and Majka, *Farmers' and Farmworkers'*, 168 (reporting that although the UFW gathered sufficient signatures on the recall petition, the certification process was delayed until the 1974 state election was too near to schedule a recall election). Still, the UFW petition drive helped register many Latino voters and in the 1974 election Latino Raul Castro was elected governor of Arizona, serving from 1975 to 1977.

19. Tony Castro, *Chicano Power: The Emergence of Mexican America* (New York: Saturday Review Press, 1974), 91; see also Jensen and Hammerback, *Words of César Chávez*, 159 (reporting attendance at the mass as about a thousand farm workers and other supporters).

20. *Safeway Stores, Inc. v. United Farm Workers Union*, 1973 WL 17000 (Ariz. Super. Ct., 1973).

21. Harold C. White and William Gibney, "The Arizona Farm Labor Law: A Supreme Court Test," 31 *Labor Law Journal* (1980): 87, 90.

22. Lucinda Carol Pocan, "California's Attempt to End Farmworker Voicelessness: A Survey of the Agricultural Relations Act of 1975," 7 *Pacific Law Journal* (1976): 197, 225–226. A conflict soon arose between the more restrictive Arizona provisions and the California Act, which an Arizona appellate court resolved by holding that the Arizona law prohibition of secondary boycotts could not be applied to conduct of the UFW occurring in California and legal there. *Bruce Church, Inc. v. United Farm Workers of America, AFL-CIO*, 169 Ariz. 22, 816 P.2d 919 (Ct. App. 1991).

23. White and Gibney, "Arizona Farm Labor Law," 91.

24. Refugio I. Rochin, "New Perspectives on Agricultural Relations in California," 28 *Labor Law Journal* (1977): 395, 398.

25. White and Gibney, "Arizona Farm Labor Law," 92.

26. Rochin, "New Perspectives," 400 (attributing the settlement to the election victories of the UFW in the wake of the California Act).

27. Ferriss and Sandoval, *Fight in the Fields*, 173.

28. Levy, *Cesar Chavez*, 431.

29. "Fight in the Fields" video. Ethel Kennedy remarked that she was "struck by his spirituality, and his reserves of gentleness and tenderness and caring and love. He was amazing." She observed about her visit that Chávez "was in a padded cell ... like he was a lunatic or a criminal."

30. Levy, *Cesar Chavez*, 432.

31. *United Farm Workers Organizing Committee, AFL-CIO v. Superior Court of Monterey County*, 4 Cal. 3d 556, 483 P.2d 1215, 94 Cal. Rptr. 263 (1971) (holding that the preliminary injunction that effectively prohibited UFWOC from informing the public of its dispute with the grower was overly broad in violation of the First Amendment).

32. Louis Sahagun, "3 of Robert Kennedy's Children Visit Chavez to Support Protest," *Los Angeles Times*, Aug. 5, 1988.

33. Ferriss and Sandoval, *Fight in the Fields*, 246; Consuelo Rodríguez, *César Chávez* (New York: Chelsea House Publishers, 1991).

34. *Bruce Church, Inc. v. United Farm Workers of America, AFL-CIO*, 169 Ariz. 22, 816 P.2d 919 (Ct. App. 1991).

35. The judge recessed the new trial for two weeks so that union officials could attend Chávez's funeral. The new trial resulted in a jury verdict of $2.9 million, but the UFW reached a labor agreement in 1996 in which the grower dropped the lawsuit.

36. Ferriss and Sandoval, *Fight in the Fields*, 261.

37. "Thousands Join Chavez Memorial March," United Press International, Apr. 29, 1993.

38. See Mark M. Hager, "Farm Workers, Boycotts, and Free Speech," 42 *Labor Law Journal* (1991): 792.

39. See discussion in chapter 11.

40. Beatriz Johnston Hernandez, "Cesar's Ghost," *California Lawyer* (July 1993): 48, 50.

41. Ibid., 51.

42. Daniel Rothenberg, *With These Hands: The Hidden World of Migrant Farmworkers Today* (Berkeley: University of California Press, 1998), 19.

43. U.S. Life Expectancy Hits High Mark, Feb. 28, 2005, at www.cnn.com (cited Jan. 31, 2006).

44. Bender, *Greasers and Gringos*, 139 (1997 median income of individual farm workers).

45. Marc Cooper, "Sour Grapes," at Hispanicvista.com (reprint from LA Weekly) (cited Jan. 31, 2006).

46. Frank Joyce, "Fate of the Union," Feb. 22, 2005, at www.alternet.com (down from 12.9 percent in 2003); "Union Membership Drops to New Low," Jan. 29, 2007,

at www.bls.gov/news.release/union2.toc.htm (2005 and 2006 figures) (cited May 26, 2007).

47. "Union Membership Drops"; Jennifer Gordon, *Suburban Sweatshops: The Fight for Immigrant Rights* (Cambridge, MA: Belknap Press, 2005), 3.

48. Rothenberg, *With These Hands*, 267.

49. Miriam Pawel, "Farmworkers Reap Little Benefit as Union Strays from Its Roots," *Los Angeles Times*, Jan. 8, 2006; Miriam Pawel, "Linked Charities Bank on the Chavez Name," *Los Angeles Times*, Jan. 9, 2006; Miriam Pawel, "Decisions of Long Ago Shape the Union Today," *Los Angeles Times*, Jan. 10, 2006. The UFW's compelling 101-page response can be found as a Research White Paper at its website, www.ufw.org (cited Dec. 26, 2006).

50. Robert Coles, "Foreword," in Rothenberg, *With These Hands*, ix.

Notes to Chapter 8

1. Hammerback and Jensen, *Rhetorical Career*, 84. Nevertheless, César Chávez did employ symbols of Mexican pride, such as the Virgen de Guadalupe, in his organizing efforts. Ian F. Haney López, *Racism on Trial: The Chicano Fight for Justice* (Cambridge, MA: Belknap Press, 2003), 158.

2. García, *Viva Kennedy*.

3. Ibid., 84.

4. See Carlos Muñoz, Jr., *Youth, Identity, Power: The Chicano Movement* (New York: Verso, 1989), 60.

5. Mario Barrera, *Beyond Aztlan: Ethnic Autonomy in Comparative Perspective* (Notre Dame, IN: University of Notre Dame Press, 1988), 37–38.

6. Carlos Ynostronza, "The Farm Worker—The Beginning of a New Awareness," 20 *American University Law Review* (1970): 39, 40–41.

7. Levy, *Cesar Chavez*, 123.

8. Del Castillo and Garcia, *Triumph of Spirit*, 154.

9. Matthiessen, *Sal Si Puedes*, 143.

10. Richard W. Etulain ed., *César Chávez: A Brief Biography with Documents* (Boston: Bedford/St. Martin's, 2002), 93 (also noting that Chávez had confronted nationalism in fighting doggedly for inclusion of blacks in the CSO, where he started his organizing career).

11. Barrera, *Beyond Aztlan*, 45.

12. Doug Shuit and Dial Torgerson, "Southland Observances Pay Final Respects to Kennedy," *Los Angeles Times*, June 9, 1968, B1.

13. Chávez, *Raza Primero*, 46.

14. Suzanne Oboler, *Ethnic Labels, Latino Lives: Identity and the Politics of (Re)Presentation in the United States* (Minneapolis: University of Minnesota Press, 1995), 63.

15. López, *Racism on Trial*, 16 (observing that by 2000, 97 percent of residents in East Los Angeles were Latino). The white flight from the East Los Angeles area took off in earnest during the years I resided there—in 1960, its Spanish-surname population was 66 percent, but by 1965, the Spanish-surname population had increased to 76 percent as the overall area population declined. Progress Report, Mexican American Study Project, Division of Research Graduate School of Business Administration, University of California, Los Angeles, June 1996.

16. López, *Racism on Trial*, 20–21; the Garfield High School Student Demands, printed on March 7, 1968, included:

1. Class size will be reduced so that teachers can be more effective in the classroom and devote more time to each student....
2. New high schools in the area to be built immediately. The present local schools should be renamed to help establish community identity.
3. All counselors should be able to speak Spanish.
   ...
12. Teachers should become more aware of the social and economic problems of the community. (Gerald Paul Rosen, *Political Ideology and the Chicano Movement: A Study of the Political Ideology of Activists in the Chicano Movement* [San Francisco: R and E Research Associates, 1975], appendix 2, 139).

Although California schools later implemented bilingual education programs, California voters in 1998 passed an anti–bilingual education initiative to eradicate bilingual programs absent a carefully prescribed parental waiver allowance.

17. Chicano! History of the Mexican American Civil Rights Movement (NLCC Educational Media, 1996), part 3. A Chicano scholar reacted negatively to Kennedy's visit as reflecting more unfulfilled promise in the barrio: "Oh, joy! Oh, happiness! Oh Nirvana! One more person listened.... Let's see now, that makes the U.S. Commission on Civil Rights ... the secretaries of the Interior, Housing, Agriculture ... and President Johnson have listened ... police departments have listened, etc., etc." García, *Chicanismo*, 41 (letter to editor by scholar Octavio Romano). One writer claims that Kennedy contributed $10,000 to the legal defense fund of thirteen students and activists charged a couple months after the East Los Angeles walkouts with the felony of conspiring to disturb the peace (Burton Moore, *Love and Riot: Oscar Zeta Acosta and the Great Mexican American Revolt* [Mountain View, CA: Floricanto Press, 2003], 39–40), charges that were later dropped when these defendants prevailed on First Amendment grounds in their appeal; see López, *Racism on Trial* and *Castro v. Superior Court*, 9 Cal. App. 3d 675, 88 Cal. Rptr. 500 (1970). Despite Kennedy's affinity for these students, any contribution seems unlikely given the timeline in which the leaders were arrested—late night Friday, May 31—and that Kennedy was killed a few days later. Carlos Muñoz, one of those arrested, remembers that Senator McCarthy did

make a sizable contribution to the defense fund. Interview with Dr. Carlos Muñoz, Jr., Oct. 1, 2005.

18. In 1968 the first campus Chicano Studies department, at California State College in Los Angeles, was founded, in response to the Mexican American student protest. Rosales, *Chicano!*, 253.

19. Quiñones, *Chicano Politics*, 123.

20. Barrera, *Beyond Aztlan*, 42.

21. Chávez, *Raza Primero*, 46 (statement of jailed Brown Beret leader David Sánchez).

22. Steven W. Bender and Keith Aoki, "Seekin' the Cause: Social Justice Movements and LatCrit Community," 81 *Oregon Law Review* (2002): 595, 610–611.

23. See Armando Morales, "The 1970–71 East Los Angeles Chicano-Police Riots," in *La Causa Politica*, 401–402 (also containing Morales's response to the editorial, which explained the "point" of the violence in addressing institutional violence in the barrio in the form of police brutality and other roots of the response).

24. Robert F. Kennedy, *To Seek a Newer World* (Garden City, NY: Doubleday, 1967), 27.

25. Ignacio M. García, *United We Win: The Rise and Fall of La Raza Unida Party* (Tucson: University of Arizona, 1989), 20 (suggesting the first La Raza Unida conference took place in El Paso in 1967 with a follow-up conference in San Antonio in 1968, although other sources suggest the political party was unnamed until 1970, including Chávez, *Raza Primero*, 82).

26. Armando Navarro, *La Raza Unida Party: A Chicano Challenge to the U.S. Two-Party Dictatorship* (Philadelphia: Temple University Press, 2000), 263; but see John C. Hammerback, Richard J. Jensen, and José Angel Gutierrez, *A War of Words: Chicano Protest in the 1960s and 1970s* (Westport, CT: Greenwood Press, 1985), 149 (detailing early Mexican American political party efforts in 1890 to form El Partido del Pueblo Unido, and in 1904 to organize the Mexican Liberal party in Missouri).

27. Navarro, *La Raza Unida*, 44; López, *Racism on Trial*, 20.

28. Navarro, *La Raza Unida*, 90.

29. Chávez, *Raza Primero*, 82.

30. Muñoz, *Youth, Identity, Power*, 121.

31. Barrera, *Beyond Aztlan*, 40.

32. García, *Viva Kennedy*, 175.

33. García, *United We Win*, 89.

34. Navarro, *La Raza Unida*, 31.

35. Muñoz, *Youth, Identity, Power*, 107; although La Raza party leaders invited both Nixon and McGovern to address their 1972 national convention, neither attended and at the convention party members voted for political independence from both party candidates rather than to endorse either candidate. "Raza Unida Won't Back Candidate," *Salinas Californian*, Sept. 4, 1972.

36. Tony Castro, "Chavez, Chicano Party in Split," *Washington Post*, Sept. 3, 1972.
37. Ibid.
38. Ibid.
39. Castro, *Chicano Power*, 24–25.
40. Ibid., 26.
41. Ibid., 103.
42. Rosales, *Chicano!*, 244.
43. Castro, *Chicano Power*, 19.
44. Santillan, *Chicano Politics*, 162.
45. Castro, *Chicano Power*, 19, 202; see also José de la Isla, *The Rise of Hispanic Political Power* (Los Angeles: Archer Books, 2003), 25–26.
46. Muñoz, *Youth, Identity, Power*, 122.

Notes to Chapter 9

1. Del Castillo and Garcia, *Triumph of Spirit*, 118.
2. George Mariscal, ed., *Aztlán and Viet Nam: Chicano and Chicana Experiences of the War* (Berkeley: University of California Press, 1999), 193.
3. López, *Racism on Trial*, 194–195.
4. Guthman and Allen, *RFK*, 342.
5. Kaiser, *1968 in America*, 120; Lorena Oropeza, *¡Raza Sí! ¡Guerra No!: Chicano Protest and Patriotism During the Viet Nam War Era* (Berkeley: University of California Press, 2005), 68.
6. Oropeza, *¡Raza Sí!*, 68–69.
7. Charley Trujillo, ed., *Soldados: Chicanos in Viet Nam* (San Jose: Chusma House Publications, 1990), vii.
8. Bender, *Greasers and Gringos*, 102. Between January 1961 and February 1967, Mexican Americans from the Southwest with Spanish surnames accounted for 19.4 percent of those killed in Vietnam at a time when Mexican Americans made up only 10 to 12 percent of the population of the Southwest region. Chávez, *Raza Primero*, 63; Trujillo, *Soldados*, vii.
9. Kaiser, *1968 in America*, 120.
10. Ibid., 21.
11. Acuña, *Occupied America*, 320.
12. Kennedy, *To Seek a Newer World*, 197.
13. Letter from Catalino Tacliban to Senator Robert F. Kennedy, Mar. 3, 1968, in JFK Library, RFK Collection, Labor-Migrant file.
14. Ibid., 194.
15. McGregor, Wathen, and Ballis, *Remembering Cesar*, 89.

16. Del Castillo and Garcia, *Triumph of Spirit*, 118.

17. Jensen and Hammerback, *Words of César Chávez*, 52.

18. O. Ricardo Pimentel, "Chavez Saw War as Proof of Failure," *Arizona Republic*, Apr. 15, 2003; see also Pitrone, *Chavez: Man of the Migrants*, 167 (noting the ultimate dismissal of the charges against Fernando for refusing the draft).

19. Letter from César E. Chávez to President [Nixon], Jan. 19, 1973, Wayne State Library, UFW Information and Research, Box 36, Folder 2.

20. "Latino Soldiers Lead in Iraq Deaths among Soldiers of Color," Mar. 23, 2007, at http://news.newamericamedia.org/news/view_article.html?article_id= b8eb7c611609c4e9b154e40d4d1f1fea (cited Mar. 30, 2007).

21. In July 2002 President Bush signed an executive order that gives noncitizen soldiers eligibility for expedited citizenship; there is also a statute permitting post-humous citizenship to those who die while on active military duty. 8. U.S.C. § 1440-1.

22. Pew Hispanic Center, The 2004 National Survey of Latinos: Politics and Civic Participation, July 2004 [hereinafter Pew 2004 Latino Survey] (conducted April to June 2004), showing that 56 percent disapproved of Bush's handling of the situation in Iraq. A separate survey at the same time found that 63 percent of registered Latino voters disapproved of the war in Iraq, an opinion shared by slightly over half of the general voting public at that time. Richard Morin and Dan Balz, "Poll Shows Kerry Leading among Registered Latinos," July 21, 2004, at washingtonpost.com (cited June 14, 2005).

23. CNN Election Results Poll, Nov. 3, 2004, at www.cnn.com/ELECTION/2004/pages/results/states/US/P/00/epolls.0.html (cited Dec. 26, 2006) [hereinafter CNN 2004 Exit Poll].

24. Poll: Support for the Iraq War Deteriorates, Mar. 19, 2007, at www.cnn.com (cited Mar. 30, 2007).

25. See Heuvel and Gwirtzman, *On His Own*, 244 n.5 (stating that Kennedy at no time publicly favored a unilateral withdrawal, but called instead for a negotiated settlement); Thilo Koch, *Fighters for a New World* (New York: G.P. Putnam's Sons, 1969), 153–154 (transcript of press conference following Kennedy's announcement of his candidacy for president in which Kennedy stated that he favored de-escalating the struggle, stopping bombing to lure the North Vietnamese to the negotiating table, and having the South Vietnamese take over more of the war effort). One Kennedy campaign brochure stated on the subject of Vietnam that "I do not want to simply withdraw or surrender in Viet Nam" (Kennedy for President brochure [undated]).

26. Howard Zinn, *A People's History of the United States: 1492–Present* (New York: HarperCollins, 1999), 483.

27. MacAfee, *Gospel According to RFK*, 5.

28. Heymann, *RFK*, 475.

29. David and David, *Bobby Kennedy*, 321.

Notes to Chapter 10

1. Del Castillo and Garcia, *Triumph of Spirit*, 116.

2. Guthman and Allen, *RFK*, 204 (speech written for Kansas State University but never delivered).

3. Witcover, *85 Days*, 17.

4. Oropeza, *¡Raza Sí!*, 57. Head Start was the most visible national program that emerged from the War on Poverty agenda. See generally Irwin Unger, *The Best of Intentions: The Triumphs and Failures of the Great Society under Kennedy, Johnson, and Nixon* (New York: Doubleday, 1996), 185.

5. Newfield, *Robert F. Kennedy*, 310.

6. Jack Jones, "Revolt in the Barrios: Social Ferment Stirs Mexican Americans," *Los Angeles Times*, May 8, 1966, C1.

7. Ibid.

8. Progress Report, Mexican American Study Project, Division of Research, Graduate School of Business Administration, University of California, Los Angeles, June 1996.

9. Ibid.

10. MacAfee, *Gospel According to RFK*, 64. By 1969, the average income of Latino families in the United States was $5,600, about 70 percent of the income of families of other backgrounds. Senator Joseph M. Montoya, "Woe unto Those Who Have Ears but Do Not Hear," in *La Causa Politica*, 3, 7.

11. Violence broke out in Spanish Harlem in the summer of 1967. Schlesinger, *Robert Kennedy*, 797.

12. Rosales, *Chicano!*, 200–206.

13. Matthiessen, *Sal Si Puedes*, 1. Robert Kennedy acknowledged this connection in observing that "[i]f we are to ... enable people to remain in their own homes if they choose, we will have to devote as much attention to rural community development as we do to our cities." Kennedy, *To Seek a Newer World*, 24.

14. Heymann, *RFK*, 15–19.

15. Ibid., 9.

16. Ferriss and Sandoval, *Fight in the Fields*, 12–21.

17. "Fight in the Fields" video.

18. Ferriss and Sandoval, *Fight in the Fields*, 28–29.

19. Heymann, *RFK*, 25–29

20. Castro, *Chicano Power*, 87.

21. Dalton, *Moral Vision*, 104.

22. Ibid., 100–101.

23. Day, *Forty Acres*, 62.

24. Schlesinger, *Robert Kennedy*, 799.

25. Levy, *Cesar Chavez*, 449.

26. Beran, *Last Patrician*, 101.
27. Schulman, *Robert F. Kennedy*, 70.
28. Guthman and Allen, *RFK*, 203.
29. Kennedy, *To Seek a Newer World*, 32.
30. Schlesinger, *Robert Kennedy*, 783.
31. MacAfee, *Gospel According to RFK*, 65.
32. Schlesinger, *Robert Kennedy*, 784. Kennedy's criticism of the welfare system in lieu of creating jobs, with statements such as "We can't have the federal government in here telling people what's good for them," led future president Ronald Reagan to joke: "I get the feeling I've been writing some of his speeches." Beran, *Last Patrician*, 202. As one commentator observed in the forging of a Kennedy coalition across political lines: "[I]n deploring 'welfare' handouts and calling on private business and local government to substitute jobs and job training for the disdained 'dole,' Kennedy could make points with everybody." Witcover, *85 Days*, 153.
33. Kennedy, *To Seek a Newer World*, 33.
34. Ibid., 23.
35. Ibid., 39.
36. Schlesinger, *Robert Kennedy*, 784.
37. Kennedy, *To Seek a Newer World*, 44. Kennedy also cited the Puerto Rico Operation Bootstrap program, a system of federal tax incentives that from 1948 to 1967 established over eleven hundred factories, helping to grow the island's economy at a rate surpassing that in the United States. Ibid., 43–44.
38. Newfield, *Robert F. Kennedy*, 106.
39. Kennedy, *To Seek a Newer World*, 51 (noting that 10 percent of the residents were Puerto Rican and 80 percent African American). Although Bedford-Stuyvesant was not the poorest district in New York, its rates of unemployment and infant mortality were among the state's highest. Margaret Laing, *Robert Kennedy* (London: Macdonald, 1968), 223.
40. MacAfee, *Gospel According to RFK*, 105–106.
41. Kennedy, *To Seek a Newer World*, 23.
42. Amending Migratory Labor Laws, 362.
43. Statement of Senator Robert F. Kennedy, A Program for the Urban Crisis, May 30, 1968, at JFK Library, RFK Collection.
44. Lyndon B. Johnson, "Message to Congress on the Economic Opportunity Act," in Gwendolyn Mink and Rickie Solinger, eds., *Welfare: A Documentary History of U.S. Policy and Politics* (New York: NYU Press, 2003), 223; see also Edelman, *Searching for America's Heart*, 97; Michael Givel, *The War on Poverty Revisited: The Community Services Block Grant Program in the Reagan Years* (New York: Lanham, 1991), 81–82. In 1965, Dolores Huerta went to Washington, D.C., and succeeded in obtaining an OEO grant for the farm workers union to train migrant workers in money management and citizenship. Dan La Botz, *César Chávez and La Causa* (New York: Pearson Longman, 2006), 75.

45. James B. Stewart, "Understanding the Future: Toward a Strategy for Black and Latino Survival and Liberation in the Twenty-First Century," in John J. Betancur and Douglas C. Gills, eds. *The Collaborative City: Opportunities and Struggles for Blacks and Latinos in U.S. Cities* (New York: Garland, 2000), 237.

46. See Mink and Solinger, *Welfare: A Documentary History*, 301 (reprinting a 1967 speech by Reagan, then governor of California, where he remarked "what about the right of those who work and earn, and share the fruit of their toil to make welfare possible.... [T]hese same people are now providing medical care for their fellow citizens, more comprehensive than they can afford for themselves").

47. Ibid., 339 (noting that a researcher found in 1972 and 1973 that 75 percent of people depicted in stories about welfare were black, even though in 1971 blacks represented about 46 percent of welfare recipients).

48. Richard Nixon initiated the states' rights strategy, calling in a 1969 speech on welfare reform for a "new federalism in which power, funds and responsibility will flow from Washington to the states and to the people" (Ibid., 313, 314). Reagan's state of the union address in 1988 suggested that "some years ago, the federal government declared war on poverty, and poverty won." He announced a welfare strategy that looked to the states for inspiration: "States have begun to show us the way.... Let's give the states even more flexibility and encourage more reforms" (Ibid., 509).

49. Bender, *Greasers and Gringos*, 79 (noting that in 1997 Congress did restore Social Security and Medicaid benefits to elderly and disabled documented immigrants).

50. Mink and Solinger, *Welfare: A Documentary History*, 659.

51. Ibid.

52. Statement of Senator Robert F. Kennedy, A Program for the Urban Crisis, May 30, 1968, at JFK Library, RFK Collection.

53. John Kerry and John Edwards, *Our Plan for America: Stronger at Home, Respected in the World* (New York: Public Affairs, 2004), 3.

54. Jennifer Kerr, "U.S. Poverty Rises 4th Year in a Row," *Eugene Register-Guard*, Aug. 31, 2005.

55. David K. Shipler, *The Working Poor: Invisible in America* (New York: Vintage Books, 2004), 9 (arguing that the federal poverty line is based on a multiplier of a "thrifty food basket" that is based on outdated times when the average family spent one-third of its income on food; today, the average family spends one-sixth of its budget on food).

56. See "Income Climbs, Poverty Stabilizes, Uninsured Rate Increases," Aug. 29, 2006, at www.census.gov/Press-Release/www/releases/archives/income_wealth/007419.html (cited Sept. 15, 2006); see also Victor M. Rodriguez, "'Browning' the 'Greens': Building the Long-Term Incorporation of Latinos into the Political System," Sept. 17, 2004, at www.hispanicvista.com (cited Mar. 20, 2005) (22.5 poverty

rate for Latinos in 2003). A 1995 study broke down the poverty levels by ethnicity and found that of the 27 percent of Latino families in poverty, 28 percent of Mexican families lived in poverty, as did 36 percent of Puerto Rican families. The poverty rate for Cuban Americans was lower, at 16 percent. John A. García, *Latino Politics in America: Community, Culture, and Interests* (Lanham, MD: Rowman and Littlefield, 2003), 47.

57. Rodriguez, "'Browning' the 'Greens.'"

58. "Latino Labor Report 2006: Strong Gains in Employment," Sept. 27, 2006, at http://pewhispanic.org/topics/index.php?TopicID=2 (cited Oct. 5, 2006).

59. Bill Richardson, "Seeking the Latino Vote," *Hispanic*, Feb. 2004: 84.

60. Rakesh Kochlar, "The Wealth of Hispanic Households: 1996 to 2002," Oct. 2004, available at www.pewhispanic.com (cited Mar. 20, 2005) (median wealth of Latino and black households is one-tenth as much as white households; in 2002 the median net worth of Latino households was only $7,932, with the median wealth of Anglo households at $88,651 and home ownership as the single most important asset factor in the calculations. Twenty-six percent of Latino households had a negative or zero net worth).

61. Cooper, "Sour Grapes."

62. Ibid.

63. Kaiser Commission Report, 1–2 (85 percent are uninsured, 10 percent have private health coverage, and 5 percent have public health coverage).

64. National Agricultural Workers Survey 2001–2002, U.S. Department of Labor, Office of the Assistant Secretary for Policy, Research Report No. 9, Mar. 2005.

65. Kaiser Commission Report, 1 (2000 National Agricultural Workers Survey).

66. Cooper, "Sour Grapes" (quoting economist Rick Mines).

67. Pew 2004 Latino Survey, chart 3 (the remaining percentage consisted of voters who didn't know or refused a response).

68. Jorge Ramos, *The Latino Wave: How Hispanics Will Elect the Next American President* (New York: HarperCollins, 2004), 231.

69. See Harry P. Pachon, "Latino Politics in the Golden State: Ready for the 21st Century?" in Michael B. Preston, Bruce E. Cain, and Sandra Bass, eds., *Racial and Ethnic Politics in California* (Berkeley, CA: Institute of Governmental Studies Press, 1998). See also Jack Citrin and Benjamin Highton, *How Race, Ethnicity, and Immigration Shape the California Electorate* (San Francisco: Public Policy Institute of California, 2002), vii; reporting the results of the study as: "The lower electoral participation of Latinos is due almost completely to three factors: their lower citizenship rate, their relative youth, and their lower socioeconomic status. These findings belie arguments that Latino residents are intrinsically less interested in elections or are more disengaged from the political process."

70. William P. Quigley, *Ending Poverty as We Know It: Guaranteeing a Right to a Job at a Living Wage* (Philadelphia: Temple University Press, 2003), 27.
71. Shipler, *Working Poor,* 287.
72. Schlesinger, *Robert Kennedy,* 674.
73. Newfield, *Robert F. Kennedy,* 155.
74. Ibid., 279.
75. Steel, *In Love with Night,* 172–173.
76. Ibid., 173. Despite the law and order rhetoric, Kennedy was sympathetic to the situation of African Americans in the burning ghettos. When former president Eisenhower suggested that the Watts riots stemmed from a "policy of lawlessness," demanding the solution of "greater respect for the law," Kennedy retorted that "There is no point in telling Negroes to obey the law. To many Negroes the law is the enemy" (Schlesinger, *Robert Kennedy,* 780). In his book *To Seek a Newer World,* Kennedy explained further that "effective law enforcement, moreover, is just the beginning. We should not delude ourselves. Punishment is not prevention. History offers cold comfort to those who think grievance and despair can be subdued by force.... The riots are not crises that can be resolved as suddenly as they arose. They are a condition that has been with us for 300 years, now worsened and intensified under the strains of modern life" (Kennedy, *To Seek a Newer World,* 21).
77. Witcover, *85 Days,* 178.
78. Ibid., 174–175.
79. Heuvel and Gwirtzman, *On His Own,* 348–349.
80. Ibid.
81. Dooley, *Robert Kennedy,* 128.
82. W. J. Rorabaugh, *Berkeley at War: The 1960s* (New York: Oxford University Press, 1989), 184.
83. Steel, *In Love with Night,* 173.
84. Ibid., 176.
85. Ibid., 173.
86. Palermo, *In His Own Right,* 216.
87. Ibid.
88. Schlesinger, *Robert Kennedy,* 906.
89. Heymann, *RFK,* 481.
90. Newfield, *Robert F. Kennedy,* 322.
91. Palermo, *In His Own Right,* 244; but see Heuvel and Gwirtzman, *On His Own,* 379 (listing final totals as 1,472,166 for Kennedy and 1,322,608 for McCarthy).
92. Steel, *In Love with Night,* 187.
93. Heuvel and Gwirtzman, *On His Own,* 379–380 n.26 (noting Kennedy drew even with Jewish voters in California, but did better among the older Jewish voters in California than with the younger, better-educated Jewish population).

94. Palermo, *In His Own Right,* 244. See also Richard Bergholz, "Kennedy Wins Race," *Los Angeles Times,* June 5, 1968, 1 ("All observers agree that Kennedy was piling up big leads with the low-income voters, with Negroes and Mexican Americans. By contrast, McCarthy's strength was with middle and high income voters").

95. Heuvel and Gwirtzman, *On His Own,* 386.

96. Hammerback and Jensen, *Rhetorical Career,* 90; Bender and Aoki, "Seekin' the Cause," 613.

97. Jensen and Hammerback, *Words of César Chávez,* 17–18.

98. Castro, *Chicano Power,* 83–84.

99. Dooley, *Robert Kennedy,* 43, 146 (documenting the role of Kennedy in the genesis of the campaign). Chávez received several telegrams from organizers of the Poor People's Campaign asking him to participate in the Poor People's March to Washington, D.C., in the spring of 1968. He was sympathetic, but he remarked to an aide that they were asking him to do "exactly the same thing as asking the Memphis garbage men to put aside their strike and come to Delano to help the farm workers" (Matthiessen, *Sal Si Puedes,* 242–243). Two icons of the Chicano Movement, Rodolfo "Corky" Gonzales and Reies López Tijerina, led the Mexican American contingent in the Poor People's March, but separatist politics fractured the potential for interracial and ethnic coalition on issues of poverty.

100. Jennifer Frost, *"An Interracial Movement of the Poor": Community Organizing and the New Left in the 1960s* (New York: New York University Press, 2001).

101. Ibid., 152–153.

102. Ibid., 153.

103. See George Yancey, *Who Is White? Latinos, Asians, and the New Black/Nonblack Divide* (Boulder, CO: Lynne Rienner Publishers, 2003), 116 (suggesting that today Jackson's Rainbow Coalition is not possible because "a significant portion of nonblack minority racial groups would fight against, rather than for, social change," leaving the supposed coalition with one dominant color, black).

104. G. William Domhoff, *Changing the Powers that Be: How the Left Can Stop Losing and Win* (Lanham, MD: Rowman and Littlefield, 2003), 74; Patricia C. McKissack, *Jesse Jackson: A Biography* (New York: Scholastic, 1989), 61.

105. See Domhoff, *Changing the Powers,* 74; McKissack, *Jesse Jackson,* 78–79; Geron, *Latino Political Power,* 74 (Jackson won the popular vote in New York City in 1988 with strong support from Puerto Rican voters; but Jackson received only 21 percent of the Mexican American vote in the 1988 Texas primary).

106. Barbara Ehrenreich, *Nickel and Dimed: On (Not) Getting By in America* (New York: Henry Holt and Company, 2001).

107. Quigley, *Ending Poverty,* 22–23.

108. David Swanson, "Thirty One States and DC Take Action on Minimum Wage," Mar. 3, 2005, at hispanicvista.com (cited June 14, 2005).

109. "Senate Defeats Minimum-Wage Plans," Mar. 7, 2005, at www.cnn.com (cited Mar. 20, 2005).

110. Ehrenreich, *Nickel and Dimed*, 220.

111. Mark Robert Rank, *One Nation, Underprivileged: Why American Poverty Affects Us All* (New York: Oxford University Press, 2004), 239.

112. Chris Zappone, "Congress OKs Minimum Wage Boost," May 24, 2007, at www.cnn.com (cited May 27, 2007).

113. "Hispanic and African American Adults Are Uninsured at Rates One-and-a Half to Three Times Higher Than White Adults," Aug. 1, 2006, at http://www.commonwealthfund.org/newsroom/newsroom_show.htm?doc_id=386212 (cited Aug. 8, 2007) (finding a vastly lower but still troublesome rate of 20 percent for white working-age adults).

114. MacAfee, *Gospel According to RFK*, 119.

115. Bender, *Greasers and Gringos*, 166–167.

116. Richard Delgado and Jean Stefancic, "The Racial Double Helix: Watson, Crick, and *Brown v. Board of Education* (Our No-Bell Prize Award Speech)," 47 *Howard Law Journal* (2004): 473, 483.

117. Bender, *Greasers and Gringos*, 164.

118. Victor Davis Hanson, *Mexifornia: A State of Becoming* (San Francisco: Encounter Books, 2003), 44–45. One could reply to this idiotic logic that it is nice to be a homeowner with a lawn to mow, to take vacations and have the summer off from teaching, to have family health insurance and a retirement account (although given the life expectancy of farm workers and the accident rate of the construction industry it may not be needed), as well as to point out that Mexican immigrant kids have teeth that may need braces too.

119. Ibid., 50. Hanson also observes: "I live in one of the poorest sections of the poorest counties in California, and people of all sorts are just not starving. Wal-Mart is packed. The local Blockbuster [video] store is teeming" (Ibid., 56). Consider the cogent observation of Barbara Ehrenreich that thanks to consignment stores and Wal-Mart, "the poor are usually able to disguise themselves as members of the more comfortable classes" (Ehrenreich, *Nickel and Dimed*, 216). Back in the 1960s, in his pathbreaking study of U.S. poverty, Michael Harrington observed that "clothes make the poor invisible too: America has the best-dressed poverty the world has ever known. For a variety of reasons, the benefits of mass production have been spread much more evenly in this area than in many others. It is much easier in the United States to be decently dressed than it is to be decently housed, fed, or doctored. Even people with terribly depressed incomes can look prosperous" (Michael Harrington, *The Other America: Poverty in the United States* [New York: Macmillan, 1964], 5).

120. Hanson, *Mexifornia*, 67.

121. Hugh Heclo, "The Political Foundations of Antipoverty Policy," in Sheldon H. Danziger and Daniel H. Weinberg, eds., *Fighting Poverty: What Works and What Doesn't* (Cambridge, MA: Harvard University Press, 1986), 312, 323.

122. Frost, *Interracial Movement,* 159 (and noting the impact on welfare budgets of the Vietnam War).

123. See Sharon Hays, *Flat Broke with Children: Women in the Age of Welfare Reform* (New York: Oxford University Press, 2003), 11 (observing that 38 percent of welfare recipients are African American, 24.5 percent Hispanic, and 30 percent white).

124. Barack Obama, *The Audacity of Hope: Thoughts on Reclaiming the American Dream* (New York: Crown Publishers, 2006), 252–253.

Notes to Chapter 11

1. Bob Fitch, "Tilting the System: An Interview with César Chávez," in *La Causa Politica,* 360, 361.

2. Patrick J. Buchanan, *State of Emergency: The Third World Invasion and Conquest of America* (New York: St. Martin's Press, 2006) (back jacket).

3. Meister and Loftis, *Long Time Coming,* 206.

4. For example, in the 1990s, the Latino population in Memphis, Tennessee, grew nearly 300 percent. Kevin R. Johnson, "The End of 'Civil Rights' As We Know It? Immigration and Civil Rights in the New Millennium," 49 *UCLA Law Review* (2002): 1481 (also reporting that Mexican immigrants swelled the ranks of poultry and meat packing workers in the Midwest and Southeast). In the 1990s, Spanish-speaking residents in North Carolina increased 449 percent, with huge percentage increases in states like Arkansas, Georgia, Tennessee, South Carolina, and Alabama. Samuel Huntington, *Who Are We? The Challenges to America's National Identity* (New York: Simon and Schuster, 2004), 226.

5. Hanson, *Mexifornia,* 63.

6. Ibid., 17.

7. Ibid., 64.

8. Ibid., 42.

9. Ibid., 68.

10. Ibid., 70.

11. Huntington, *Who Are We?* 232.

12. Ibid. (translated from Spanish), 254.

13. John Kennedy blasted the quota system in his book *A Nation of Immigrants,* stating that the immigration laws in effect in 1958 were based on the "assumption that there is some reason for keeping the origins of our population in exactly the same proportion as they existed in 1920," a bias Kennedy contended was "at complete variance with the American traditions and principles that the qualifications of an immigrant do not depend on the country of his birth, and [one that] violates the spirit expressed in the Declaration of Independence that 'all men are created equal.'" Kennedy, *Nation of Immigrants,* 75.

14. Before the repeal in 1965 of the Western Hemisphere exclusion, there were numerous congressional efforts to impose quotas generally on the Western Hemisphere and specifically on Mexican immigration. Acuña, *Occupied America*, 185–189.

15. See generally Lorenzo A. Alvarado, "A Lesson from My Grandfather, The Bracero," 22 *Chicano-Latino Law Review* (2001): 55 (detailing abuses by employers of bracero workers).

16. Gilbert Paul Carrasco, "Latinos in the United States: Invitation and Exile," in Juan F. Perea, ed., *Immigrants Out! The New Nativism and the Anti-Immigrant Impulse in the United States* (New York: New York University Press, 1997), 190–195.

17. Among the requirements for lawful immigration were the payment of a fee, providing certain documents such as immunization records and a birth certificate, and undergoing screening for such circumstances as membership in the Communist Party or the presence of mental or moral defects. Notes, "Commuters, Illegals and American Farmworkers: The Need for a Broader Approach to Domestic Farm Labor Problems," 48 *New York University Law Review* (1973): 439, 480 n.273.

18. Letter from César Chávez to Assemblyman Richard Alatorre, Jan. 6, 1975, Wayne State Library, UFW Information and Research Part 1, Box 4, Folder 38.

19. Christopher David Ruiz Cameron, "Borderline Decisions: Hoffman Plastic Compounds, the New Bracero Program, and the Supreme Court's Role in Making Federal Labor Policy," 51 *UCLA Law Review* (2003): 1, 3; see also Steve Allen, *The Ground Is Our Table* (Garden City, NY: Doubleday and Company, 1966), 56–59 (famous comedian/activist detailing abuses in the bracero program).

20. David G. Gutiérrez, *Walls and Mirrors: Mexican Americans, Mexican Immigrants, and the Politics of Ethnicity* (Berkeley: University of California Press, 1995), 182.

21. By 1976, in addition to the overall quota, Western Hemisphere countries such as Mexico were also subjected to a 20,000 per country annual limit. Pub. L. No. 94-571, 90 Stat. 2703 (1976); see generally James F. Smith, Symposium, "United States Immigration Policy—A History of Prejudice and Economic Scapegoatism? A Nation that Welcomes Immigrants? An Historical Examination of United States Immigration Policy," 1 *University of California at Davis Journal of International Law and Policy* (1995): 227.

22. Kevin R. Johnson, *The "Huddled Masses" Myth: Immigration and Civil Rights* (Philadelphia: Temple University Press, 2004), 25.

23. Congressional Record, Sept. 20, 1965, at 24483. Senator Edward Kennedy also opposed the act's imposition of a ceiling on Western Hemisphere immigration, citing the "unique relationship" among its nations and arguing that:

The existence [until 1965] of a nonquota status for nationals of the Western Hemisphere has never been considered a form of discrimination against the other nations of the world, for the distinction was not based on race, religion, or ethnic origin. It was a firm indication of our esteem for our good neighbors

and our pride in the special solidarity that exists among the people of this hemisphere. Now, despite the absence of any real immigration problem, and the presence of more stringent qualitative controls on entry to this country, it is proposed that we take this historic step backward in our otherwise progressive Western Hemisphere policies.

We consider this decision by the Senate Immigration Subcommittee [to add the Western Hemisphere restriction] to be most regrettable. The majority of the hemisphere immigrants come to us from our closest neighbors—Canada and Mexico. We have long welcomed especially the contributions of these nations to our culture and society. (Senate Report 89-748, 89th Cong., 1st Sess., 1965 [joint remarks of Edward M. Kennedy, Philip A. Hart, and Jacob K. Javits]).

24. See Letter from Abba P. Schwartz to Bob [Kennedy], Sept. 20, 1965, and Letter from Robert F. Kennedy to Abba P. Schwartz, Department of State Administrator, Sept. 24, 1965, in JFK Library, RFK Collection, Immigration file. See also Smith, "U.S. Immigration Policy," 234 (noting that the Johnson administration opposed the Western Hemisphere limitation). Among the reasons for the enactment of the quota in the face of this opposition were concerns over spiraling immigration from other Central and South American countries than Mexico—in 1965 and 1964, the total number of immigrants (81,395) from countries such as Cuba, the Dominican Republic, and Colombia exceeded the total coming from both Mexico and Canada (76,296 in 1965), with Western Hemisphere immigration in 1965 totaling 157,691. Progress Report, Mexican American Study Project, Division of Research, Graduate School of Business Administration, University of California, Los Angeles (June 1966), 5.

25. Gutiérrez, *Walls and Mirrors*, 182.

26. Conservative Latino commentator Raoul Lowery Contreras lays the blame for "today's problems with illegal immigration from Mexico" on the "Kennedys personally," based on his contention that President Kennedy was spear-carrying for the AFL-CIO union in securing the termination of the Bracero Program. Raoul Lowery Contreras, *The New American Majority: Hispanics, Republicans and George Bush: Accession to the White House* (Lincoln, NE: Writer's Showcase, 2002), 95. But this view carelessly omits consideration of the imposition of a quota on Western Hemisphere immigration, a move that Senators Edward and Robert Kennedy opposed, and that President Kennedy could not have anticipated and likely would have opposed. In his 1958 book *A Nation of Immigrants*, published two years before his presidency, John Kennedy proposed elimination of the quota system that became the basis of the 1965 reform, but urged expansion of the Western Hemisphere exception to encompass immigrants from the newly independent nations of Jamaica, Trinidad, and Tobago (Kennedy, *Nation of Immigrants*, 105, 106). Therefore, Kennedy could not have foreseen the elimination, rather than the expansion, of the Western Hemisphere exception,

and subsequent individual country quotas placed on Mexico, that, combined with the end of the Bracero Program, created the current situation where employer demand exceeds immigration limits and lures undocumented immigrants.

27. Samuel W. Bettwy, "A Proposed Legislative Scheme to Solve the Mexican Immigration Problem," 2 *San Diego International Law Journal* (2001): 93, 109. See also *Diaz v. Kay-Dix Ranch*, 9 Cal. App. 3d 588, 88 Cal. Rptr. 443 (1970) (discussing INS annual reports and noting that 96.7 percent of the INS removals from California in 1969 were of Mexican undocumented immigrants).

28. Gutiérrez, *Walls and Mirrors*, 188.

29. Richard K. Park, Note, "Illegal Entrants: The Wetback Problem in American Farm Labor," 2 *University of California at Davis Law Review* (1970): 55, 58.

30. Harrn Bernstein, "Surplus of Farm Hands in State, Tieburg Reports," *Los Angeles Times*, Mar. 14, 1966, A3.

31. Del Castillo and Garcia, *Triumph of Spirit*, 159–160 (apparently some of these Mexican workers were green card holders).

32. *RFK*, Fox Television Studios (2003).

33. *Oral History*, 9.

34. Telegram from César Chávez to Robert F. Kennedy Senator, Aug. 11, 1967, JFK Library, RFK Collection, RFK Senate Papers, Migratory Labor: California.

35. Memo from Peter [Edelman] to RFK, Aug. 25, 1967, in JFK Library, RFK Collection, Migratory Labor.

36. Ibid. (date of the strike certification obtained from subsequent litigation by Giumarra company).

37. Letter from Jerome Cohen to Hon. Robert F. Kennedy, Mar. 20, 1968, JFK Library, RFK Collection.

38. Senate Bill 2790, 90th Congress, 1st Session. Responding by letter to an interested Californian, Robert Kennedy explained his support of this legislation because it "would provide that holders of green cards would not use what is a continuing privilege in such a way as to adversely affect the wages and working conditions of workers in the United States similarly employed." Letter from Robert F. Kennedy to Glen L. Andersen, Apr. 15, 1968, JFK Library, Labor/Migrant Collection.

39. *Giumarra Vineyards Corp. v. Farrell*, 431 F.2d 923 (9th Cir. 1970) (noting that the federal government stated that its interpretation of the regulation was that it only applied to aliens whose actual residence was outside the United States).

40. *Sam Andrews' Sons v. Mitchell*, 457 F.2d 745 (9th Cir. 1972); see also *Saxbe v. Bustos*, 419 U.S. 65 (1974) (rejecting the UFWOC contention that alien commuter workers are not lawfully admitted for permanent residence; interpreting permanent residence based on eligibility for permanent residence rather than actual establishment of permanent residence in the United States).

41. Del Castillo and Garcia, *Triumph of Spirit*, 160; Neil Parse, "UFW Pickets Abandon Vineyards to Protest against Border Patrol," *Daily Enterprises (Riverside Cty.)*, July 11, 1973. Complementing the efforts of the UFW, farm workers filed individual and class action lawsuits against San Joaquin Valley growers seeking to enjoin employment of undocumented workers. See, e.g., *DeCanas v. Bica*, 424 U.S. 351 (1976) (in action by farm workers against farm labor contractors alleging that contractors violated California law prohibiting employment of undocumented immigrants, the Supreme Court held that the lower court had erred in striking down the state statute as preempted by federal law); *Larez v. Oberti*, 23 Cal. App. 3d 217, 100 Cal. Rptr. 57 (1972) (holding that the federal Immigration and Nationality Act did not create a private cause of action for resident farm workers to sue employers of "wetbacks"); and *Diaz v. Kay-Dix Ranch*, 9 Cal. App. 3d 588, 88 Cal. Rptr. 443 (1970) (refusing to issue injunction against growers knowingly hiring undocumented immigrants, as it was more orderly and effectual for the federal government to redeem its commitment to enforce the immigration laws).

42. Del Castillo and Garcia, *Triumph of Spirit*, 161–162.

43. Ibid., 164–165; Ferriss and Sandoval, *Fight in the Fields*, 244 (discussing allegations that some union members assaulted strikebreaking undocumented immigrants and carried weapons).

44. Interview with Dolores Huerta, Apr. 9, 2007.

45. La Botz, *César Chávez*, 83–84 (describing dissention from the Chicano Movement).

46. Letter from César Chávez to Paul Pumphrey, June 27, 1974, in Wayne State Library, UFW Information and Research, Box 39, File 6.

47. Meister and Loftis, *Long Time Coming*, 206; Del Castillo and Garcia, *Triumph of Spirit*, 162. Similar allegations still exist today. See Marisa Arrona, "The Face of the Frontier," Apr. 17, 2005, at alternet.org (cited July 11, 2005). ("When farms in the Imperial Valley need extra pickers and workers, the Border Patrol is ordered not to catch crossing immigrants. The Border Patrol turns a blind eye and allows immigrants to enter the U.S. until the farms have enough workers, and then they bear down again when they are told to do so"; summarizing conclusions from Luis Alberto Urrea, *The Devil's Highway*).

48. Press Statement of César Chávez, July 1, 1974, Wayne State Library, UFW Information and Research, Box 39, Folder 1.

49. Letter from James F. Greene [Deputy Commissioner of the INS] to César Chávez, Oct. 25, 1974, Wayne State Library, UFW Information and Research, Box 39, Folder 5.

50. Gutiérrez, *Walls and Mirrors*, 197.

51. The Rodino Bill: UFW Legislative Position on H.R. 982, Wayne State Library, UFW Information and Research, Box 38, Folder 8.

52. Letter from César E. Chávez to Senator Edward Kennedy, June 24, 1968, Wayne State Library, UFW Office of the President, Box 5, Folder 2.

53. César E. Chávez, Letter to Editor, *San Francisco Examiner*, Nov. 27, 1974, 28.

54. Meister and Loftis, *Long Time Coming*, 207.

55. Rodolfo F. Acuña, *Anything But Mexican: Chicanos in Contemporary Los Angeles* (London: Verso, 1996), 115 (noting that the legislation was introduced by a Democratic congressman from Pennsylvania).

56. Christine Marie Sierra, "In Search of National Power: Chicanos Working the System on Immigration Reform, 1976–1986," in David Montejano, ed., *Chicano Politics and Society in the Late Twentieth Century* (Austin: University of Texas Press, 1999), 132–133 (describing the opposition of the UFW to Democratic president Carter's immigration plan, which aimed to reduce undocumented immigration).

57. Del Castillo and Garcia, *Triumph of Spirit*, 167.

58. Carrasco, "Latinos in the United States," 199.

59. Huntington, *Who Are We?* 225 (noting the unrealized dual objective of the 1986 act to reduce future undocumented immigration).

60. Hernandez, "Cesar's Ghost."

61. Ibid.

62. Kelé Onyejekwe, "The Irrelevance of the Report of the Commission on Agricultural Workers: A Review of the Report of the Commission on Agricultural Workers," 21 *Lincoln Law Review* (1993): 95, 106 (UFW vice president Dolores Huerta's statement on the commission argued against enhanced border controls as they "increase the violence, militarization, and human rights abuses at the border," and her statement denounced the still-in-effect H-2A guest worker program for farm workers as "institutionalized slavery").

63. Gordon, *Suburban Sweatshops*, 50–51.

64. Peter Szekely, "AFL-CIO Rejects US Guest Worker Proposals," Feb. 28, 2006, Reuters news service; Statement by AFL-CIO president John Sweeney on the Senate's Immigration Bill, May 26, 2006 ("We are also greatly disappointed that the Senate adopted the greedy corporate model of addressing our nation's future needs for workers—guestworker programs—instead of crafting a mechanism to ensure that future foreign workers come into the U.S. with full rights and as full social partners").

65. David Bacon, "How US Corporations Won the Debate over Immigration," Oct. 11, 2004 (e-mail on file with author).

66. "Bush Calls for Changes on Illegal Workers," Jan. 7, 2004, at www.cnn.com (cited Feb. 2, 2005).

67. Harold Meyerson, "Bush's Retreat on Immigration Reform," *Washington Post*, July 21, 2004, A19.

68. Michael Doyle, "Groups Support AgJobs Measure," *Fresno Bee,* Feb. 11, 2005, www.fresnobee.com (cited Mar. 20, 2005).

69. Available at www.minutemanproject.com (cited Mar. 30, 2005).

70. Ibid. (cited May 25, 2005).

71. UFW action alert, e-mail received by the author Apr. 5, 2005.

72. Transcript, *Lou Dobbs Tonight,* Mar. 27, 2006, at www.cnn.com (cited Apr. 3, 2006); see also Buchanan, *State of Emergency,* 241–242 (subchapter titled "Cesar Chavez, Minuteman").

73. Interview with Richard Chávez, Apr. 9, 2007.

74. David Bacon, "The Border Is a Common Ground between Us," Dec. 19, 2005, at www.truthout.org_2005/121905G.shtml (cited Dec. 26, 2005).

75. Available at http://clinton.senate.gov/issues/immigration/ (cited May 23, 2007).

76. Available at www.barackobama.com/issues/immigration_and_the_border/ (cited May 23, 2007).

77. Available at www.teamtancredo.com/tancredo_issues_index.asp (cited May 23, 2007).

78. Field Institute, Voting in the 1994 General Election (Jan. 1995): 5.

79. See generally Acuña, *Anything But Mexican,* 162 (noting that Latinos voted only 23 percent for Wilson after supporting him at 40 percent in 1990, and suggesting that his support of Proposition 187 alienated many Latino voters).

80. Peter Andreas, *Border Games: Policing the U.S.-Mexico Divide* (Ithaca, NY: Cornell University Press, 2000), 87.

81. Rebecca Thatcher Murcia, *Dolores Huerta* (Bear, DE: Mitchell Lane Publishers, 2003), 39.

82. Most of California Proposition 187's provisions were gutted in court action that relied on constitutional doctrines of supremacy and equal protection. Bender, *Greasers and Gringos,* 253 n.60.

83. Marcelo Ballve, "Recall Election Fires Up California's Powerful Hispanic Media," Pacific News Service, Aug. 14, 2003.

84. Vicki Haddock, "Recall: Politics and Race," *San Francisco Chronicle,* Sept. 28, 2003.

85. Ibid.

86. "Special Report: California Recall," Oct. 7, 2003, at www.cnn.com (cited Mar. 20, 2005).

87. See generally Kevin R. Johnson, "Driver's Licenses and Undocumented Immigrants: The Future of Civil Rights Law?" 5 *Nevada Law Review* (2004): 213.

88. Debra J. Saunders, "Gov. Schwarzenegger," *San Francisco Chronicle,* Oct. 9, 2003.

89. Matea Gold, "Bustamante Goes Left to Take on Schwarzenegger," *Los Angeles Times,* Sept. 10, 2003.

90. "Bustamante Won't Renounce Ties to Chicano Student Group," Aug. 28, 2003, at foxnews.com (cited Mar. 20, 2005).

91. Kathryn Jean López, "Independence Day: Latinos Didn't Conform to Either Party's Expectations in California's Special Election," *Hispanic,* Dec. 2003: 24, 25.

92. Gold, "Bustamante Goes Left."

93. Ibid.

94. Ibid.

95. Robert F. Kennedy, introduction to Kennedy, *Nation of Immigrants,* ix. Note that some Latino scholars and activists have questioned the assertion that the United States is a "nation of immigrants," contending with some persuasive force that this slogan fails to acknowledge the country's indigenous heritage.

96. Ibid., 63.

97. Ibid., 68.

98. Ross, *Robert F. Kennedy,* 348–349.

99. Ibid., 336 (Statement of Robert Kennedy, Subcommittee on Immigration of the Senate Judiciary Committee, Mar. 4, 1965); see also Robert F. Kennedy, *The Pursuit of Justice* (New York: Harper and Row, 1964), 71 (arguing that increased diversity of heritage enlarges our democracy).

100. *Oral History,* 20.

101. Congress amended the act in 1975 to require bilingual ballots anywhere in the United States where certain language minority thresholds are met. This multilingual assistance provision applies only to specified racial and ethnic minority groups.

102. James Crawford, *Hold Your Tongue: Bilingualism and the Politics of English Only* (Reading, MA: Addison-Wesley, 1992), 193.

103. Statement of Senator Kennedy, U.S. Senate, Apr. 5, 1965, in JFK Library, RFK Collection.

104. See *Katzenbach v. Morgan,* 384 U.S. 641 (1966) (upholding the constitutionality of the Kennedy provision). In 2006 Congress reauthorized the Voting Rights Act for twenty-five years. In a scathing article published in *The New Republic* in 1965, law professor Alexander Bickel criticized the Kennedy provision as "irresponsible" because it violated principles of federalism: "[I]t is well to begin by asking why the two Senators from New York did not direct their reforming effort at the state legislature, which is currently in session.... This is too big and diverse a country to be governed in every detail from Washington. All encompassing national government will be insufficiently responsive, and finally, despite appearances, undemocratic.... [Federalism] will become fully obsolete if every time a couple of Senators take a notion to institute a reform in their home state, their first recourse is to amend some handy bill before them; the more so if the notion concerns the very structure of the state government" (Alexander M. Bickel, "The Kennedy-Javits Voting Amendment," *The New Republic,* June 5, 1965: 10).

105. Unless, for example, those voters were schooled in the United States in a bilingual education program in which they ultimately did not gain sufficient English proficiency to pass a voter literacy test, perhaps because they did not complete their education after the sixth grade.

106. *Castro v. State*, 466 P.2d 244 (Cal. 1970).

107. Bilingual Education Act, Pub. L. No. 90-247; see generally Rachel F. Moran, "Bilingual Education as a Status Conflict," 75 *California Law Review* (1987): 321.

108. Robert A. Reveles, *The Arizona Newsletter on Mexican American Affairs*, Feb. 29, 1968, in JFK Library, RFK Collection.

109. James Crawford, "Obituary, The Bilingual Education Act 1968–2002" (Spring 2002), at http://ourworld.compuserve.com/homepages/JWCRAWFORD/T7obit.htm (cited July 11, 2005).

110. Ibid.

111. Raymond Tatalovich, *Nativism Reborn? The Official English Language Movement and the American States* (Lexington: University Press of Kentucky, 1995), 109.

Notes to Chapter 12

1. Schulman, *Robert F. Kennedy*, 97.

2. Ramos, *Latino Wave*, 238.

3. Ibid., xxii.

4. Exit poll statistics from 1960 until 1976 counted only Mexican American voters, with a switch in 1976 to count the broader Latino voting participation.

5. At the time, Texas voted heavily Democratic. In 1960, Kennedy received 91 percent of the Texas Latino (mostly Mexican American) vote. John P. Schmal, "Electing the President: The Latino Electorate (1960–2000)," Apr. 17, 2004, at www. hispanicvista.com (cited May 10, 2005). Even as late as 1969, a survey of the Texas electorate generally found that 70 percent identified themselves as strong or weak Democrats, with 86 percent of Texas Latinos so identifying. Only 6 percent of the Texas electorate generally identified themselves as strong Republicans, with 1 percent of Latino voters so identifying. Clifton McCleskey and Bruce Merrill, "Mexican American Political Behavior in Texas," in *La Causa Politica*, 134.

6. José de la Isla, *The Rise of Hispanic Political Power* (Los Angeles: Archer Books, 2003), 23. Johnson received 86 percent of the Puerto Rican vote in 1964. Schmal, "Electing the President."

7. Louis DeSipio, *Counting on the Latino Vote: Latinos as a New Electorate* (Charlottesville: University Press of Virginia, 1996), 31. Nixon received 15 percent of the Puerto Rican vote in 1968. Schmal, "Electing the President."

8. One commentator credits Nixon in 1972 as receiving 35 percent of the overall Latino vote (Schmal, "Electing the President"). Another reports that Nixon received

31 percent of the Latino vote in 1972 (de la Isla, *Rise of Hispanic Political Power*, 50). CBS polls concluded that Nixon received 31 percent of the Spanish-speaking vote nationally. Castro, *Chicano Power*, 212 (noting that Nixon made sweeping gains in previously Democratic Texas, carrying 49 percent of the Spanish-speaking vote there and also 49 percent among Florida's Cuban-oriented Latino population, but only 11 percent in California).

9. DeSipio, *Counting on the Latino Vote*, 31.

10. Schmal, "Electing the President" (*Los Angeles Times* exit poll apparently for national Latinos).

11. For example, the CBS/*New York Times* poll gave Reagan 35 percent of the Latino vote but the *Los Angeles Times* poll credited Reagan with 47 percent of the Latino vote in 1984. Ibid.

12. For example, the CBS/*New York Times* exit poll had Bush with 31 percent and the *Los Angeles Times* exit poll gave 33 percent of the Latino vote to Bush. Ibid.

13. Voter Research and Surveys had Clinton with 62 percent of the Latino vote. De la Isla, *Rise of Hispanic Political Power*, 235.

14. Voter News Source exit poll, *New York Times* (crediting Dole with 21 percent of the Latino vote in 1996 and Perot with 6 percent); see also Schmal, "Electing the President."

15. Quiñones, *Chicano Politics*, 93–94.

16. Letter from César E. Chávez to President Lyndon B. Johnson, Jan. 8, 1968, JFK Library, RFK Collection.

17. Quiñones, *Chicano Politics*, 161; see also Acuña, *Occupied America*, 379 (noting that in 1973 Nixon appointed an Anglo to the post of aide on domestic Hispanic affairs; apparently she was qualified as a ranch owner in Texas in an area of extensive Mexican American population).

18. See discussion in chapter 7.

19. Acuña, *Occupied America*, 364; see also de la Isla, *Rise of Hispanic Political Power*, 34 (criticizing the Nixon "New Federalism" policy).

20. De la Isla, *Rise of Hispanic Political Power*, 55–56.

21. Raymond Tatalovich, "Official English as Nativist Backlash," in *Immigrants Out!* 78, 98.

22. Bender, *Greasers and Gringos*, 79.

23. Ibid., ch. 8.

24. Ramos, *Latino Wave*, 129–130 (although states can opt out of the federal law with new legislation, the federal legislation put the onus on states to enact this legislation).

25. Schmal, "Electing the President" (reporting that 31 percent of Latino votes went to Bush and 67 percent to Gore in 2000).

26. There was some variation in exit polling—for example, the CNN poll had Bush with 44 percent, but the National Annenberg Election Survey of pre- and post-

election polling found Bush garnering 41 percent of the vote (that poll had determined that Bush obtained 35 percent of the vote in 2000). A *Los Angeles Times* exit poll gave Bush 45 percent of the national Latino vote. By all accounts, despite the variation in polling, Bush made substantial gains in 2004 among Latino voters. See generally John Wildermuth, "Latino Growth Not Reflected in Polls," *San Francisco Chronicle,* June 28, 2005 (suggesting through later study that Bush's share of the Latino vote was closer to 40 percent than the 44 percent originally shown by national exit polls, but acknowledging nonetheless the dramatic boost seen for Republicans).

27. Raoul Lowery Contreras, "Hispanics, Morality, Values and Republicans," at www.hispanicvista.com (cited Feb. 2, 2005).

28. Patrick Osio Jr., "Hispanics/Latinos Didn't Vote Republican—They Voted for Bush," at www.hispanicvista.com (cited Feb. 2, 2005).

29. Raoul Lowery Contreras, "Hispanic Male Voters Flock to the President!" at www.hispanicvista.com (cited Feb. 2, 2005).

30. Pew Hispanic Center Report, "Hispanics and the 2004 Election: Population, Electorate and Voters," June 27, 2005 [hereinafter Pew 2004 Election Report].

31. CNN 2004 Exit Poll.

32. Ibid.

33. Contreras, "Hispanic Male Voters."

34. Stephen Dinan, "Hispanic Men Moved to Bush," *Washington Times,* Dec. 22, 2004.

35. Ibid.

36. Pew 2004 Election Report.

37. See chapter 13 for a discussion of Catholic voting.

38. Richard Morin and Dan Balz, "Poll Shows Kerry Leading among Registered Latinos," July 21, 2004, at washingtonpost.com.

39. Pew 2004 Latino Survey, 24.

40. A separate poll in 2005 found that 62 percent of Hispanic voters opposed gay marriage. National Latino Survey, 2005, the Latino Coalition [hereinafter Latino Coalition Survey, 2005].

41. *Lawrence v. Texas,* 539 U.S. 558 (2003).

42. Adam Nagourney and Janet Elder, "Latinos Surveyed on Politics," *New York Times,* Aug. 3, 2003.

43. CNN 2004 Exit Poll.

44. Ibid.

45. Antoinette Sedillo Lopez, "Hispanics 'Wedged,'" *Albuquerque Tribune,* Nov. 11, 2004.

46. During the 2004 election season, I received a mass mailing containing the allegedly nonpartisan 2004 Christian Coalition Voter Guide, which showcased the moral issues of abortion (separated into three issues: support for unrestricted abortion on demand, banning partial-birth abortions, and public financing of abortions) and

gay rights (in two issues, support for passage of a federal marriage protection amendment, and adoption of children by homosexuals). Bush's positions listed on all these select moral issues stood in sharp contrast to Kerry's positions.

47. Lopez, "Hispanics 'Wedged.'"

48. "Latino Groups Endorse President George W. Bush," Oct. 27, 2004, www.usnewswire.com (cited Dec. 27, 2006).

49. Steven Thomma, "Catholics Divided on Bush, Kerry," *Oregonian*, June 4, 2004, A2.

50. Mary Jo McConahay and Elena Shore, "Republican Appeal to Latinos' Conservative Side Helped Bush," www.pacificnews.com (cited Mar. 20, 2005).

51. Brian DeBose, "Bush Share of Hispanic Vote Rose to 44 Percent," at www.hispanicvista.com (cited Mar. 20, 2005).

52. Pete Martinez, "Bush Got Latinos to Vote for Him in Spite of Latino 'Nonpartisan' Organizations," at www.hispanicvista.com (cited Feb. 2, 2005); see also Ramos, *Latino Wave*, 224. A 2005 survey on the question of which Latino public figure living today was most admired found that well over half of those surveyed gave no answer, and of those who did, Los Angeles mayor Antonio Villaraigosa came out on top with only 4.3 percent of the respondents, followed by entertainer Jennifer Lopez with 2.2 percent. Latino Coalition Survey, 2005.

53. Raoul Lowery Contreras, "Hispanics, Morality, Values and Republicans," at www.hispanicvista.com (cited Feb. 2, 2005).

54. Ibid.

55. George Wallace and Nixon began the code-speak in the 1968 campaign, with Wallace using language of law and order, running your own schools, and protecting property rights: "Nixon spoke in the same stilted code where 'bloc vote' meant 'black vote' and 'neighborhood schools' meant 'all-white schools.' 'Hard-core unemployed,' 'welfare cheats,' and 'laggards,' and 'muggers' and 'rapists' and assorted other 'street punks' meant black people generally" (Kenneth O'Reilly, *Nixon's Piano: Presidents and Racial Politics from Washington to Clinton* [New York: Free Press, 1995], 281).

56. Michelle Malkin, *Invasion: How America Still Welcomes Terrorists, Criminals, and Other Foreign Menaces to Our Shores* (Washington, DC: Regnery Publishing, 2002), 39, 45.

57. Pew 2004 Latino Survey, chart 20 (of registered Latino voters, 26 percent were born in another country).

58. Ramos, *Latino Wave*, 125.

59. Ibid.

60. Pew 2004 Latino Survey, 26. The same survey found that the vast majority (84 percent) of registered Latino voters favored the proposal endorsed by John Kerry in the 2004 campaign that created a pathway to citizenship for undocumented immigrants, with only 13 percent of registered Latinos opposing the proposal. Ibid., 8; a 2005 survey confirmed the percentage of support for a citizenship plan. Pew

Hispanic Center Report, "Attitudes toward Immigrants and Immigration Policy: Surveys among Latinos in the U.S. and in Mexico," Aug. 16, 2005 [hereinafter Pew Immigration Survey].

61. Bender, *Greasers and Gringos*, 139.

62. Steven W. Bender, "Sight, Sound, and Stereotype: The War on Terrorism and Its Consequences for Latinas/os," 81 *Oregon Law Review* (2002): 1153; Johnson, "Driver's Licenses and Undocumented Immigrants."

63. Pew 2004 Latino Survey, chart 23 (figures given are for Latino adults).

64. Ibid., 7.

65. *Negron v. State of New York*, 434 F.2d 386 (2nd Cir. 1970).

66. Georgie Anne Geyer, "Illegal Immigration Shows Up at Core of California Angst," *Oregonian*, Oct. 27, 2003, B7.

67. Harold Meyerson, "Bush's Retreat on Immigration Reform," *Washington Post*, July 21, 2004, A19; Steven Ginsberg, "Demonstrators Swarm around Rove's Home," *Washington Post*, Mar. 29, 2004, B1.

68. Latino Coalition Survey, 2005 (49.6 to 19.3 percent on issue of job creation, 50.1 to 19.8 percent on issue of improving education, 54.5 to 15 percent on health care, 45.8 to 16.5 percent on immigration views, and 56.5 to 16.3 percent on being in touch with the Latino community; the Republican Party did fare slightly better than the Democratic Party on the question of which party better kept the United States safe from terrorism, 29.8 to 29.5 percent).

69. Pew 2004 Latino Survey.

70. Kerry and Edwards, *Plan for America*, 246 (citing 1.9 million lost private-sector jobs, presumably during Bush's first term in office).

71. Arian Campo-Flores and Howard Fineman, "A Latin Power Surge," *Newsweek*, May 30, 2005: 26.

72. Roberto Suro, "Latino Power? It Will Take Time for the Population Boom to Translate," June 26, 2005, B1, at washingtonpost.com (cited Sept. 6, 2005); Pew 2004 Election Report.

73. Pew 2004 Election Report, 6.

74. Ibid.

75. Ibid.

76. Newfield, *Robert F. Kennedy*, 320.

77. Dr. Victor M. Rodriguez, "Republicans Develop a Three-Pronged Latino Strategy: Democrats Practice Benign Neglect," Jan. 9, 2004, at hispanicvista.com (cited Sept. 6, 2005). Still, Arnold Schwarzenegger lured a significant number of Latino voters with a platform and background combining conservative economic policies with liberal social values.

78. *Oral History*, 39–40.

79. National Annenberg Election Survey, Dec. 21, 2004, at www.annenbergpublicpolicycenter.org/Downloads/Political_Communication/naes/2004_

03_hispanic-data-12_21_pr.pdf (cited May 26, 2007) (revealing that Latinos of South American and Central American background, although identifying primarily as Democrats, were respectively 40 and 26 percent Independent, as compared to Mexican Americans, who identified 22 percent as Independent).

80. La Botz, *César Chávez*, 179.

Notes to Chapter 13

1. Schulman, *Robert F. Kennedy*, xi.

2. Luís D. León, "César Chávez and Mexican American Civil Religion," in Espinosa, Elizondo, and Miranda, *Latino Religions*, 53.

3. García, *Latino Politics*, 25.

4. Available at www.facsnet.org/issues/faith/espinoza.php (cited Jan. 5, 2006).

5. Jon Lewis, *From This Earth ... of the Delano Grape Strike* (n.p., 1969).

6. García, *Chicanismo*, 88; Dalton, *Moral Vision*, 35.

7. Dalton, *Moral Vision*, 40.

8. Ibid., 46.

9. Hammerback and Jensen, *Rhetorical Career*, 85; Taylor, *Chavez*, 167.

10. César Chávez, "The Mexican American and the Church," in *La Causa Política*, 143, 144.

11. Harry Bernstein, "Catholic Leaders Urge Bargaining at Delano," *Los Angeles Times*, Mar. 17, 1966, A4.

12. "Amending Migratory Labor Laws," 633.

13. Dick Meister, "Catholic Bishops Back Farm Unions," *San Francisco Chronicle*, Mar. 17, 1966, A1.

14. Ibid.

15. Bernstein, "Catholic Leaders."

16. Dalton, *Moral Vision*, 56.

17. Statement of the National Conference of Catholic Bishops, Wayne State Library, UFW Information and Research Part 1, Box 3, Folder 16.

18. Father Richard Humphrys, A Position Paper for Churchmen with Regard to the Farm Labor Issue, May 1974, Wayne State Library, UFW Information and Research Part 1, Box 3, Folder 16.

19. Statement by Pope Paul VI at Private Audience for César Chávez and Party, Sept. 25, 1974, in Wayne State Library, UFW Information and Research Part 1, Box 3, Folder 16.

20. CNN 2004 Exit Poll.

21. Steven Thomma, "Catholics Divided on Bush, Kerry," *Oregonian*, June 4, 2004, A2; William B. Prendergast, *The Catholic Voter in American Politics: The*

Passing of the Democratic Monolith (Washington, DC: Georgetown University Press, 1999), 223; see also Lawrence H. Fuchs, *John F. Kennedy and American Catholicism* (New York: Meredith Press, 1967), 186 ("Also, by 1960, large numbers of Catholics had moved to the suburbs, away from their lower-class and lower-middle-class origins and presumably were more vulnerable to Republican appeals on domestic issues").

22. Thomas J. Carty, *A Catholic in the White House? Religion, Politics, and John F. Kennedy's Presidential Campaign* (New York: Palgrave Macmillan, 2004), 95.

23. Ibid., 162.

24. Konstantin Sidorenko, *Robert F. Kennedy: A Spiritual Biography* (New York: Crossroad Publishing Company, 2000), 111; Kennedy, *To Seek a Newer World,* 105 ("I believe we should provide assistance to any nation that decides family planning and population control are in its national interest, as well as accelerate our research into population control devices and techniques").

25. Sydney H. Schanberg, "Javits Calls on Legislature to Pass Abortion Reform," *New York Times,* Feb. 20, 1967, 1.

26. Ibid.

27. Letter from Robert F. Kennedy to Gary S. Ellis, Jan. 12, 1968, JFK Library, Health: Birth Control file.

28. In 1972, the state legislature repealed the liberalized abortion law, but Governor Rockefeller vetoed the repeal as it would reactivate the "backroom abortion mill trade."

29. Carty, *A Catholic in the White House?* 162–163. At the same time, many Catholics were highly supportive of the war effort and taken aback by violence in the antiwar movement. Prendergast, *The Catholic Voter,* 30.

30. Prendergast, *The Catholic Voter,* 157 (noting that the Michigan Survey Research Center found an even stronger Catholic vote for Nixon in 1972 at 60 percent).

31. N.E.H. Hull and Peter Charles Hoffer, *Roe v. Wade: The Abortion Rights Controversy in American History* (Lawrence: University Press of Kansas, 2001), 163–164.

32. Prendergast, *The Catholic Voter,* 162.

33. *Roe v. Wade,* 410 U.S. 113 (1973) (recognizing a right to privacy that prevents most state regulation of abortion in the first trimester, permits state regulation that protects maternal health in the second trimester, and allows states to prohibit abortion in the third trimester but with exceptions to preserve the life and health of the mother).

34. Philip R. Fileri and Jeffery S. Sabin, "The Politics of Abortion in New York State" (undergraduate honors thesis, Cornell University, May 15, 1974).

35. Hull and Hoffer, *Roe v. Wade,* 186.

36. Carty, *A Catholic in the White House?* 166.

37. Ibid., 169.

38. Thomma, "Catholics Divided."

39. Pope John Paul II, *Memory and Identity: Conversations at the Dawn of a Millennium* (New York: Rizzoli, 2005).

40. Walter L. Williams and Yolanda Retter, eds., *Gay and Lesbian Rights in the United States: A Documentary History* (Westport, CT: Greenwood Press, 2003), 180.

41. *Shared Catholic Social Teaching: Challenges and Directions, Reflections of U.S. Catholic Bishops* (Washington, DC: U.S. Catholic Conference, 1998), 5.

42. Michael Pennock, *Catholic Social Teaching: Learning and Living Justice* (Notre Dame, IN: Ave Maria Press, 2000), 191.

43. Manuel G. Gonzales and Richard Delgado, *The Politics of Fear: How Republicans Use Money, Race, and the Media to Win* (Boulder, CO: Paradigm Publishers, 2006), 96.

44. Lopez, "Hispanics 'Wedged.'"

45. See generally Terry Coonan, "There Are No Strangers among Us: Catholic Social Teachings and U.S. Immigration Law," *Catholic Lawyer*, v. 40 (2000): 105.

46. House Bill Denounced by a Range of Leaders, at hispanicvista.com (cited July 11, 2005) (noting that the Old Testament contains references to protecting aliens, who are vulnerable to exploitation).

47. Deal W. Hudson, "Is Cardinal Mahony Right on Immigration?" Mar. 15, 2006, The Window, an e-mail publication of the Morley Institute for Church and Culture.

48. David Rieff, "Nuevo Catholics," *New York Times*, Dec. 24, 2006.

49. Alexander Zaitchik, "Who Would Jesus Deport?" Jan. 29, 2007, www.alternet.org (cited Feb. 3, 2007).

50. Rachel Zoll, "Immigration Reform Splits Catholics, GOP," *Seattle Post-Intelligencer*, Apr. 21, 2006.

51. Available at www.facsnet.org/issues/faith/espinoza.php (cited Jan. 5, 2006).

52. Oropeza, *Raza Sí*, 164.

53. George Mariscal, ed., *Aztlán and Viet Nam: Chicano and Chicana Experiences of the War* (Berkeley: University of California Press, 1999), 191.

54. Chávez, "The Mexican American" (emphasis in original).

55. Lawrence J. Mosqueda, *Chicanos, Catholicism and Political Ideology* (Lanham, MD: University Press of America, 1986), 138.

56. CNN 2004 Exit Poll.

57. Deal W. Hudson, "Immigration Threatens GOP Hispanic Outreach," Mar. 31, 2006, Morley Institute for Church and Culture.

58. Available at www.facsnet.org/issues/faith/espinoza.php (cited Jan. 5, 2006).

59. Pew 2004 Election Report.

60. Ibid., 13, n.1 (reporting that preelection surveys show that the bulk of the Latino non-Catholic, Christian voters are evangelical or born-again Christians, as opposed to mainline Protestants).

61. Ibid.

62. Gastón Espinosa, "Latino Clergy and Churches in Faith-Based Political and Social Action in the United States," in Espinosa, Elizondo, and Miranda, *Latino Religions*, 299.

63. Pew 2004 Election Report, 10.

64. Ibid.

65. Espinosa, "Latino Clergy," 282–283.

66. Etulain, *César Chávez*, 23.

67. Rank, *One Nation, Underprivileged*, 125.

Notes to Chapter 14

1. Telegram from Martin Luther King, Jr. to César Cháve[z], Mar. 5, 1968, in Wayne State Library, UFW Office of the President, Box 30, Folder 13.

2. Telegram from César E. Chávez to Mrs. Martin Luther King, Jr., in Wayne State Library, *El Malcriado*, vol. 2, Feb. 1968–Feb. 1969. A letter to Robert Kennedy in March 1968 accused Chávez of adhering to the politics of the Black Power advocates, contending that Chávez wanted a "marriage between the Americans of Mexican descent and the militant radicals like Stokely Carmichael who wants to burn America down … [and] DESTROY White America." Letter from Alfred Ramirez to Senator Robert Kennedy, Mar. 24, 1968, JFK Library, RFK Collection. In contrast to these absurd allegations, Chávez steadfastly followed the same path of nonviolence as Kennedy and King.

3. Jensen and Hammerback, *Words of César Chávez*, 96.

4. Witcover, *85 Days*, 143.

5. Etulain, *César Chávez*, 81.

6. Schlesinger, *Robert Kennedy*, 779.

7. *Boynton v. Virginia*, 364 U.S. 454 (1960).

8. Schlesinger, *Robert Kennedy*, 873.

9. Ibid.

10. Ibid., 878.

11. David Halberstam, *The Unfinished Odyssey of Robert Kennedy* (New York: Random House, 1968), 198.

12. Bender and Aoki, "Seekin' the Cause," 610.

13. Ian F. Haney López, "Protest, Repression, and Race: Legal Violence and the Chicano Movement," 150 *University of Pennsylvania Law Review* (2001): 205, 217.

14. Schlesinger, *Robert Kennedy*, 781.

15. Bender, *Greasers and Gringos*, 165–166.

16. Raquel L. Swarns, "Growing Unease for Some Blacks on Immigration," *New York Times*, May 4, 2006.

17. Mayer, *Running on Race*, 94.

18. James Dao, "G.O.P. Backs Blacks to Run to Lure Votes," *New York Times*, July 1, 2005.

19. Paula D. McClain and Joseph Stewart, Jr., *"Can We All Get Along?" Racial and Ethnic Minorities in American Politics* (Boulder, CO: Westview Press, 2002, 3d. ed.), 97.

20. CNN 2004 Exit Poll.

21. Steven Bender, Sylvia R. Lazos Vargas, and Keith Aoki, "Race and the California Recall: A Top Ten List of Ironies," 16 *Berkeley La Raza Law Journal* (2005): 11, 16. But the Asian American vote in California went to the Republican candidates, who pulled 60 percent of the Asian American vote.

22. Once in office, Hahn alienated the African American community when he refused to support the reappointment of the city's black police chief, and Villaraigosa claimed the mayor's office in the 2005 election.

23. Mayer, *Running on Race*, 16–17.

24. National Latino Congreso Resolution 1.2 (adopted Sept. 6, 2006).

Notes to Chapter 15

1. Hopkins, *Rights for Americans*, 229 (speech delivered May 20, 1964, to Young Israel of Pelham Parkway, New York City).

2. David Bacon, "Uniting African-Americans and Immigrants," Aug. 26, 2005, at truthout.com (cited Aug. 15, 2006).

3. "Numbers," *Time*, Jan. 19, 2004.

4. Philip A. Klinkner, "Bill Clinton and the Politics of the New Liberalism," in Adolph Reed Jr., ed., *Without Justice for All: The New Liberalism and Our Retreat from Racial Equality* (Boulder, CO: Westview Press, 1999), 12.

5. Field Institute, "Voting in the 1994 General Election" (Jan. 1995), 3.

6. Angela D. Dillard, *Guess Who's Coming to Dinner Now? Multicultural Conservatism in America* (New York: NYU Press, 2001), 176.

7. See Bruce E. Cain and Karin MacDonald, "Race and Party Politics in the 1996 U.S. Presidential Election," in Preston, Cain, and Bass, *Racial and Ethnic Politics in California*, 201.

8. Bender, Lazos, and Aoki, "Race and the California Recall," 20: "Nowhere was this electoral immigration dichotomy of 'good' and 'bad' immigrants more evident than in Schwarzenegger's campaign ads. To the Spanish-language media went ads

proclaiming Arnold's background as an immigrant, but to mainstream media and Anglo voters Schwarzenegger's ads decried California's law allowing undocumented immigrants to obtain driver's licenses."

9. Carla Marinucci and Mark Martin, "Governor Endorses Minutemen on Border," Apr. 29, 2005, at www.sfgate.com (cited Sept. 6, 2005).

10. Robert Salladay, "Polls Push Governor to the Border," Apr. 30, 2005, at www.latimes.com (cited June 14, 2005).

11. Arianna Huffington, "And Now for Something Completely Different: Real Moral Values," Nov. 10, 2004, at hispanicvista.com (cited June 14, 2005); see also Arianna Huffington, *Fanatics and Fools: The Game Plan for Winning Back America* (New York: Hyperion, 2004).

12. Jim Wallis, *God's Politics: Why the Right Gets It Wrong and the Left Doesn't Get It* (New York: HarperSanFrancisco, 2005) (commenting that poverty has fallen off the national social and political agenda).

13. Huffington, *Fanatics and Fools*, 253.

14. In a 5 to 4 decision in 1982, the Supreme Court recognized a constitutional basis for undocumented school-age children to attend public school. *Plyler v. Doe*, 457 U.S. 202 (1982). Congress codified *Plyler* in the Personal Responsibility and Work Opportunity Reconciliation Act of 1996 by prohibiting states from denying children access to public elementary schools. See 8 U.S.C. § 1643(a)(2).

15. Marc Cooper, "Beyond the Borders of Hypocrisy," at http://www.huffingtonpost.com/theblog/archive/marc-cooper/beyond-the-borders-of-hyp_1492.html (cited June 14, 2005).

16. See Peter Laufer, *Wetback Nation: The Case for Opening the Mexican–American Border* (Chicago: Ivan R. Dee, 2004) (arguing that open borders will enable the Border Patrol to concentrate on drug traffickers and terrorists).

17. *America the Beautiful: In the Words of Robert F. Kennedy* (New York: G.P. Putnam's Sons, 1968), 24 (excerpting Robert Kennedy's speech June 6, 1965, at State University College, Plattsburgh, New York).

18. Kennedy, *To Seek a Newer World*, 65.

19. Robert F. Kennedy, *Thirteen Days: A Memoir of the Cuban Missile Crisis* (New York: W.W. Norton and Company, 1969), 51, 120–121.

20. José Luis Morín, *Latino/a Rights and Justice in the United States: Perspectives and Approaches* (Durham, NC: Carolina Academic Press, 2005), 34 (noting that as a result of the 1980s intervention, hundreds of thousands of Central Americans became refugees, and that by the early 1990s, more than a million Salvadorans and 200,000 Guatemalan refugees resided in the United States).

21. Laufer, *Wetback Nation*, 205.

22. For example, Calderón implored "[t]he only solution to the basic problem of emigration is to multiply job opportunities in this country and open doors to investment in Mexico." *Hispanic*, Feb. 2007: 11.

23. "Senator Kennedy Outlines Concerns with Chairman Specter's Immigration Proposal," Feb. 28, 2006, at www.americanchronicle.com/articles/viewArticle.asp?articleID=637 8 (cited Aug. 8, 2007).

24. "Immigration Bill Debate Could Last a 'Couple of Weeks,'" May 21, 2007, at www.cnn.com (cited May 26, 2007).

25. Richardson, "Seeking the Latino Vote."

26. Ann Radelat, "Election 2004: Up for Grabs," *Hispanic*, Oct. 2004: 16, 17.

27. Pew Immigration Survey.

28. Mitchell Landsberg, "L.A. Mayor Sees Dropout Rate as 'Civil Rights Issue,'" *Los Angeles Times*, Mar. 2, 2006.

29. Aurelio Rojas, "Blacks, Latinos Try to Find Unity in L.A.," July 23, 2006, at www.sacbee.com/content/politics (cited Aug. 15, 2006).

30. Senator John F. Kerry, "I Am More in Touch," *Hispanic*, Oct. 2004: 25.

31. President George W. Bush, "My Record Stands," *Hispanic*, Oct. 2004: 20.

32. Pachon, "Latino Politics in the Golden State," 418.

33. Lance T. Izumi, "California Teachers Association Members Should Join Minutemen," May 18, 2005, at www.pacificresearch.org/pub/cap/2005/cap_05-05-18.html (cited Dec. 27, 2006).

34. Darryl Fears, "Latinos Express Election Concern: Bush, Kerry Teams Reassure Group," June 26, 2004, A6, at washingtonpost.com (cited July 11, 2005) (remarks of professor Leobardo Estrada).

35. Robert Kennedy's legacy is marked in many schools, including the Colegio Robert F. Kennedy, a private Catholic school in Atizapán, Mexico.

36. Kennedy, *To Seek a Newer World*, 82.

37. Viva Kennedy, in Wayne State Library, UFW Office of the President, Box 48, File 14.

38. Jensen and Hammerback, *Words of César Chávez*, 150–151.

39. Castro, *Chicano Power*, 3–4.

Notes to the Conclusion

1. Pitrone, *Chavez: Man of the Migrants*, 166.

Index

Abortion, 148–149; Catholic Church and, 149, 150, 151, 154; constitutional limits on, 147; Latinos and, 131, 132, 133, 134, 138, 139, 143, 153; RFK and, 147–148

Acosta, Oscar "Zeta": on Kennedy, 52

Activism, 69; Catholic Church and, 153; Latino, 140

Acuña, Rodolfo, 9

Affirmative action, 97, 99, 116, 135; education and, 174; at University of Michigan, 137

AFL-CIO, 27, 38, 54, 105; immigrant legalization and, 112; UFWOC and, 37

African Americans: antipoverty agenda and, 95; Chávez and, 160; Chicano Movement and, 69; Democratic Party and, 91, 138, 147, 159, 160, 161, 163; economic status of, 82; National Latino Congreso and, 162; Nixon and, 55; population of, 162; racial profiling and, 97; Republican Party and, 160, 161; RFK and, 42, 43, 92, 93, 158, 160; undocumented immigrants and, 159; urban unrest and, 53, 81, 82; Vietnam War and, 77; voter turnout by, 47, 49

AgJOBS. *See* Agricultural Jobs, Opportunity, Benefits, and Security bill

Agricultural industry, Latinos and, 135

Agricultural Jobs, Opportunity, Benefits, and Security bill (AgJOBS), 112, 113, 114, 166, 170, 171

Agricultural Workers Organizing Committee (AWOC), 9, 12, 27, 68

Aid to Families with Dependent Children, 87

Allen, Steve, 94

Alliance for Progress, 168

American Farm Bureau Federation, 11

American Law Institute Model Penal Code, 147–148

Amigos de Goldwater, 10

Amnesty, 111, 116, 129, 166; granting, 112; opposition to, 115

Anti-immigrant sentiment, 45, 74, 101, 102, 116, 118–119, 129, 134, 137, 140, 151, 164–165, 171, 172, 173, 176; Democratic Party and, 165; Republican Party and, 165

Anti-Mexican sentiment, 45, 102, 116, 117, 118–119

Antipoverty coalition, 93, 95, 98, 161, 162; focus of, 97; goals of, 96; health care and, 96; nurturing, 90; RFK and, 91, 92, 96

Antipoverty policy, 81, 99, 168

Anti-Spanish laws, 137

Antle, Bud: boycott and, 62, 63

AP, poll by, 132

Arizona State Game Commission, mock guidelines from, 113

Arizona Taxpayer and Citizen Protection Act (2004), 116

Arriba Goldwater, 10
Asian Americans: antipoverty agenda
and, 95; Democratic Party and, 160
Assimilationism, 70, 113–114
Aviation and Transportation Security Act
(2001), 136
AWOC. *See* Agricultural Workers
Organizing Committee

Barrios, 45, 66, 158; life in, 82, 88;
poverty in, 4, 82
Bell, Derrick, 97
Berle, Milton, 47
Bilingual education, 69, 121, 134; end
of, 120, 122, 129; opposition to, 116,
122, 135
Bilingual Education Act (1967), 121, 122,
128
Birth control, 147, 148, 152
Bishop's Committee on Farm Labor, 145,
146
Black-brown alliance, 159, 160–162
Black Power, 70, 158, 159
Bond, Julian, 56
Border patrol, 101, 110, 167
Border Protection, Anti-Terrorism, and
Illegal Immigration Control Act
(2005), 115, 151, 171
Border security, 114, 115–116, 167, 171
Boycotts, 10, 53, 65, 76, 128, 146; Chávez
and, 24, 59, 60–61, 83; eluding, 25;
farm workers and, 54, 145; RFK and,
24, 36, 60, 145; secondary, 54, 59, 60,
61, 62, 63; support for, 54
Bracero Program, 107, 111–112, 123,
172; abuses of, 104–105; end of, 106;
opposition to, 170
Branigan, Roger, 91
Brown, Edmund "Jerry," 55, 61, 141
Brown, Kathleen, 116
Brown, Pat, 22
Brown, Rap, 71
Brown Berets, 68, 70

Buchanan, Patrick: abortion issue and,
148; anti-immigrant sentiment and,
45; Latinos/welfare abuse and, 99; on
Mexican immigration, 101
Bush, George H. W., 127, 160
Bush, George W.: African American
vote for, 159–160; agribusiness and,
170; Asian American vote for, 160;
backlash against, 165; border security
and, 116; Catholic vote for, 147,
150, 153; economic plans of, 88; Fox
negotiations with, 112; guest worker
program and, 168; immigration reform
and, 104, 112, 129, 151, 164; Latino
vote for, 90, 127, 129, 130, 132–133,
153, 159, 173; Minutemen Project and,
165; No Child Left Behind and, 121,
173; REAL ID Act and, 151
Bustamante, Cruz, 133, 160; criticism
of, 117–118; Latino vote for, 90, 126,
127; UFW and, 118; undocumented
immigration and, 117

Calderón, Felipe: immigration reform
and, 169
California Agricultural Relations Act
(1975), 62, 64
California primary: Chávez and, 43, 47,
48; Mexican Americans and, 46, 48,
49, 97; RFK and, 42, 43, 44, 45, 47,
48, 49
California Supreme Court, 63, 121
California Teachers Association, 173
Carter, Jimmy, 55, 87, 149
Casa Avila, 6
Castro, Tony: on Kennedys/Mexican
Americans, 73
Catholic Church: abortion issue and, 149,
150, 151, 154; activism of, 153; birth
control and, 152; Chávez and, 146,
152–153; Democratic Party and, 146,
147, 149, 150; farm labor movement
and, 144, 145; gay marriage and,

15, 150, 151; immigration reform
and, 151; Latinos and, 132, 143;
Republican Party and, 149; social
justice and, 150, 151, 152
Chávez, César, v; candlelight mass
for, 62–63; Communist allegations
against, 20–21; contempt charges
against, 28; criticism of, 21; death of,
63, 64, 65, 83; health problems of,
56, 57; honoring, 33, 34; interview
of, 177; pilgrimage by, 22; praise for,
42; presidential campaign and, 4–5,
37–38, 39; on RFK, 27, 36, 143; RFK
death and, 50; RFK friendship with,
2, 7, 11, 15–16, 20–21, 26, 34–35, 46,
135, 145; testimony of, 12; vision of,
155, 162; youth of, 2–3, 83
Chávez, Fernando, 79
Chávez, Helen, 2, 9, 31, 63; arrest of, 16,
17
Chávez, Richard, 8, 63; on farm workers/
RFK, 36; on fruits/vegetables, 58; on
RFK, 34, 36, 120; on strikebreakers,
115
Chicano Liberation Front, 70
Chicano Moratorium, 77, 78
Chicano Movement, 68, 71, 134, 158;
African Americans and, 69; antiwar
march and, 77; Chávez and, 46,
72–73; decline of, 74; emergence of,
66–67, 70; manifesto of, 67; Mexican
Americans and, 46; nationalism of, 67;
school "blowouts" and, 69
Chicano Studies, 70
Chicano Youth Liberation Conference, 70
Child labor, 11, 13, 63
Citizen militia, 113, 116
Citizenship, 110, 113; airport screeners
and, 136; barriers to, 102; classes for,
56, 139; Latinos and, 135; pathway
to, 3, 112, 116, 137, 168, 170, 171,
172; proof of, 122; requirements for,
111; test for, 111; UFW and, 115;

undocumented workers and, 115, 116,
140
Civil liberties, 17, 134
Civil rights, 10, 21, 133, 158, 163; Chávez
and, 155; laws, 91; reform, 122, 161;
RFK and, 155
Civil Rights Act (1964), 133
Civil Rights Movement, 79, 99, 106,
155; Chávez and, 78; Communist
involvement in, 158; King and, 157,
158–159; rural justice and, 157
Clinton, Bill, 136, 164; Asian American
vote for, 160; border security and, 114,
167; immigration and, 129; Latino
issues and, 128–129; Latino vote for,
127; RFK and, 88; welfare and, 88,
129
Clinton, Hillary, 113, 116
CNN, 114, 165
CNN poll, on Iraq War, 80
Collective bargaining, 33, 145;
farm workers and, 23, 62; illegal
immigrants and, 101
Colson, Charles, 148
Commonweal, 147, 148
Commonwealth Club, 58
Communism, 21, 25
Community development corporations,
86
Community Service Organization
(CSO), 50, 67; Chávez and, 3, 4, 8,
10; convention of, 8; farm worker
organization and, 9; Viva Kennedy
and, 6; voter registration and, 6, 38
Commuter workers, 108
Congressional Black Caucus, 163
Contreras, Raoul Lowery, 130
Corona, Bert, 41, 46, 48
Coyotes, 167
Craig, Larry: AgJOBS and, 113
Crawford, James: Bilingual Education
Act and, 122
Criminal justice system, Latinos and, 136

Kennedy, Robert, v; assassination of,
10, 46, 49, 50, 55, 56, 78, 87, 88;
Chávez friendship with, 2, 7, 11,
15–16, 20–21, 26, 34–35, 46, 135, 145;
Chávez on, 26; criticism of, 20, 35;
election of, 11; JFK campaign and, 5;
memorial for, 55–56, 61; presidential
campaign of, 2, 4–5, 37–38, 40, 41,
42–44, 45–46, 48–49, 81–82; support
for, 91, 92–93; vision of, 155, 177;
youth of, 83
Kerry, John: abortion issue and, 132,
149–150; African American vote
for, 159; AgJOBS and, 113; Asian
American vote for, 160; Catholic vote
for, 147; Dream Act and, 112–113;
education and, 173; gay marriage
and, 132; immigration proposal and,
112–113; Iraq War and, 80; Latino
vote for, 129, 130, 131, 132, 137, 159;
platform of, 88
King, Coretta Scott, 56, 63, 156
King, Martin Luther, Jr., 15, 46, 62,
69; African American vote and,
161; assassination of, 133, 156–157;
Chávez and, 155, 157; civil rights
and, 155; Civil Rights Movement
and, 157; class-based coalitions and,
94; farm worker movement and, 157;
fast and, 155–156; Hoover and, 158;
Nixon and, 161; nonviolence and,
155, 156–157; RFK and, 157, 158;
Vietnam War and, 77, 158; vision of,
154, 162

Labor camps, 14, 84
Labor issues, 13–14, 107, 141
Labor laws, 54, 74
Labor market economics, 22
Labor reform, 11–12, 13, 22, 123
Landrum-Griffin Act (1959), 59
Latino Coalition, National Hispanic
Survey from, 132–133

Latino immigrants, 97, 135; employment
of, 102; origins of, 142; Proposition
187 and, 98
Latinos: Catholic Church and, 132, 143;
Democratic Party and, 10, 89–90,
127, 130, 131, 135, 136, 138, 139,
140, 141, 143; health insurance and,
89; household income for, 90; Iraq
War and, 79; moral issues and, 131,
132; patriotism of, 135; political
prominence of, 58, 142; population of,
162; poverty and, 89; Protestantism
and, 153; racial profiling and, 97;
Republican Party and, 89–90, 127,
131, 132, 136, 138, 139, 140, 141,
163, 172; RFK and, 138, 147, 160;
unemployment of, 89; Vietnam War
and, 79; voting behavior of, 90;
welfare abuse and, 99
Latino vote, 139, 141, 161; capturing,
126; gender gap in, 130; income and,
130
Lawson, Patricia Kennedy: remembrances
and, 56–57
League of United Latin American
Citizens (LULAC), 112, 158
Lee, Sheila Jackson, 163
Limited-English proficiency (LEP)
students, 121, 128
Literacy tests, 120, 121
London, Jack, 15
López Tijerina, Reies, 70, 74
Los Angeles County, Mexican population
of, 4
Los Angeles Times, 65, 68, 77, 145, 176; on
barrios, 82; on Bracero Program, 106;
on Bustamante, 118; on Chávez fast,
30; on JFK, 6
Los Lobos, quote from, 45
Lungren, Dan, 164

Mahony, Roger, 64, 151
Malcolm X, 70

Malcriado, El, 38, 46, 52
Malkin, Michelle: on driver's licenses/
undocumented workers, 134
Mann, Horace, 174
MAPA. *See* Mexican American Political
Association
Marriage, defining, 131. *See also* Gay
marriage
Martin Luther King Nonviolent Peace
Award, 156
McCain, John, 113, 172
McCarrick, Theodore, 151
McCarthy, Eugene, 52; boycott and, 54,
60; presidential campaign and, 37, 38,
39, 42; support for, 39, 47, 49, 91, 92,
93; Vietnam War and, 41, 147
McClintock, Tom, 90, 117, 126
McGovern, George: abortion issue and,
148–149; boycott and, 60; Chávez and,
72, 73; La Raza Unida and, 74
McIntyre, Cardinal, 145
Meany, George, 37
MEChA. *See* Movimiento Estudiantil
Chicano de Aztlán
Medicaid, 87
Medicare, 98, 172
Memorial Park, mass/ceremony at, 30
"Mexican American and the Church,
The" (Chávez), 144
Mexican American community, 2,
66; California primary and, 46,
48, 49, 97; Chávez and, 36, 159,
161; Chicano Movement and, 46;
Democratic Party and, 55, 89, 126,
127, 133, 135, 140, 153, 159; East Los
Angeles and, 85; economic status of,
82; equality for, 176; human rights
and, 176; Humphrey and, 55; JFK
campaign and, 5; nationalism and,
68; Nixon and, 55, 73; presidential
campaign and, 43–44, 47; racism and,
5; Republican Party and, 126, 141,
147, 153, 160; respect for, 71; RFK

and, 36, 39, 41, 42, 43, 50, 69, 72,
73, 92, 93, 158; struggles of, 67–68;
undocumented immigrants and, 159;
Vietnam War and, 69, 76, 77, 82;
voting by, 7, 26, 47, 49; work ethic of,
103
Mexican American Political Association
(MAPA), 6, 41, 54
Mexican immigrants: attacks on, 103,
167; equal privilege of, 98; influx
of, 101, 153; opposition to, 116;
organization of, 110; origins of, 142;
restrictions on, 104, 105, 106; RFK
and, 118–119
Mexican Revolution (1910), 144
Mexifornia: A State of Becoming (Hanson),
102, 118, 164
Minimum wage, 11, 13, 84, 145; farm
workers and, 22, 33; increases in, 95,
96, 136
Minutemen Project, 113, 164, 165, 169,
171; border security and, 115; cultural
heritage and, 119; UFW and, 114
Mission District, 43
Mondale, Walter, 149
Moral issues, 101, 150, 151; Democratic
Party and, 165–166; economic issues
and, 165; Latinos and, 131, 132,
137–138, 141
Movimiento Estudiantil Chicano de
Aztlán (MEChA), 118
Murphy, George, 12, 14, 16, 17–18
Muskie, Edmund, 148

NAACP. *See* National Association for the
Advancement of Colored People
NAFTA, 169
Napolitano, Janet, 165
National Association for the
Advancement of Colored People
(NAACP), 158, 161
National Conference of Catholic Bishops,
145, 149

National Council of La Raza, 112

National Farm Workers Association (NFWA), 9, 27, 68; grape strike and, 12; Johnson and, 10; picketing by, 23

National Hispanic Survey, 132

Nationalism, 46, 67; cultural, 70; La Raza Unida and, 71–72; Mexican American community and, 68

National Labor Relations Act (NLRA), 14, 61, 86, 128; boycott and, 60; child labor laws and, 11; farm workers and, 11, 23, 53, 54, 145; organizational rights and, 59; RFK and, 33; unionizing protections of, 13; Williams and, 22

National Labor Relations Board (NLRB), 60, 61

National Latino Congreso, 162

Nation of Immigrants, A (Kennedy), 119

New Democrat Network, 138

New Liberalism, 163, 164

New York Times, 53, 77

New York Times/CBS News poll, 131

NFWA. *See* National Farm Workers Association

Nickel and Dimed (Ehrenreich), 95–96

Nixon, Richard, 7, 52, 80; African Americans and, 55, 159; agribusiness and, 170; boycott and, 54, 60; Catholic vote for, 148, 149; Chávez and, 21, 79, 170; civil rights and, 53–54, 161; *corrido* of, 54; economic/social policies of, 128; farm workers and, 46, 55; Hoffa and, 25; King and, 161; La Raza Unida and, 74; Latino vote for, 53, 128; "law and order" campaign by, 53–54; Mexican Americans and, 55, 73, 127, 129; support for, 54, 55, 92; Teamsters and, 25; undocumented workers and, 110; Vietnam War and, 80; War on Poverty and, 128; welfare reform and, 87

NLRA. *See* National Labor Relations Act

NLRB. *See* National Labor Relations Board

Noble, Charles, 99

No Child Left Behind Act, 121, 129, 137, 173

Nonviolence, 14–15, 35; Chávez and, 33, 71, 76, 78, 155, 175; commitment to, 28, 33, 76, 156–157; faith in, 79; fast and, 28–29, 32, 175; RFK and, 71, 175

Obama, Barack, 175; AgJOBS and, 113; border security and, 116; compassion and, 99; on individualism/connection, 174

Office of Economic Opportunity (OEO), 81, 87

Olvera Street, 6, 42, 85

"One Time, One Night" (Los Lobos), 45

Operation Gatekeeper, 129, 153

Operation Wetback, 104

Other America, The (Harrington), 12, 100

Our Plan for America: Stronger at Home, Respected in the World (Kerry and Edwards), 88

Pacific Research Institute, 173

Patriotism, Latino, 135

Paul VI, Pope, 146, 147

Perot, Ross, 127

Personal Responsibility and Work Opportunity Reconciliation Act (1996), 87, 164, 167

Pesticides, 64, 83

Pew Hispanic Center, 79, 89, 160, 172, 173; survey by, 90, 130, 131, 135; on undocumented workers/work force, 112

Pfaff, William, 71

"Plan de Santa Barbara," 70

"Plan Espiritual de Aztlán," 67, 70

"Plan of Delano, The" (farm union), 93

Plimpton, George, 47

Poor People's Campaign, 94, 157

About the Author

Steven Bender is the James and Ilene Hershner Professor of Law at the University of Oregon School of Law. He is coauthor of *Everyday Law for Latino/as* (Paradigm 2008) and author of *Greasers and Gringos: Latinos, Law, and the American Imagination* (NYU Press 2003). He has written extensively in diverse subject areas such as race relations, politics, and film studies. He is active in international, national, and local academic and social service–based Latino/a organizations and causes.